SUBJECTS AND UNIVERSAL GRAMMAR

The "subject" of a sentence is a concept that presents great challenges to linguists. Most languages have something which looks like a subject, but subjects differ across languages in their nature and properties, making them an interesting phenomenon for those seeking linguistic universals. This pioneering volume takes a new approach to subjects, addressing their nature from a simultaneously formal and typological perspective. Dividing the subject into two distinct grammatical functions, it shows how the nature of these functions explains their respective properties, and argues that the split in properties shown in "ergative" languages (whereby the subject of intransitive verbs is marked as an object) results from the functions being assigned to different elements of the clause. Drawing on data from a typologically wide variety of languages, and examining a range of constructions, this book explains why, even in the case of very different languages, certain core properties can be found.

YEHUDA N. FALK is Senior Lecturer in the Department of English, The Hebrew University of Jerusalem. He has also been a Visiting Scholar at Stanford University (1999–2000). He has previously published *Lexical-Functional Grammar: An Introduction to Parallel, Constraint-based Syntax* (2001), and has contributed to a variety of journals including *Language* and the *Journal of Linguistics*.

In this series

74 ALICE C. HARRIS and LYLE CAMPBELL: *Historical syntax in cross-linguistic perspective*
75 LILIANE HAEGEMAN: *The syntax of negation*
76 PAUL GORRELL: *Syntax and parsing*
77 GUGLIELMO CINQUE: *Italian syntax and universal grammar*
78 HENRY SMITH: *Restrictiveness in case theory*
79 D. ROBERT LADD: *Intonational morphology*
80 ANDREA MORO: *The raising of predicates: predicative noun phrases and the theory of clause structure*
81 ROGER LASS: *Historical linguistics and language change*
82 JOHN M. ANDERSON: *A notional theory of syntactic categories*
83 BERND HEINE: *Possession: cognitive sources, forces and grammaticalization*
84 NOMI ERTESCHIK-SHIR: *The dynamics of focus structure*
85 JOHN COLEMAN: *Phonological representations: their names, forms and powers*
86 CHRISTINA Y. BETHIN: *Slavic prosody: language change and phonological theory*
87 BARBARA DANCYGIER: *Conditionals and prediction*
88 CLAIRE LEFEBVRE: *Creole genesis and the acquisition of grammar: the case of Haitian creole*
89 HEINZ GIEGERICH: *Lexical strata in English*
90 KEREN RICE: *Morpheme order and semantic scope*
91 APRIL McMAHON: *Lexical phonology and the history of English*
92 MATTHEW Y. CHEN: *Tone Sandhi: patterns across Chinese dialects*
93 GREGORY T. STUMP: *Inflectional morphology: a theory of paradigm structure*
94 JOAN BYBEE: *Phonology and language use*
95 LAURIE BAUER: *Morphological productivity*
96 THOMAS ERNST: *The syntax of adjuncts*
97 ELIZABETH CLOSS TRAUGOTT and RICHARD B. DASHER: *Regularity in semantic change*
98 MAYA HICKMANN: *Children's discourse: Person, space and time across languages*
99 DIANE BLAKEMORE: *Relevance and linguistic meaning: the semantics and pragmatics of discourse markers*
100 IAN ROBERTS and ANNA ROUSSOU: *Syntactic change: a minimalist approach to grammaticalization*
101 DONKA MINKOVA: *Alliteration and sound change in early English*
102 MARK C. BAKER: *Lexical categories: verbs, nouns and adjectives*
103 CARLOTA S. SMITH: *Modes of discourse: the local structure of texts*
104 ROCHELLE LIEBER: *Morphology and lexical semantics*
105 HOLGER DIESSEL: *The acquisition of complex sentences*
106 SHARON INKELAS and CHERYL ZOLL: *Reduplication: doubling in morphology*
107 SUSAN EDWARDS: *Fluent aphasia*
108 BARBARA DANCYGIER and EVE SWEETSER: *Mental spaces in grammar: conditional constructions*
109 MATTHEW BAERMAN, DUNSTAN BROWN and GREVILLE G. CORBETT: *The syntax–morphology interface: a study of syncretism*
110 MARCUS TOMALIN: *Linguistics and the Formal Sciences: the origins of generative grammar*
111 SAMUEL D. EPSTEIN and T. DANIEL SEELY: *Derivations in Minimalism*
112 PAUL DE LACY: *Markedness: reduction and preservation in phonology*
113 YEHUDA N. FALK: *Subjects and Universal Grammar: An explanatory theory*

Earlier issues not listed are also available

CAMBRIDGE STUDIES IN LINGUISTICS

General editors: PETER AUSTIN, JOAN BRESNAN,
BERNARD COMRIE, STEPHEN CRAIN,
WOLFGANG DRESSLER, COLIN EWEN, ROGER LASS,
DAVID LIGHTFOOT, KEREN RICE, IAN ROBERTS,
SUZANNE ROMAINE, NEIL SMITH

Subjects and Universal Grammar

An Explanatory Theory

SUBJECTS AND UNIVERSAL GRAMMAR

AN EXPLANATORY THEORY

YEHUDA N. FALK
The Hebrew University of Jerusalem

CAMBRIDGE
UNIVERSITY PRESS

CAMBRIDGE UNIVERSITY PRESS
Cambridge, New York, Melbourne, Madrid, Cape Town, Singapore, São Paulo

Cambridge University Press
The Edinburgh Building, Cambridge CB2 2RU, UK

Published in the United States of America by Cambridge University Press, New York

www.cambridge.org
Information on this title: www.cambridge.org/9780521858540

© Yehuda N. Falk 2006

This publication is in copyright. Subject to statutory exception
and to the provisions of relevant collective licensing agreements,
no reproduction of any part may take place without
the written permission of Cambridge University Press.

First published 2006

Printed in the United Kingdom at the University Press, Cambridge

A catalogue record for this publication is available from the British Library

ISBN-13 978-0-521-85854-0 hardback
ISBN-10 0-521-85854-2 hardback

Cambridge University Press has no responsibility for the persistence or accuracy of URLs for external or third-party internet websites referred to in this publication, and does not guarantee that any content on such websites is, or will remain, accurate or appropriate.

To the people responsible for my linguistic career:
   my late grandmother
   Barbara Klima ז׳ל
who first introduced me to a language other than English
   and my parents
   Paul and Eva Falk יבל׳א
who encouraged my mishegas with languages.

(Who would have thought that those Berlitz records would lead to this?)

Contents

	Preface	*page* xiii
	Notes on the text	xvi
	List of abbreviations used in glosses	xvii
1	**On subjects and explanation**	**1**
1.1	Overview	1
1.2	Subject properties	2
	1.2.1 First approximation	2
	1.2.2 Case and subjects	7
	1.2.3 Second approximation	12
1.3	On explanation	16
	1.3.1 General considerations	16
	1.3.2 Subject as structural position	16
	1.3.3 Subject as grammatical relation	19
	1.3.4 Subject as grammatical function	21
1.4	The formal framework	24
1.5	A look ahead	28
2	**Most prominent argument**	**30**
2.1	Argumenthood	30
	2.1.1 First approximation	30
	2.1.2 Argument structure and hierarchies	32
	2.1.3 Most prominent argument	36
	2.1.4 Mismatches between argument structure and grammatical functions	39
	2.1.5 Mapping in mixed-subject languages	44
	2.1.6 Further thoughts on argument mapping	46
2.2	Specification of argument properties	47
	2.2.1 Introductory remarks	47
	2.2.2 Null arguments	49
	2.2.3 Imperative addressee	59

x   Contents

2.3	Anaphora	60
	2.3.1 Anaphoric prominence	60
	2.3.2 Switch-reference	66
2.4	Summary	72

3   Pivot — 73

3.1	The pivot function	73
	3.1.1 The concept	73
	3.1.2 Formalization: the Pivot Condition	76
3.2	Uniform subjects and mixed subjects	78
3.3	Pivothood and constructions	83
	3.3.1 Types of constructions	83
	3.3.2 Distinguishing formal constructions	89
	3.3.3 Multiple pivots	92
3.4	Clause-internal PIV properties	95
	3.4.1 External position	95
	3.4.2 Other clause-internal properties	98
3.5	Some morphology	100
3.6	Forthcoming attractions	105

4   Long-distance dependencies — 106

4.1	About long-distance dependencies	106
	4.1.1 Functional uncertainty	107
	4.1.2 Pivots and non-pivots	110
	4.1.3 Matrix subjects	119
4.2	Across-the-board extraction	122
4.3	The *that*-trace effect	128
4.4	Summary	134

5   Control constructions — 135

5.1	Overview of the issues	135
5.2	The semantic basis of control	137
5.3	Syntactic types of control	140
5.4	Subjecthood and control	142
	5.4.1 General	142
	5.4.2 Case study: Tagalog	147
	5.4.3 A non-problem in Balinese	152
5.5	Other control constructions	154
	5.5.1 Non-complement equi	154
	5.5.2 Raising	155
5.6	Conclusion	161

6	**Universality**	**163**
6.1	Non-subject languages	163
6.2	The realization of arguments	166
6.3	Universality of the Pivot Function	170
	6.3.1 Case study: Acehnese	170
	6.3.2 Topic prominence	175
	6.3.3 Pivotless languages	178
6.4	Conclusion	195
7	**Competing theories**	**197**
7.1	Other approaches	197
7.2	Typological approach	198
7.3	Functionalism	201
7.4	Inverse mapping and multistratal subjects	203
7.5	Constituent structure approaches	208
7.6	Final thoughts	219
	References	222
	Language index	231
	Author index	233
	General index	235

Preface

According to the biblical book of Kohelet (Ecclesiastes), "the making of many books is without end." I don't know about "many books," but the making of this book has sometimes appeared to be without end. It began some forgotten day in the late 1980s when the idle thought crossed my mind: "How might one redesign GB Case theory to account for ergative languages?" A very early exploration of the issues in this book, in the guise of GB Case theory, was published in *Linguistics* in 1991, under the title "Case: Abstract and Morphological." I also presented several papers on Case, ergativity, and such at conferences of the Israel Association for Theoretical Linguistics in the 1990s. But in the course of trying to understand ergative languages I began to realize that the GB framework was missing something. What this "something" was started to become clearer to me when I started considering Philippine-type languages, because it was obvious to me that direct reference to grammatical functions was necessary to account for the "voice" morphology.

This realization led me back to LFG, the theoretical framework in which I had begun my linguistic career. I began reframing the work that I had been doing in terms of LFG. A presentation at the 1999 conference of the Austronesian Formal Linguistics Association received encouraging responses. In the fall semester of the 1999–2000 academic year, I was fortunate to be able to spend a sabbatical as a Visiting Scholar at Stanford University, hosted by Joan Bresnan. I spent incredible amounts of time in the Green Library with my laptop, taking notes from books not available in Jerusalem. Based on my reading, and with enthusiastic encouragement from Joan, I started focusing my attention on issues of subjecthood, and started to take seriously languages I hadn't considered before and constructions that I didn't really understand earlier. It was also as a result of Joan's encouragement that I began to think of writing a book. The core of this book was presented at the LFG 2000 conference, and I have presented this material in departmental colloquia at the Hebrew University of Jerusalem and Tel Aviv University. However, this book took a back seat to another project that grew out of my sabbatical, my LFG textbook *Lexical-Functional Grammar: An*

Introduction to Parallel Constraint-Based Syntax (2001). Finally I was able to complete the manuscript, only to be faced with two major rewrites as a result of comments by readers for Cambridge University Press.

There are many people who have had a hand in helping me complete this book. In the first place, this book would not exist without the fieldworkers who have collected the data on which this book is based. While I know very few of them personally, I am forever indebted to these hardy souls. They have forever enriched the database on which linguistics works and, if generative linguistics is to be the search for the nature of Universal Grammar, it is only through their continued efforts that the field will be able to progress.

Joan Bresnan, as my sponsor at Stanford, has provided immeasurable input into this study and much invaluable moral support, as well as being my role model as a descriptive/theoretical linguist. Ron Kaplan, the keeper of the LFG formalism, helped me out on a couple of occasions when I couldn't find the right way to express something. My Hebrew University colleague Yael Ziv has helped me realize the importance of pragmatics in language, and given me a new appreciation for the insights (if not the formulations) of functionalists. Ray Jackendoff, from whom I first learned transformational syntax back in 1976, encouraged me to abandon the transformational model; the influence of his views on language should be apparent to all. Other people who have commented on portions of the material here and/or helped me with data include Alex Alsina, I Wayan Arka, Aaron Broadwell, Elizabeth Coppock, Mary Dalrymple, Edit Doron, Mike Dukes (my officemate at Stanford), Fred Landman, Paul Kroeger, Chris Manning, Irit Meir, Anita Mittwoch, Asya Pereltsvaig, Ivan Sag, Jane Simpson, the late Joe Taglicht, Lisa Travis, and Annie Zaenen. Participants in the conferences and colloquia at which I have presented this material have been very helpful. I am also grateful to the students who have taken graduate seminars in which this material has been covered in one form or another, in 1996, 1998, 2000, 2001, and 2003. In teaching the material to them I was better able to formulate the half-baked ideas that were swirling around in my mind. Andrew Winnard at Cambridge University Press has been very helpful and encouraging, and the Press's anonymous readers forced me to go over the material again and again, first fleshing out the points I have tried to make, then strengthening the argumentation. Thanks to their comments, the book is much better than the first manuscript that I submitted. For making my Stanford sabbatical more enjoyable, I would like to thank the Palo Alto Jewish community, especially Rabbi Shelly Lewis and the rest of the folks at Congregation Kol Emeth.

My wife Brandel, a longtime La Leche League leader, has, as always, been an inspiration with her dedication. My sons, all now either in or approaching adulthood, have enriched my life in various ways which have helped me complete this project: Eli with his interest in academic endeavor; Yoni with his fierceness of conviction; Mati with his unbridled enthusiasm; and Gabi with his still-open-minded childlike innocence. And my baby daughter Pnina has helped me rediscover what an incredible journey of exploration life is (and how fascinating language is).

My maternal grandmother, Barbara Klima, passed away while this book was under review. A survivor of the Holocaust, she made a new life for herself and her daughter (my mother), and lived to age 98, seeing seven great-grandchildren. Her strength of spirit was inspirational. I miss her terribly.

Notes on the text

Dyirbal and Yidin^y examples are presented using the practical orthography currently employed by Australianists (as in Dixon 1994). The examples from Dixon's grammars (1972 for Dyirbal and 1977 for Yidin^y) have been updated accordingly: ɲ has been changed to n^y, ḍ to j, ṭ to r, and r to rr.

Except for section 1.2.2 on Case marking, absolutive and nominative case are only glossed when there are overt markers.

I follow the typographical convention of capitalizing the word "Case". This notation was introduced in early Government/Binding theory as a device for disambiguating the word "case", a word which happens to have a wide-ranging set of meanings: "I will follow the practice of capitalizing 'Case' when it is used in the technical sense, to avoid confusion with informal use, as in 'the unmarked case,' etc." (Chomsky 1980: 13 fn. 18). The distinction is a useful one; in fact, taking Chomsky's own example, one wants to distinguish between "unmarked case" (i.e. unmarked situation) and "unmarked Case" (unmarked morphological form of a noun). It is in this spirit that the capitalization is being used here. This notation has, over the years, acquired an unfortunate sense of distinguishing some abstract, theoretical notion of Case from ordinary morphological Case. In the present study, Case refers to morphological marking.

Abbreviations used in glosses

numbers	(in examples from Bantu languages) noun class
ABL	ablative case
ABS	absolutive case or agreement
ACC	accusative case
ACT	actor "voice" (nominative = A argument) in Philippine-type languages
ADJ	adjective
ADNOM	adnominal
AGT	agent agreement
ALL	allative case
APASS	antipassive
APPL	applicative
ASP	aspectual marker
AUX	auxiliary
BEN	benefactive "voice" (nominative = benefactive) in Philippine-type languages
CAUS	causative
CLASS	classifier
CNTMP	contemplated tense
COMP	complementizer
COMPL	completive
DAT	dative case
DECL	declarative
DEF	definite
DEICT	deictic
DIFF	different subject (in switch-reference systems)
DIR	directional
DIRS	directional suffix
DIST	distal realis

Abbreviations used in glosses

DO	direct-object "voice" (nominative = P argument) in Philippine-type languages
DU	dual
ERG	ergative case or agreement
EXCL	exclusive
F	feminine
FSG	feminine singular
FOC	focus
FUT	future tense
GEN	genitive case
GER	gerund
IMM	immediate
IMP	imperative
IMPERF	imperfect(ive)
IMPLIC	implicated clause
INCH	inchoative
INCL	inclusive
IND	indicative
INF	infinitive
INS	instrumental "voice" (nominative = instrument) in Philippine-type languages
INSTR	instrumental case
INTR	intransitive
IO	indirect-object "voice" (nominative = indirect object, locative, or directional) in Philippine-type languages
IRR	irrealis
LNK	linker
LOC	locative case
M	masculine
MSG	masculine singular
NEG	negative
NFUT	non-future
NMNL	nominalizer
NOM	nominative case
NONVOL	non-volitive mood
NPST	non-past
OBJ	object agreement marker or case
OBL	oblique
OCONTR	object "control" in Walpiri

PART	participle
PASS	passive
PAT	patient agreement
PERF	perfect(ive)
PERS	noun referring to a person
PL	plural
POL	polite
POSS	possessive
PRES	present tense
PRON	pronoun
PROP	proper noun
PSPRT	passive participle
PST	past tense
Q	question
REAL	realis
REC	recent past tense
RECIP	reciprocal
REFL	reflexive
REL	relative
SAME	same subject (in switch-reference systems)
SBJCT	subjunctive
SCONTR	subject "control" (same subject) in Warlpiri
SG	singular
STAT	stative
SUBJ	subject agreement marker
SUFF	suffix
TNS	tense
TOP	topic
TR	transitive
TRANSL	translative case
VWL	vowel (thematic or similar phonological augment)

1 On subjects and explanation

1.1 Overview

Explaining subjects and their properties is an important challenge in contemporary linguistics. For formalist approaches to linguistics, the clustering of properties that subjects display necessitates some special representational properties unique to subjects. Without such representational uniqueness, the properties of subjects that set them apart from other elements of the clause are mysterious. However, this only pushes the need for explanation back one level: such special representation itself calls out for explanation. For functionalist approaches, similar issues are raised, as it is not clear what the functional properties of subjects are that set them apart. From a typological perspective, the mystery of subjects is even deeper, as different language types appear to deploy subject properties in different (but systematic) ways. As a result of the discoveries of ergative languages, Philippine-type languages, active languages, and the like, interesting questions have been raised about the properties of subjects, the representation of subjects, and even the cross-linguistic validity of "subject" as an element of linguistic description.

The concept of "subject" is one with a long history in linguistics. As with most other such concepts, contemporary linguistics did not invent the subject. Instead, it has taken a traditional concept and attempted to provide it with theoretical content. Problems have arisen because the concept "subject" originates in traditional studies of classical Indo-European languages such as Greek and Latin, languages which are closely related genetically, areally, and typologically. Investing "subject" with theoretical content thus usually depends on either focusing on languages which are typologically similar to classical Indo-European languages or attempting to extend an Indo-European notion to languages which have very different typological properties. As a result, different researchers take varying positions on which languages are examined, and in some languages which element (if any) is to be identified as the subject. Much of the literature on such topics as ergativity and active languages focuses on debates such as these. These issues need to be clarified if a true understanding of subjects and their properties is to be achieved.

All contemporary approaches to linguistics – formalist, functionalist, typological, etc. – appropriately take the goal of linguistics to be the explanation of linguistic phenomena. As such, they depart from merely being satisfied with describing linguistic facts, although proper description is, of course, a prerequisite for explanation. In the realm of subjecthood, this means that simply stipulating the properties of subjects is not sufficient: the properties should follow from a proper characterization of the nature of subjects. Since explanation is possible only in the context of a theory of the linguistic domain in question, the attempts that have been made at explaining subjects have been as varied as schools of linguistics, and have mirrored the drawbacks of the theoretical assumptions made by the researchers. Formal accounts tend to be characterized by a disregard for functional factors and often by inadequate cross-linguistic coverage. Functionalist and typological accounts are typically based on superficial surveys of languages and disregard the nature of the formal devices involved in syntax.

It is the thesis of this study that a truly explanatory theory of subjects has yet to be constructed, and its goal is the proposal of such a theory. A theory of subjects must be formally grounded, functionally aware, and achieve sufficiently broad typological coverage, including all of the types of languages which are potentially problematic. Unlike previous accounts, the theory of subjects to be proposed here meets all of these criteria. Naturally, it draws on insights of earlier approaches, but it synthesizes them in a way which results in true explanation of the properties of subjects as they are revealed in cross-linguistic study.

In this first chapter, we will enumerate the properties generally thought to be subject properties. We will also discuss typological issues related to subjecthood. Finally, we will discuss different types of approaches to subjects.

1.2   Subject properties

1.2.1   First approximation

As mentioned above, subjects display an array of properties which must be accounted for by a theory of subjecthood. Properties of subjects have been enumerated in studies like Keenan (1976) and Andrews (1985). We will review them here briefly, primarily using examples from English. However, before we discuss the properties of subjects, it is necessary to take heed of the following observation by Andrews (1985: 104):

At the outset we must note that there are no properties which in all languages are always exhibited by subjects and only exhibited by them. There may be some properties that are universally restricted to subjects [fn. omitted], but there are certainly none that they always have. Rather, we find properties that are exhibited by subjects in a wide range of languages, and which may be plausibly argued to be restricted to subjects in some of them.

This observation is not surprising – it is in line with the way typological properties typically apply (Comrie 1989). However, it violates the usual formalist preference for absolute universals, and thus is an important caveat for any formally based theory of subjects. In addition, the fact that typological properties typically emerge as tendencies rather than absolutes is itself something that needs to be explained.

The first property is that if a verb has an Agent argument, the Agent is realized as subject.

(1)   a. Predicate: 'eat'; Agent: 'the kid'; Patient: 'the sandwich'
      b. The kid ate the sandwich
      c. *The sandwich ate´ the kid.

A verb like the putative *eat´* in (1c), in which the Patient is realized syntactically as subject and the Agent as object, is disallowed. Of course, while all Agent arguments are subjects, not all subjects are Agents. If the verb does not have an Agent argument, the subject will express some other thematic role. A special case of this is the passive construction, in which the Agent loses its expressed-argument status (Chomsky 1981, Bresnan 2001).

Another property of subjects is that the addressee of an imperative is a subject. This can be seen in each of the following imperatives: the addressee can have a variety of thematic roles, not necessarily Agent, but it must have the syntactic status of subject.

(2)   a. Eat the sandwich!
      b. Go to school!
      c. Freeze, if that's what you want! (Parent to child who refuses to put on a coat in freezing weather)
      d. Be happy!
      e. Be arrested by the municipal police, not the state police!

Another property which is apparent in the English imperative examples, although more clearly in other languages, is that the subject is more susceptible to being realized as a covert (null or empty) pronoun. It is telling that the empty-pronoun construction (or pro-drop) is often referred to in the theoretical literature as the null-subject construction, a name which is based on this higher susceptibility. We will discuss the facts in more detail in Chapter 2.

A frequently discussed property of subjects is anaphoric prominence. The exact details vary from language to language (as will be discussed in Chapter 2), but one clear consequence which can be seen in all languages with reflexive pronouns[1] is that, in a transitive clause in which the subject and object are coreferential, it is the subject which is expressed as a full NP and the object as the reflexive pronoun.

(3)   a. Pnina saw herself.
       b. *Herself saw Pnina.

In some languages the antecedent of a reflexive must be a subject, while in others (like English) it just has to have higher prominence, but in either case the most prominent element of the clause is the subject.

An anaphoric construction which does not exist in English, but in which the greater prominence of the subject is again apparent, is the switch-reference construction, in which a clause marks the anaphoric relation (coreference or disjoint reference) between its own subject and the subject of a superordinate and/or coordinate clause. This is exemplified in the following Diyari sentences (Austin 1981).

(4)   a. Karna wapa- rna   warrayi, jukudu   nanda- lha.
            man   go-   PART   AUX   kangaroo kill-   IMPLIC.SAME
            'The man went to kill a kangaroo.'
       b. Karna- li   marda matha- rna   warrayi, thalara
            man-   ERG   stone bite-   PART   AUX   rain
            kurda- rnanthu.
            fall-   IMPLIC.DIFF
            'The man bit the stone so the rain would fall.'

In (4a), the clauses have coreferential subjects, so the "same" morpheme is used in the subordinate clause. In (4b), on the other hand, the subjects are disjoint in reference, and the "different" morpheme is used.

---

1 An anonymous reviewer suggests that the data from Samoan in Chapin (1970) may be a counterexample. Chapin observes that there is no subject/non-subject asymmetry for a pronoun with a reflexive interpretation; the only condition is that the antecedent must precede the pronoun. However, he also notes that there are no distinct reflexive pronouns in the language. Since the Samoan forms are simply undifferentiated anaphoric elements, there is no reason to expect a restriction to subject.

Even in a language like English, which has no switch-reference system, subjects have a special status in coordination and subordination. In coordinated clauses, if the subjects of both clauses are identical, the subject can be omitted in the second clause. The object cannot be involved in this kind of relation.

(5) a. Mati kissed Pnina and hugged Yoni. (= Mati hugged Yoni; ≠ Pnina hugged Yoni)
     b. *Mati kissed Pnina and Yoni hugged. (intended reading: ... hugged Pnina)

More frequently discussed in the theoretical literature is the subordination construction known as control (or equi). In the control construction, the subordinate subject is covert (and modeled as a special null nominal called PRO in the transformational literature) if it is identical to an element of the main clause. While the coreferential main clause element need not be subject, the subordinate clause element must be.

(6) a. They persuaded the starship captain [to kiss the alien woman].
     b. *They persuaded the alien woman [(for) the starship captain to kiss].
     c. They persuaded the alien woman [to be kissed by the starship captain].

A similar construction is raising,[2] in which an element which is a thematic (semantic) argument of the subordinate clause is expressed as part of the main clause, in which it is not a thematic argument. The only kind of subordinate clause element which can be raised in this fashion is the subject.

(7) a. It seems [that lions eat zebras].
     b. Lions seem [to eat zebras].
     c. *Zebras seem [(for) lions to eat].
     d. Zebras seem [to be eaten by lions].

Coordination, control, and raising are thus constructions in which the subject has a special status.

Subjecthood interacts in various ways with long-distance (*wh*) dependencies. One of the best-known cases is the fact, originally observed in Keenan and Comrie's (1977) classical study of relative clauses, that subjects are more prone to *wh*-movement cross-linguistically than other elements. In English, paradoxically, subjects appear to be more resistant to *wh*-movement than other elements of the clause: non-subjects can be extracted from a clause with an overt complementizer while subjects cannot (the *that*-trace effect).

---

2 Also known as matrix coding (Van Valin and LaPolla 1997).

(8) a. Pnina thinks that Yoni gave the ball to Gabi.
b. *Who does Pnina think that gave the ball to Gabi?
c. What does Pnina think that Yoni gave to Gabi?
d. Who does Pnina think that Yoni gave the ball to?

There are other subjecthood-related aspects to long-distance dependency constructions, to be discussed in detail in Chapter 4.

There are other properties that are unique to subjects. For example, many languages require every sentence to have a subject (either overt or covert), a property enshrined in transformational theory's Extended Projection Principle (and analogous principles in other contemporary theories of syntax). Another property which has been built into the transformational model is that subjects often occupy a special "external" structural position (e.g., outside of VP), a position which provides them with structural prominence relative to other arguments of the verb. Subjects also have semantic and pragmatic prominence. For example, subjects are often definite. They also take wide scope over other elements of the clause.

(9) a. A student didn't take my course. (*a* takes wide scope over negation)
b. I didn't see a student. (ambiguous)

Finally, the subject is usually the discourse topic.

We can summarize these subject properties in the following list.

(10) Agent argument in the active voice
Most likely covert/empty argument
The addressee of an imperative
Anaphoric prominence
Switch-reference systems
Shared argument in coordinated clauses
Controlled argument (PRO)
Raising
Extraction properties
Obligatory element
"External" structural position
Definiteness or wide scope
Discourse topic

This catalog of properties[3] represents the reason for the continued interest in the nature of subjects. There is no obvious pretheoretical reason for a single

---

3 Another construction which is often mentioned in the context of subject properties is Quantifier Float. While the ability to launch floating quantifiers is limited to subjects in some languages, it is clearly not true universally. We suspect that Quantifier Float is not a uniform syntactic construction cross-linguistically, but will not attempt to account for its properties here.

element of the sentence to have all these properties; the fact that one does in many languages calls out for explanation.

1.2.2 Case and subjects

To sharpen the conception of subject properties that we outlined in the previous section, we need to consider the relationship between subjecthood and morphological marking: Case[4] and, to a lesser extent, agreement. Subjects in many languages are realized with either no overt Case marking or with the same Case marking that is used with citation forms, two situations we can unify under the heading "unmarked Case." This unmarked Case, often called nominative, is sometimes taken to be a defining property of subjects in Case-marking languages. However, typological study has shown that this is an overly simplistic view of the situation. We will outline the relevant facts in this section. Similarly, it is often stated that subjects have a special status in terms of agreement. Here again, the facts appear to be more complicated. We will return to the question of Case and agreement in Chapter 3.

Since we need to be able to refer to clausal participants without committing to their status as subjects and objects, we will follow much of the typological literature (see, for example, Comrie 1978, 1989) in using the following terminology:

(11)   Sole argument of intransitive verb: S
       Agent-like argument of transitive: A
       Patient-like argument of transitive: P   (sometimes called O)

The most common (and most familiar) situation is one where S and A have unmarked Case (traditionally called nominative) and P has a marked Case (traditionally called accusative). Such a language is called nominative-accusative. In a nominative-accusative language, the traditional identification of S/A as "subject" and the hypothesis that subjects have the unmarked Case coincide.

However, in some languages, it is the S and P that have unmarked Case. The S/P unmarked Case is usually called absolutive rather than nominative. In this kind of language, the A has a marked Case which is called ergative. For this reason, these languages are usually referred to as ergative languages. As observed by Dixon (1994), ergative languages are found almost everywhere around the globe, including many languages of Australia (Dyirbal, Warlpiri,

---

4 See "Notes on the text" on page xvi for an explanatory of the capitalization of the word "Case".

Diyari, Yidin^y, etc.), Eskimo languages (Inuit, Yupik), Basque, Georgian, Avar, Chukchee, Hindi-Urdu, Tongan, Samoan, and many others.[5]

(12) **Dyirbal** (Dixon 1994)
 a. Ḍuma banaga- n^yu
 father.ABS return- NFUT
 'Father returned.'

 b. Ḍuma yabu- ŋgu bura- n
 father.ABS mother- ERG see- NFUT
 'Mother saw father.'

(13) **Greenlandic Inuit** (Marantz 1984)
 a. Anut- ip arnaq taku- vaa.
 man- ERG woman.ABS see- IND3SG.3SG
 'The man saw the woman.'

 b. Anut autlar- puq.
 man.ABS go.away- IND3SG
 'The man went away.'

(14) **Basque** (Bittner and Hale 1996b)
 a. Miren- ek ni jo n- au.
 Miren- ERG me.ABS hit 1SG- have.3SG
 'Miren hit me.'

 b. Miren erori d- a.
 Miren.ABS fallen 3SG- be
 'Miren fell.'

(15) **Avar** (Mallinson and Blake 1981)
 a. Či v- ač?- ula.
 man.ABS he- come- PRES
 'The man comes.'

 b. Ebél- alda či v- at̰- ula.
 mother- ERG man.ABS he- discover- PST
 'Mother discovers the man.'

---

5 Some of these (such as Dyirbal) are split ergative, meaning that some types of NPs display an ergative pattern and others a nominative-accusative pattern. Languages of that type have distinct ergative and accusative Cases, showing that the marked Cases differ from each other. There are also a few languages ("three-way" languages) in which all NPs are marked ergative in A function and accusative in P function. It has been claimed by Woolford (1997) that there are also four-way languages, in which two distinct markings are possible for P. However, in the languages she brings as examples, Nez Perce (in which the A may also be unmarked) and Kalkatungu, one of these P Cases is unmarked morphologically. Apparently she wants to distinguish unmarked P from unmarked S (or A in Nez Perce) because unmarked S and A trigger subject agreement (as does ergative A), while unmarked P triggers no agreement. However, while Case and agreement are both methods of identifying the arguments of verbs, there is no reason (outside of a particular theory of Case and/or agreement) to expect a straightforward relation between head marking (agreement) and dependent marking (Case).

The term "ergative language" is also generally used for languages, such as the Mayan languages, in which there is no Case marking, but agreement groups S and P together as opposed to A.

(16) **Tzotzil** (Aissen 1983)
    a. Č- i- bat.
       ASP- 1ABS- go
       'I'm going.'
    b. L- i- s- ma.
       ASP- 1ABS- 3ERG- hit
       'He hit me.'
    c. Ta- ∅- h- mah.
       ASP- 3ABS- 1ERG- hit
       'I'm going to hit him.'

On the other hand, some ergative languages, like Warlpiri, have ergative Case marking but nominative–accusative agreement.

(17) **Warlpiri** (Simpson 1983)
    a. Ngaju ka- rna parnka- mi.
       I.ABS PRES- 1SGSUBJ run- NPST
       'I am running.'
    b. Ngajulu- rlu ka- rna- ∅ nya- nyi kurdu.
       I- ERG PRES- 1SG.SUBJ- 3SG.OBJ see- NPST child.
       'I see the child.'
    c. Kurdu- ngku ka- ∅- ju nya- nyi ngaju.
       child- ERG PRES- 3SG.SUBJ- 1SG.OBJ see- NPST I.ABS
       'The child sees me.'

As noted above, nominative-accusative languages are plausibly analyzed by calling S/A the subject, and associating subject status with unmarked Case. One way to understand ergative languages would be to hypothesize that the absolutive argument, S/P, is subject instead of S/A. But if P is subject in ergative languages, it should have subject properties. Investigation has shown that things are not that simple. In some ergative languages, such as Basque and Warlpiri, the P argument of a transitive clause has no subject properties. For languages of this kind, called "morphologically ergative," P is clearly not the subject. (For now, we leave it open whether S/A is the subject in such languages, or whether such languages can be said to have no subject. We will discuss one morphologically ergative language, Warlpiri, in Chapter 6.) It is clear, however, that in morphologically ergative languages unmarked Case cannot be said to be a subject property. For other ergative languages, such as Dyirbal and Inuit, subject properties are split. Some subject properties are properties of (S and) A, just as in English. Other subject properties are S/P (absolutive) properties. So in some sense A and P are both subject-like in these languages, but in different ways. Since the ergative Case marking seems to be in some sense related to syntactic properties, these languages are said to be "syntactically ergative." We will return to syntactically ergative languages in the next section.

In another class of languages, the Philippine-type languages, any element of the clause can have unmarked Case (usually referred to as nominative); the verb is marked with an affix designating one of its arguments as the nominative. The nominative nominal is referred to by Philippinists as the topic, but as observed by Schachter (1976) it is not a topic in the sense that the term is usually used in linguistics.[6]

(18)   **Tagalog** (Schachter 1987)
      a. Mag- aalis ang tindero ng bigas sa sako para
         ACT- take.out NOM storekeeper ACC rice DAT sack for
         sa babae.
         DAT woman
         'The storekeeper will take some rice out of a/the sack for a/the woman.'

      b. Aalis- in ng tindero ang bigas sa sako para
         take.out- DO ERG storekeeper NOM rice DAT sack for
         sa babae.
         DAT woman
         'A/The storekeeper will take the rice out of a/the sack for a/the woman.'

      c. Aalis- an ng tindero ng bigas ang sako para
         take.out- IO ERG storekeeper ACC rice NOM sack for
         sa babae.
         DAT woman
         'A/The storekeeper will take some rice out of the sack for a/the woman.'

      d. Ipag- aalis ng tindero ng bigas sa sako
         BEN- take.out ERG storekeeper ACC rice DAT sack
         ang babae.
         NOM woman
         'A/The storekeeper will take some rice out of a/the sack for the woman.'

      e. Ipang- aalis ng tindero ng bigas sa sako
         INS- take.out ERG storekeeper ACC rice DAT sack
         ang sandok.
         NOM scoop
         'A/The storekeeper will take some rice out of a/the sack with the scoop.'

---

[6] The morphological Case marking for non-nominative A arguments, which is often glossed as genitive, we consider to be ergative Case and gloss it accordingly. Verbal aspect is not glossed.

As with the term "ergative language," the term "Philippine-type language" can also be used for languages that lack Case marking but have a similar system of marking the verb to designate one of the arguments as having a special status. These other Philippine-type languages are typically Western Austronesian languages not spoken in the Philippines, and with a less extensive marking system than the core case of Tagalog-type languages. One such language is Balinese, where the specially designated argument is preverbal.

(19) **Balinese** (Arka 1998)
    a. Nyoman ejuk polisi.
       Nyoman DO.arrest police
       'A policeman arrested Nyoman.'
    b. Polisi ng- ejuk Nyoman.
       police ACT- arrest Nyoman
       'A policeman arrested Nyoman.'

The same question can be asked for Philippine-type languages as for syntactically ergative languages concerning subjecthood and, as we will see in the next section, the answers are similar as well: the A has some subject properties, and the specially designated (nominative) argument has others.

Finally, there are languages in which S is not treated uniformly. Instead, agentive Ss are Case marked like A or trigger agreement like A and patientive Ss are Case marked like P or trigger agreement like P.

(20) **Manipuri** (intransitive examples from Dixon 1994, transitive from Bhat and Ningomba 1997)
    a. əy- nə celli
       I- ERG ran
       'I ran.'
    b. əy sawwi
       I got.angry
       'I got angry.'
    c. Nuŋsit- nə ce cèlli.
       wind- ERG paper carried
       'The wind carried away the paper.'

(21) **Lakhota** (Mallinson and Blake 1981)
    a. Wa- i'.
       1SG.AGT- arrive
       'I arrived.'
    b. Ma- si'ca.
       1SG.PAT- bad
       'I am bad.'

c. Ma-   ya-   kte.
   1SG.PAT- 2SG.AGT-   kill
   'You kill me.'

(22) **Acehnese** (Durie 1985)
   a. Gopnyan ka=   geu=   jak u= keude.
      he   already   3.AGT go   to market
      'He went to market.'
   b. Gopnyan sakêt= geuh.
      he   sick   3.PAT
      'He is sick.'
   c. Ji=   kap=   keuh.
      3.AGT bite   2.PAT
      'It'll bite you.'

These are often called active languages. It has been claimed that concepts like "subject" are irrelevant in active languages, because the realization and properties of arguments are determined on the basis of thematic roles. We will refer to these languages provisionally as "non-subject" languages. A theory of subjecthood must address the question of whether non-subject languages truly lack subjects, and, if it is determined that they do not, why they appear to exhibit different properties from other types of languages. It is insufficient to simply deal with languages that have one or two elements with subject properties. We will return to non-subject languages in Chapter 6.

1.2.3   Second approximation

The subject properties in (10) can be motivated for a wide range of languages, including nominative-accusative languages and possibly at least some morphologically ergative languages. We will henceforth refer to these as "uniform-subject languages." However, as alluded to in the previous section, the situation is more complicated in syntactically ergative and Philippine-type languages. In these languages, which we will call "mixed-subject languages," the subject properties are divided between two elements.

For example, consider West Greenlandic Inuit, a syntactically ergative language exemplified in (13) above. The antecedent of a possessive reflexive can be S or A (i.e., subject in the familiar sense) but not P (the Inuit examples in this section from Manning 1996).

(23)   a. Ataata- ni   Juuna- p   tatig(i- v)aa.
          father- REFL.POSS Juuna- ERG trust- IND.TR.3SG.3SG
          'Juuna$_i$ trusts his$_i$ father.'

b. Aani illu- mi- nut ingerla- vo- q.
Anne house- REFL.POSS- DAT go- IND.INTR- 3SG
'Anne is going to her house.'

c. *Anaana- mi Piita nagligi- janga.
mother- REFL.POSS(ERG) Piita love- 3SG.3SG
'His$_i$ mother loves Piita$_i$.'[7]

In control constructions, the controllee is S or A, not P.

(24) a. Miiqqat [Juuna ikiu- ssa- llu- gu] niriursui- pp- u- t.
children Juuna help- FUT- INF- 3SG promise- IND- INTR- 3PL
'The children promised to help Juuna.'

b. Miiqqat [qiti- ssa- llu- tik] niriursui- pp- u- t.
children dance- FUT- INF- REFL.PL promise- IND- INTR- 3PL
'The children promised to dance.'

On the other hand, the P is accessible to extraction (in relative clauses), as is the S. The A is not.

(25) a. nanuq [Piita- p tuqu- ta- a]
polar.bear Peter- ERG kill- TR.PART- 3SG
'a polar bear that Peter killed'

b. miiraq [kamat- tu- q]
child angry- REL.INTR- SG
'the child who is angry'

c. *angut [aallaat tigu- sima- sa- a]
man gun take- PERF- REL.TR- 3SG
'the man who took the gun'

As discussed by Bittner (1994), the S and P arguments obligatorily take wide scope over sentential operators such as negation, while the A need not.

(26) a. Atuartu- p ataasi- p Juuna uqaluqatigi- sima- nngi-
student- ERG one- ERG Juuna talk.to- PERF- NEG-
la- a.
IND- 3SG.3SG
(i) 'No student has talked to Juuna (yet).'
(ii) 'One student hasn't talked to Juuna (yet).'

b. Atuagaq ataasiq tikis- sima- nngi- la- q.
book one come- PERF- NEG- IND- 3SG
'One book hasn't come (yet).'

---

7 This example is from the closely related language Inuktitut, spoken in Canada.

c. Juuna- p   atuagaq ataasiq tigu- sima- nngi- la-   a.
   Juuna- ERG book   one   get- PERF- NEG- IND- 3SG.3SG
   'There is a book which Juuna hasn't got (yet).'

Thus, Inuit displays a split in subject properties, with some, as in English, as properties of the S and A arguments, and others as properties of the S and P arguments.

Another language which exhibits a split in subject properties is Tagalog, as first observed in the seminal study of Schachter (1976). Tagalog is a Philippine-type language, and is exemplified above in (18). Here the split is between those subject properties which are properties of the S or A regardless of verbal morphology, and those which are properties of the nominative. As the examples in (18) show, the A argument (thematically Agent in cases like this, where the verb takes an Agent argument) is the nominative when the verb has Agent-nominative marking; otherwise it is marked with what we are glossing as ergative Case. S arguments involve the same markings as A arguments. The A argument is the one that can act as antecedent for reflexives in Tagalog.

(27)   (Schachter 1976)
        a. Sinakt- an ng   babae ang kaniyang sarili.
           hurt-   IO ERG woman NOM her   self
           'A/The woman hurt herself.'

        b. Iniisip   nila   ang kanilang sarili.
           think.about.DO   they.ERG NOM their   self
           'They think about themselves.'

        c. Nag- iisip   sila   sa   kanilang sarili.
           ACT- think.about they.NOM DAT their   self
           'They think about themselves.'

The A is the addressee of an imperative, regardless of nominativity.

(28)   (Schachter 1987)
        a. Mag-   alis   ka   ng   bigas sa   sako.
           ACT.INF- take.out you.NOM   ACC rice   DAT sack
           'Take some rice out of the/a sack.'

        b. Basah- in   mo   nga   ang libro- ng   ito.
           read-   DO.INF   you.ERG   please NOM book-   LNK   this
           'Please read this book.'

On the other hand, it is the nominative that is accessible to extraction.

(29)   (Guilfoyle et al. 1992)
        a. Sino ang   bumili   ng   damit para sa   bata?
           who   COMP ACT.bought   ACC dress for   DAT child

  b. *Sino ang binili   para sa bata' ang damit?
    who COMP DO.bought for   DAT child NOM dress
  c. *Sino ang ibinili   ng   damit ang bata'?
    who COMP BEN.bought ACC dress NOM child
    'who bought the dress for the child?'

(30) a. *Ano ang bumili   para sa bata ang tao?
    what COMP ACT.bought for   DAT child NOM man
  b. Ano ang binili   ng   tao para sa bata?
    what COMP DO.bought ERG man for   DAT child
  c. *Ano ang ibinili   ng   tao ang bata?
    what COMP BEN.bought ERG man NOM child
    'What was bought for the child by the man?'

(31) a. *Sino ang bumili   ng   damit ang tao?
    who COMP ACT.bought ACC dress NOM man
  b. *Sino ang binili   ng   tao ang damit?
    who COMP DO.bought ERG man NOM dress
  c. Sino ang ibinili   ng   tao ng damit?
    who COMP BEN.bought ERG man ACC dress
    'Who was bought the dress (for) by the man?'

The nominative is also the argument that undergoes Raising.

(32) (Kroeger 1993)
  a. Pinang- aakalaan si   Fidel [na
    IMPERF- think.IO NOM Fidel COMP

    makakagawa   ng   mabute].
    ACT.NONVOL.FUT.do ACC good
    'Fidel is thought to be able to do something good.'
  b. Malapit   na   si   Manuel [na hulihin
    STAT.close already NOM Manuel COMP catch.DO

    ng   polis].
    ERG police
    'Manuel is about to be arrested by the police.'

And, as shown by the translations of (18), the nominative is interpreted as definite.

  Inuit and Tagalog are thus mixed-subject languages, Inuit exemplifying the syntactically ergative subclass, and Tagalog the Philippine-type subclass. A survey of the literature on these types of languages reveals that the split in subject properties in mixed-subject languages is not random. Rather, it transpires that the set of subject properties can be universally divided into what we can call Type 1 properties and Type 2 properties.

(33)   a. <u>Type 1 subject properties (S/A)</u>
Agent argument in the active voice
Most likely covert/empty argument
The addressee of an imperative
Anaphoric prominence
Switch-reference systems
Controlled argument (PRO) (in some languages)
Discourse topic

        b. <u>Type 2 subject properties
(S/P in syntactically ergative languages; nominative in Philippine-type languages)</u>
Shared argument in coordinated clauses
Controlled argument (PRO) (in some languages)
Raising
Extraction properties
Obligatory element
"External" structural position
Definiteness or wide scope

In other words, the split in subject properties in mixed-subject languages is systematic. A theory of subjects thus needs to explain not only why subjects have the properties they do, but also why they split in this way in mixed-subject languages.

1.3   On explanation

1.3.1   *General considerations*

In order to develop an explanatory theory of subjects, first we need to determine what kind of entity a subject is. In the history of contemporary theoretical syntax, several approaches have been taken. In this section, we discuss the three primary views: subject as structural position, subject as grammatical relation, and subject as grammatical function.[8] We show that the last of these is the most promising approach in which to develop an explanatory theory of subjects.

1.3.2   *Subject as structural position*

What is probably the leading view of subjects in formalist syntax is the one which is standard in transformational theory. Under such an approach, what

---

8 Of course, the term "subject" has also been used outside of syntax, either as a semantic function or a discourse pragmatic function. While there are interesting relationships between subject in the syntactic sense and subject in these other senses, and we will discuss these, our primary interest is in subject as a syntactic notion.

distinguishes subjects from objects is their position in constituent structure. Objects, like other arguments of the verb, occupy a structural position in the verb's "domain": VP or V′, depending on the exact version of the theory. The subject, on the other hand, occupies a unique structural position outside of the verb's domain: under S, in specifier of IP, or in specifier of VP, depending on the precise implementation. Schematically:

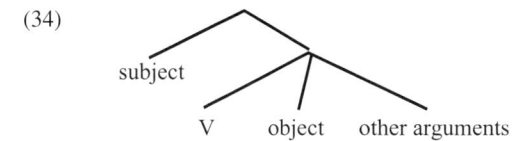

(34)
```
        /\
       /  \
  subject  /\
          /  \
         V  object  other arguments
```

It is by virtue of properties stipulated for this special structural position that subjects have their unique characteristics.

Consider, for example, the structural explanation of why only subjects can raise (Chomsky 1981, 2000).[9] Subjects, by virtue of their special structural position, have their Case assigned/checked by Infl/Tense (which is assumed to occupy a structural position as the head of an IP/TP which takes VP as its complement) rather than by the verb. Depending on the version of the theory, the Case-checking domain is defined either in terms of the structural relation of government (1981) or in terms of the SPEC–head relation (2000). The Infl/Tense element in a raising infinitive (*to* in English) is stipulated to be defective in some way, thus preventing it from assigning/checking the subject's Case. In the 1981 version of the theory, the same defectiveness was attributed to the superficially identical Infl of equi (control) infinitives, but in the 2000 version the Tense of an equi infinitive assigns/checks a special "null Case" which, by stipulation, can only be carried by PRO. The subject of the raising infinitive moves in order to have its Case checked (or to have Case assigned to it). Since other elements of the clause are not in the government/checking domain of Infl/Tense (but rather of the verb), their Cases are assigned/checked in raising clauses the same way as in other clause types. Thus, the subject moves out of its clause while other arguments do not.

Structural accounts of subjecthood are claimed to be explanatory (Marantz 1982) because they do not directly attribute properties to an entity called "subject." Instead, these allegedly independent structural properties result in the subject having certain characteristics. However, there is a circularity to this kind of argumentation. The special government properties of infinitival *to* (or

---

9 While many of the details differ, the approaches of Government/Binding theory (Chomsky 1981) and the Minimalist Program (Chomsky 2000) are fundamentally the same. The discussion here includes both: the analysis in terms of Infl and Case assignment is GB; Tense and Case checking are MP.

18 *Subjects and their properties*

their Minimalist equivalents), the null Case carried by PRO,[10] etc., are stipulated because they are needed to explain various facts about subjects; they have no independent justification. Since these structural properties are hypothesized in order to account for the facts, it cannot be said that they explain the facts.

Constituent-structure-based approaches to subjecthood are also often derivational, or multistratal. While it is not clear that this is a necessary property of such approaches, it does represent the major school of thought. As discussed by McCloskey (1997), a multistratal constituent-based approach treats subjects not in terms of a single structural position, but rather as a derivationally linked series of such positions. The machinery required to produce the movements of the subject-to-be tends to be rather arcane. We will return to this in Chapter 7.

Another problem, often downplayed (or perhaps misunderstood) by proponents of a structural approach (e.g., Baker 1997), is that the proposed structure is not appropriate for all languages. There are languages, often referred to as non-configurational languages, in which the subject and object appear to be sisters, and thus not distinguishable in terms of constituent-structure position. In fact, as discussed for Warlpiri by Simpson (1991) and Wambaya by Nordlinger (1998), there is evidence against the verb+object constituent in languages which put the auxiliary in second position, after a single arbitrary initial constituent. The putative VP in such languages does not count as a first constituent, casting doubts on its existence.[11] Nevertheless, such languages display subject properties just as much as configurational languages do.

Finally, it is not really true that structuralist accounts do not attribute any properties to an entity called "subject." The external position is such a property.

10 If anything, the situation is worse for the earlier account of PRO, under which it is simultaneously a pronoun and a reflexive ("anaphor"). PRO does not have any reflexive-like properties – in particular, it need not have a syntactic antecedent. Arbitrary PRO, which has no antecedent, is an obvious problem for any theory that claims a reflexive-like status for PRO. Even when not arbitrary, PRO can, under certain conditions, have discourse antecedents. This analysis, which was once trumpeted as the paradigm example of the explanatory power of GB theory, is completely arbitrary and stipulative.
11 Attempts have been made in the structurally oriented literature to discover indirect arguments for VP in non-configurational languages; one recent example is Legate (2001) on Warlpiri. Typically, these studies demonstrate that non-configurational languages have subject/non-subject asymmetries in some area of the grammar, such as anaphora, and then argue that such asymmetries require a VP node. However, this argumentation is circular: nobody denies the existence of subject/non-subject asymmetries – the disagreement is over how best to express them formally. Since the basic intuition behind constituent structure is that sentences are built out of hierarchically arranged "pieces" (constituents), what is missing is direct evidence for the VP as a "piece" of structure. While it is true that absence of evidence is not evidence of absence, the absence of such evidence in the literature – despite the theoretical importance of demonstrating that non-configurational languages have a VP – is, to my mind, significant.

Since structural theories of subjecthood define the subject by its external position (going so far as to call it an "external argument"), the external position is stipulated and not explained. Nor is it explained by claiming, as Chomsky (1995) does, that the Agent role is assigned not by the verb itself but by a light verb v which takes the main VP as its complement. This simply changes the domain in which the explanation is required. The same is true of theories based on the concept that the VP is a syntactic predicate which must take an argument (e.g. Williams 1984); the predicate status of the VP is a stipulated property which is itself in need of explanation.

Thus, despite its leading position in formalist work, we reject the notion of subject as a structural position. The rhetoric of explanation that often accompanies expositions of the structural approach is not matched by its actual achievements.

1.3.3 Subject as grammatical relation

An alternative view of subjecthood sees it as a grammatical relation: a relation which is relevant to the syntax (taking "grammatical" here to mean "syntactic"). This view is most clearly represented by Relational Grammar, in which it is further claimed that grammatical relations like subject are primitive concepts of syntactic theory. We will argue here that this approach is also not a promising one for explaining the properties of subjects.

What does it mean to say that "subject" is a "grammatical relation"? Taken literally, it means that it is some sort of relationship relevant to the syntax. There are many such relations. For example, c-command is a grammatical relation, a relation relevant to the syntax. Johnson and Postal (1980) consider linear precedence to be a grammatical relation on par with such relations as subject. It is unclear what is gained by calling subject a grammatical relation. That it is a grammatical relation is clear; the question revolves around the nature of the relation.

This vagueness of the concept "grammatical relation" does not reflect the actual use of the concept. In practice, grammatical relations are identified by their properties. Much argumentation in Relational Grammar consists of arguments for an analysis in terms of multistratal relational networks on the basis of splits in grammatical relation–related properties. In one such study, Perlmutter (1984) argues against monostratal accounts of passivization on the grounds that what are claimed to be properties of subjects sometimes appear as properties of elements which are not surface subjects. For example, in Russian the antecedent of a reflexive in a passive clause can be either the Patient (the "derived" or surface subject) or the Agent (the deep subject; passive chômeur in RG terminology).

(35) a. Rebenok$_i$ byl otpravlen k svoim$_i$ roditeljam.
         child.NOM was sent   to REFL.GEN parents
         'The child was sent to his (self's) parents.'
      b. Èta kniga   byla kuplena Borisom$_i$ dlja sebja$_i$.
         this book.NOM was bought   Boris.INSTR for REFL
         'This book was bought by Boris for himself.'

He argues on this basis that both the Agent and the Patient must be subjects (1s in RG terminology), and therefore a multistratal theory of subjecthood (and of passivization) is needed. A passive sentence such as (36a) is analyzed as having the sequence of grammatical relations represented by the stratal diagram (36b).

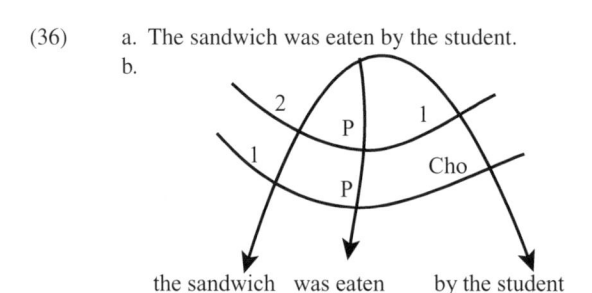

(36) a. The sandwich was eaten by the student.
      b.

[Stratal diagram showing arcs labeled 2, P, 1, Cho, 1, P pointing down to "the sandwich was eaten by the student"]

Nowhere does Perlmutter explain why the antecedent of a reflexive needs to be the subject; he simply assumes that this is a property which identifies subjects in Russian. Other properties of subjects (and other grammatical relations) are treated similarly. Since splits in properties are common, this kind of approach to notions like subject seems to lead invariably to multistratal analyses.

Treating grammatical relations as being essentially defined by their properties is not limited to Relational Grammar, but is in fact found widely. This is, for example, the approach of Role and Reference Grammar (RRG), as presented in Van Valin and LaPolla (1997). Van Valin and LaPolla identify grammatical relations with what they call "restricted neutralizations" of semantic and pragmatic relations. In their view, a grammatical relation can only be motivated for a particular language if there is some set of elements that cannot be defined in semantic or pragmatic terms which displays some property. They use this view of grammatical relations to argue that grammatical relations are not universal. Since, in their view, semantic and pragmatic relations are needed independently, grammatical relations are to be invoked only as a last resort. Grammatical relations like subject are thus no more than ad hoc clusterings of construction-based properties.

A different, but equally problematic, implementation of the grammatical relations approach is that of Palmer (1994). Palmer takes the position that, because properties differ in nominative-accusative languages and in ergative languages, the two types of languages use different sets of grammatical relations: subject and object in nominative-accusative languages and ergative and absolutive in ergative languages. While this may be useful for a preliminary description of the facts, it does not hold any possibility of explaining the cross-linguistic properties of subjects.

The inadequacy of the grammatical relations approach has been noted in the structural literature.[12] For example, Marantz (1982) notes that undefined grammatical relations cannot serve as a basis for explaining properties such as the subject properties discussed earlier in this chapter. At best, properties of this kind need to be stipulated as part of Universal Grammar. In a similar vein, Williams (1984) notes that, in the absence of some definitional characterization of what makes subjects different from other elements in the clause, the subject/non-subject distinction is no different from any other arbitrary distinction (such as indirect object/non-indirect object). Given that subjects display an impressive list of unique properties, the grammatical relations approach is flawed.

It should be clear that the notion of grammatical relation, under any implementation, is not a fruitful one for explaining the properties of subjects. If "subject" means "entity with some subset of subject properties," there can be no explanation why subjects have the properties they do. The problem is even worse than that faced by the structural approach. For the structural approach, the external position of the subject is a defining, and thus stipulated, property. For the grammatical relations approach, all properties are stipulated as defining the subject.

1.3.4 Subject as grammatical function

There is a third way to approach the nature of subjects, which we will refer to as the grammatical function approach. It is based on the idea that a syntactic structure is defined both in terms of the constituents of which it is composed

---

12 These studies usually confuse grammatical relations, as discussed here, with grammatical functions, to be discussed in the next section. They therefore incorrectly take their arguments to apply against the approach of Lexical-Functional Grammar, and to support a structural account.

and the function(s), or purpose(s), they serve in the structure. For example, the italicized element of the sentence in (37a) serves both of the functions listed in (37b); the names we will give these functions are listed in parentheses.

(37)   a. *What* did you put on the shelf?
       b. introducing a new element into the discourse (FOCUS)
          expressing the Theme argument of the verb *put* (OBJ)

At the level of constituent structure, *what* will be a DP in the specifier position of the matrix CP. However, the representation of the functionality of elements in the sentence, functional structure, will show that *what* has the two functions noted above:

(38) $$\begin{bmatrix} \begin{Bmatrix} \text{FOCUS} \\ \text{OBJ} \end{Bmatrix} & [\text{``what''}] \\ \text{TENSE} & \text{PAST} \\ \text{SUBJ} & [\text{``you''}] \\ \text{PRED} & \text{`put} \langle \text{SUBJ}, \text{OBJ}, \text{OBL}_{\text{Loc}} \rangle \text{'} \\ \text{OBL}_{\text{Loc}} & [\text{``on the shelf''}] \end{bmatrix}$$

Constituent structure and functional structure are parallel linguistic representations, related to each other by universally constrained language-specific rules of mapping. Other dimensions of language (pragmatic, thematic, phonological, morphological, and so on) will be represented by other types of representations, each with its own vocabulary, geometry, and primitives.

Although it is often supposed that "grammatical function" is synonymous with "grammatical relation," there is a significant difference between them. As we have seen, grammatical relations are, by their very nature, unexplanatory. Grammatical relations have no inherent properties, and therefore all of their properties are stipulated. Grammatical functions are something quite different: they are the purposes that grammatical elements serve. Properly understood, the functions that elements have are the basis for their properties. If we can properly identify the functions, the properties should follow.

Grammatical functions differ from grammatical relations also in that the former are necessarily monostratal. We have seen that one element can have more than one function; however, it is incoherent to say that two elements have the same function at different strata of representation. Consider the passive sentence in (36) again. Under the multistratal analysis, both *the sandwich* and *the student* are subjects. This may be an appropriate analysis under a property-driven grammatical relations approach, if it can be shown that properties that are typical of subjects in the language are shared by the two nominals. However, these two nominals clearly do not have the same function in the sentence: they express different arguments of the verb. If subjecthood is defined in functional terms, it is incoherent to speak of these two elements as both being subjects. They must have different functions. (Note, though, that it is possible, as in the case of adjuncts, for more than one entity to have a particular function, but simultaneously, not at different strata.) Where we find a split in properties, we need to determine why the properties split the way they do, not propose multiple strata of the same grammatical function and imagine that we have accounted for something.

This kind of approach to explanation in syntax requires us to break down the common arbitrary distinction between "formal" and "functional" approaches to the study of language. Like Jackendoff (1997, 2002), it rejects the syntactocentric approach to language typical of much formalist theorizing. It is based rather on the idea that formal and functional properties of language coexist. Language has formal structures which serve various functions. Among these functions, in addition to the familiar discourse-based functions, are grammatical functions, which are functions within the formal syntactic system. The formal and the functional are inextricably intertwined, and explanations of linguistic phenomena will often involve the formal properties of functions.

This kind of approach also requires us to adopt a parallel-architecture approach to syntax, as structure and function are distinct modular aspects of syntactic representation. As discussed extensively by Jackendoff (2002), parallel architecture holds numerous advantages over other potential theoretical architectures for language. One of the most important points for us is that parallel architecture, because it involves relations of correspondence between formally distinct dimensions, will necessarily involve imperfect correspondence and occasional mismatches between levels. (A similar point is made by Bresnan 2001.) The "soft" character of subject universals, noted in the citation from Andrews (1985) earlier in this chapter, will emerge as being largely the result of imperfect correspondence between levels.

Under the grammatical function approach we will pursue here, subject properties are not stipulations about the nature of subjects, as in the grammatical relations approach, nor a consequence of a series of interconnected stipulations about structural relations, as in the structural approach. Instead, subjects will be defined (or characterized) in terms of their function(s), and the properties will be derived from the function(s). Properties like anteceding reflexives and having an external structural position are not primitive properties under this view. They are observations in need of explanation, and the explanation will come from an understanding of the function(s) of subjects.

1.4 The formal framework

The subject-as-grammatical-function approach, and the consequent mixed formal-functional conceptualization of syntax, is most typical of the theoretical framework of Lexical-Functional Grammar (LFG), a theoretical framework originally developed by Joan Bresnan and Ron Kaplan in the late 1970s, and described in Bresnan (2001), Falk (2001), and Dalrymple (2001). The formal portions of the present study will therefore be couched in the notation and terminology of LFG. In this section, we will outline most of the aspects of the LFG formalism which will be relevant in this study. We will not relate to subjecthood-related issues here.

LFG is based on a parallel-architecture model of language, in which constituent structure and grammatical functions are represented as distinct dimensions of linguistic structure. The functional structure in (38) is a simplified version of the formal LFG representation of grammatical functions: the f-structure. F-structure is an "attribute-value matrix" (AVM), a table-like representation of "attributes" (grammatical functions and grammatical features) and their values.

(39) $\begin{bmatrix} \text{ATTRIBUTE 1} & \text{VALUE 1} \\ \text{ATTRIBUTE 2} & \text{VALUE 2} \\ \text{ATTRIBUTE 3} & \text{VALUE 3} \\ \text{ATTRIBUTE 4} & \text{VALUE 4} \\ \vdots & \vdots \end{bmatrix}$

As we have done in (38), where the internal structure of an f-structure element is unimportant, an orthographic representation of the element enclosed in double quotes can be used. This is the f-structure equivalent of a constituent structure triangle.

Unlike in structurally based theories, the structure–function mapping is taken to be defined by language-specific constraints (albeit constrained by universal principles; Bresnan 2001). It is these constraints which form the heart of the descriptive power of LFG. Consider the c-structure and f-structure of the sentence (40a).

(40) a. The baby will put a book on the shelf.
b.

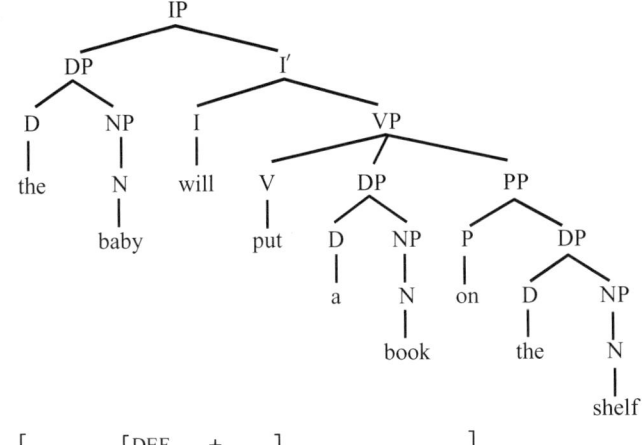

```
                    IP
                 /      \
               DP         I'
              /  \      /    \
             D   NP    I      VP
             |   |     |    /    \
            the  N    will V   /  |  \
                 |        |   DP  PP
               baby      put /  \  / \
                           D  NP P  DP
                           |  |  |  / \
                           a  N  on D  NP
                              |     |   |
                            book   the  N
                                       |
                                     shelf
```

c.
$$\begin{bmatrix}
\text{SUBJ} & \begin{bmatrix} \text{DEF} & + \\ \text{PRED} & \text{'baby'} \\ \text{NUM} & \text{SG} \end{bmatrix} \\
\text{TENSE} & \text{FUT} \\
\text{PRED} & \text{'put} \langle (\uparrow \text{SUBJ})(\uparrow \text{OBJ})(\uparrow \text{OBL}_{\text{Loc}}) \rangle \text{'} \\
\text{OBJ} & \begin{bmatrix} \text{DEF} & - \\ \text{PRED} & \text{'book'} \\ \text{NUM} & \text{SG} \end{bmatrix} \\
\text{OBL}_{\text{Loc}} & \begin{bmatrix} \text{PRED} & \text{'on} \langle (\uparrow \text{OBJ}) \rangle \text{'} \\ \text{OBJ} & \begin{bmatrix} \text{DEF} & + \\ \text{PRED} & \text{'shelf'} \\ \text{NUM} & \text{SG} \end{bmatrix} \end{bmatrix}
\end{bmatrix}$$

Elements of the c-structure and elements of the f-structure are in a relation of correspondence with each other. The correspondence function mapping from c-structure to f-structure is usually called ϕ, and the mapping relation from f-structure to c-structure is its inverse, ϕ^{-1}.

The DP *the baby* corresponds to a functional element which is the value of the attribute SUBJ, while the DP *a book* corresponds to a functional element which is the value of the attribute OBJ. Or, informally, *the baby* is the SUBJ and *a book* is the OBJ. This is because *the baby* is a daughter of the IP node and *a book* is a daughter of the VP node, and the grammar of English associates each of these structural positions with a particular grammatical function. Similarly, the PP under VP is associated with an oblique argument function. Unlike constituent-structure-based theories, these associations of structural positions with grammatical functions are not assumed to be universal; this allows for languages with different associations between structure and function, as in non-configurational languages.

The grammar of English therefore must include constraints of the following nature:[13]

(41) a. An IP node may dominate a DP, which functions as the value of the attribute SUBJ in the f-structure of the IP, and/or a head I'.
b. A VP node may dominate any or all of: a head V, a DP which functions as the value of the attribute OBJ in the f-structure of the VP, a PP which functions as the value of the attribute OBL in the f-structure of the VP,[14] etc.

The formal expression of constraints licensing c-structure configurations has traditionally been the phrase structure rule. In LFG, this is enriched by adding functional annotations to the elements on the right-hand side of the phrase structure rule. These annotations use the symbols $\uparrow$, indicating the f-structure corresponding to the mother node, and $\downarrow$, indicating the f-structure corresponding to the daughter node.[15] For example, the DP daughter of IP will be annotated with the functional constraint (42a), which means (42b) or, more precisely, (42c).

(42) a. $(\uparrow \text{SUBJ}) = \downarrow$
b. The f-structure corresponding to the mother node (IP) includes the attribute SUBJ. The value of this attribute is the f-structure corresponding to the daughter node (DP).
c. The f-structure corresponding to the mother node (IP) includes the attribute SUBJ. There is also an f-structure corresponding to the daughter node (DP). Traversing a path through the f-structure from the f-structure corresponding to the mother node through the attribute SUBJ leads to the same f-structure element as (i.e. is equal to) the f-structure corresponding to the daughter node.

---

13 All c-structure positions are optional, including structural heads. Missing heads in LFG correspond roughly to empty heads in transformational theory.
14 Oblique arguments are more complicated than suggested by this characterization, since the exact oblique function (goal, benefactive, locative, etc.) is determined by the preposition. This is irrelevant for the present study. The full formal expression can be found in the standard LFG references mentioned at the beginning of this section.
15 The symbols $\uparrow$ and $\downarrow$ are technically defined in terms of the ϕ mapping function: if the current node of the tree is represented by *, and each of the surrounding nodes is represented by an arrowhead pointing in the appropriate direction of the tree (i.e. the mother node is $\hat{*}$, the left sister is $<*$, and the right sister is $*>$), $\downarrow$ is $\phi(*)$ and $\uparrow$ is $\phi(\hat{*})$. For more on the technical details of the formalism, see Dalrymple (2001).

Similarly, a head, like I′, is annotated (43), which expresses part of what is meant by "head."

(43)   a. ↑ = ↓
        b. The f-structure corresponding to the mother node (IP) is identical (equal) to the f-structure corresponding to the daughter node (I′).

The full formal version of (41) is thus (44):

(44)   a. IP →   DP   I′
                    (↑ SUBJ) =↓   ↑ = ↓
        b. VP → V   DP   PP   . . .
                ↑=↓ (↑ OBJ)=↓ (↑ OBL)=↓

As shown in (42c), the parenthesized expressions formally express paths through the f-structure. We will return to this in Chapters 3 and 4.

Functional constraints also appear in lexical entries. For example, the lexical entry of the word *baby* includes the following constraints:

(45)   (↑ PRED) = 'baby'
          (↑ NUM) = SG

The PRED feature is a representation of the meaningfulness of syntactic elements, which is one aspect of their functionality. For most lexical items, the value of this feature is an atomic expression, conventionally represented as the word in single quotes. Pronouns have a special value for the PRED feature, 'PRO.' In the case of argument-taking predicates, the value of the PRED feature includes a specification of the arguments selected. The lexical entries of forms of the verb *put*, for example, include:

(46)   (↑ PRED) = 'put ⟨(↑ SUBJ)(↑ OBJ)(↑ OBL$_{Loc}$)⟩'

The list of selected arguments is a projection of the verb's argument structure; we will discuss some aspects of LFG's theory of argument structure in Chapter 2. The ↑ in the specification of each argument function is a formal indication that the arguments must be local: the OBJ of *put* must be in *put*'s local f-structure, while the OBJ of *on* must be in *on*'s local f-structure. In general, each of the argument functions specified in the value of the PRED feature must be present in the local f-structure. The principle that specifies this is called the Completeness Condition. Conversely, the principle that disallows other (unlicensed) argument functions from appearing is called the Coherence Condition. Taken together, the Completeness and Coherence Conditions enforce the selectional

28 *Subjects and their properties*

properties of the predicate, and correspond approximately to the Θ Criterion of Government/Binding theory.

In addition to argument functions, LFG hypothesizes adjunct functions (primarily ADJ) and grammaticized discourse functions (such as FOCUS and TOPIC).[16] These elements are not selected, but must still be licensed as specified in an extension of the Coherence Condition. The Extended Coherence Condition requires adjuncts to modify meaningful elements. For the grammaticized discourse functions, the Extended Coherence Condition specifies that any item bearing one of those functions must also bear an argument or adjunct function. For example, in our example (38) the same item that bears the FOCUS function also bears the argument OBJ function. An element that bears only the FOCUS function is ruled out by the Extended Coherence Condition.

The f-structure in (38) is more standardly drawn as follows:

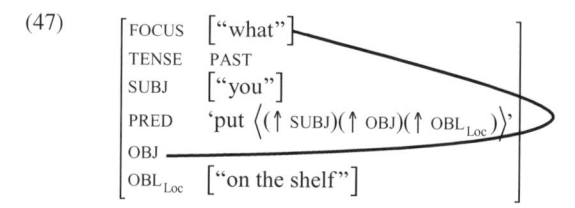

(47) $\begin{bmatrix} \text{FOCUS} & [\text{"what"}] \\ \text{TENSE} & \text{PAST} \\ \text{SUBJ} & [\text{"you"}] \\ \text{PRED} & \text{'put} \langle (\uparrow \text{SUBJ})(\uparrow \text{OBJ})(\uparrow \text{OBL}_{Loc}) \rangle\text{'} \\ \text{OBJ} & \\ \text{OBL}_{Loc} & [\text{"on the shelf"}] \end{bmatrix}$

Here, a curved line is used to show that one element has two different functions (or, more formally, is the value of two different attributes). It is more useful than the bracket we used informally earlier, as it can be used when the two functions are in two different clauses.

Formalism in linguistics provides a way to express descriptive generalizations precisely. In addition, if the formalism is well designed, properties of the formalism can themselves turn out to be part of the explanation of linguistic phenomena.

1.5   A look ahead

This book can be seen as a case study of the concept of grammatical functions, as well as an attempt to understand subjects. The analysis to be proposed here builds on ideas which have their origin in the work of Schachter (1976), Dixon

---

16 The grammaticized discourse functions should not be confused with an actual representation of such properties as topicality and focushood at the level of information structure. The grammaticized discourse functions are present only when topicality and focushood are expressed syntactically, and they are related to information structure concepts such as new information, givenness, and the like through mapping principles.

(1994), and others. We will propose that subjects in familiar uniform-subject languages have two distinct functions: the expression of the most prominent argument of the verb ($\widehat{\text{GF}}$) and the singling out of a particular clausal actant to be the element of cross-clausal continuity (PIV, or pivot). These two functions, both of which are syntactic functions represented at f-structure, will be discussed in Chapters 2 and 3. These functions are dissociated in mixed-subject languages, resulting in the (predictable) split of properties that these languages display.

Chapters 4 and 5 will focus on two families of subject-sensitive constructions: long distance dependencies and control constructions, respectively. We will show how the proposed theory of subjecthood, combined with aspects of the LFG formalism, explains the properties of these constructions. Chapter 6 will then turn to the non-subject languages, and discuss the presence of each of these two grammatical functions in such languages.

The theory of subjects proposed here differs in important respects from the previous LFG analysis of subjects – that of Manning (1996). In Manning's theory, there is one grammatical function, called either SUBJ or PIVOT. This function is characterized as an argument function, unlike the characterization of the PIV function in the present study. Manning has no direct analog of the $\widehat{\text{GF}}$ function to be proposed here, considering our $\widehat{\text{GF}}$-related properties to be based on argument structure. The theory proposed here also contrasts with functionalist and typological characterizations of the pivot function (e.g. Dixon 1994, Van Valin and LaPolla 1997), in that we view pivothood as a language-wide function rather than construction-specific. We will contrast our account with Manning's and functionalist-typological approaches throughout the book, and especially in Chapter 7. Chapter 7 will also discuss structurally based theories; it will argue that, despite the conceptual elements shared by all these theories, the implementation proposed here is superior.

2 Most prominent argument

2.1 Argumenthood

The subject is generally considered to be an argument. This is true in GB/MP, where the subject is characterized as the "external argument." It is also true in RG, where the relation 1 (subject) is a Term Relation, and LFG, where SUBJ is an argument function. In this chapter, we will examine the notion of subject as argument function. We will determine exactly what is meant by that concept, and we will see what properties follow as a result of characterizing the subject in those terms. We will also contrast the approach taken here with that of such works as Manning (1996).

2.1.1 First approximation
It is well established that (at least in the uniform-subject languages) there is a standard mapping from thematic roles to grammatical functions. A canonical transitive verb takes two arguments, one of which performs an action which affects the other. Semantically, following current terminology, these can be characterized as Agent and Patient. (We will say more about this in section 2.1.2.) These two semantic arguments are uniformly mapped into syntactic (grammatical) argument functions. Traditionally, the function that expresses Agents is called "subject" (SUBJ) and the one that expresses Patients is called "object" (OBJ). In many languages, there can be additional Patient-like arguments realized as "secondary objects" or "restricted objects" (OBJ2 or OBJ_θ). Finally, additional nominal arguments are marked (generally by prepositions or Case) to indicate the thematic role explicitly; these are called obliques (OBL_θ). With the exception of the division of labor between OBJ and OBJ2 (discussed in Dryer 1986), the syntactic realizations of semantic arguments of canonical transitive verbs is the same in all uniform-subject languages.

(1)   a. **English**
          The teacher (Agent/SUBJ) put the book (Patient/OBJ) on the shelf (Location/OBL).

b. **Hebrew**
Ha- more sam et ha- sefer al ha- madaf.
the- teacher put ACC the- book on the- shelf
Agent/SUBJ   Patient/OBJ   Location/OBL
'The teacher put the book on the shelf.'

c. **Latin** (Palmer 1994)
Puer   hominem planxit.
boy.NOM   man.ACC hit
Agent/SUBJ   Patient/OBJ
'The boy hit the man.'

Given the foregoing, we can propose our first, provisional characterization of the function of SUBJ.

(2)   The SUBJ is the element with the function of expressing the Agent argument.

Appealing though it may appear, this characterization is problematic both conceptually and empirically. It is conceptually problematic because it stipulates an arbitrary relation between a specific thematic role and a specific grammatical function. Stipulation of this kind is inherently unexplanatory: the goal should be to explain the relationship between Agenthood and subjecthood, not to stipulate it. To put it slightly differently, this stipulation of a relationship between a specific thematic role and a specific grammatical function is simply a restatement of the problem. Empirically, this characterization is too simple for most languages. Some languages allow Agents to appear as what has been argued to be object in the existential construction. Note the following example from Norwegian; it is argued by Lødrup (2000) that the Agent has the grammatical function of OBJ.

(3)   Det lekte   noen barn   i   gresset.
       it play.PST some children in grass.DEF
       'Some kids played in the grass.'
       (Literally: 'There played some kids in the grass.')

More crucially, in most languages the sole argument of an intransitive is expressed syntactically as SUBJ, regardless of its thematic role. For example, in English, where subjects have an unmarked preverbal position, take nominative Case forms, undergo Raising, and so forth, the sole argument of an intransitive verb invariably displays these properties regardless of its thematic role. This is illustrated here with position and Case. (The intended reading in [4c,d] is an inchoative reading of *broke*, meaning "They [e.g., the dishes] broke," and this is the reading under which the marking as ungrammatical holds.)

(4) a. I (*Me) broke them (*they).
    b. They (*Them) sneezed.
    c. They (*Them) broke.
    d. *(It/There/ ∅) Broke them.

In derivational and multistratal theories, such facts can be brought into line with our characterization of the SUBJ function by limiting it to the underlying representation or initial stratum. Intransitive verbs whose sole argument is non-agentive can be analyzed as involving the initial assignment of the argument to the function OBJ with a subsequent advancement to SUBJ. This analysis has its origins in the RG analysis of Perlmutter (1978), and has been adopted in GB/MP as a result of the work of Burzio (1986).[1]

(5) a.

b.

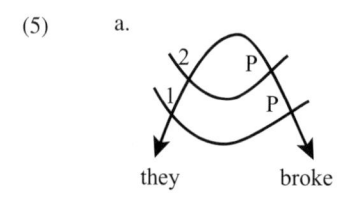

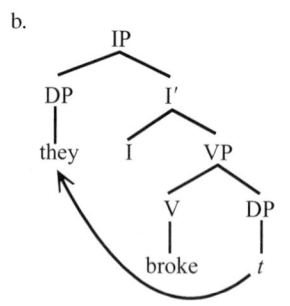

Our approach to grammatical functions is non-derivational and monostratal, and therefore does not allow such an analysis. We must therefore take a closer look at the nature of argumenthood and argument mapping, a question which has been addressed much in the literature.

2.1.2 Argument structure and hierarchies

Argumenthood lies at the interface between syntax and lexical semantics. In the usual situation, a verb (or other argument-taking predicate) selects elements

---

[1] This analysis is motivated on the basis of "object" properties that nonagentive ("unaccusative") subjects display. For discussion of the interplay between syntax and semantics, see Levin and Rappaport Hovav (1995).

syntactically based on open positions in its conceptual (or lexical semantic) representation. For example, the verb *put* selects three syntactic arguments (SUBJ, OBJ, and OBL$_{Loc}$) because its conceptual representation includes open positions for Agent, Patient/Theme, and Location. As noted above, the mapping of arguments from semantics to syntax is usually predictable from the (semantic) thematic roles: Agents typically map to SUBJ and Patients to OBJ. Since the aspect of semantic/conceptual structure that is relevant to argumenthood is thematic roles, we will refer to the semantic representation informally as thematic structure, and represent it as a list of thematic roles.

Thematic structure, in the informal approach we are adopting here, can be thought of as a list of relatively coarse-grained labels generalizing over ways in which actants can participate in an event. While such labels alone cannot account for the variety of verb meanings, it is generally accepted that these coarse-grained thematic roles are what is relevant for the syntax. In taking this kind of approach, we are abstracting away from specific theories of lexical semantic/conceptual representation, which are irrelevant to the issues here. The coarse-grained approach to thematic roles is compatible with approaches as varied as those of Jackendoff (1990), Dowty (1991), and Palmer (1994).

It is generally accepted in the literature that there is a natural hierarchy in the conceptualization of events, represented generally as a hierarchy of thematic roles (originally proposed by Jackendoff 1972). A typical transitive event includes a doer (Agent) and an undergoer (Patient, Beneficiary, or Recipient). The Agent outranks the element with an undergoer role (henceforth Patient) because it is the Agent's act that results in the Patient's affectedness. Other semantic argument types are hierarchically lower.[2] This "thematic hierarchy" is not a primitive of the linguistic system, but rather a consequence of the semantic/conceptual nature of thematic representation. As observed by Rappaport Hovav and Levin (2003), different proposals for thematic hierarchies have differed from each other because they encode different things; once one realizes that a thematic hierarchy is a derivative description rather than an actual part of language, many of the apparent conflicts between proposed thematic

---

2 This follows the thematic hierarchy as discussed in Jackendoff (1990: 258). The description of the thematic hierarchy in Bresnan (2001) places Beneficiary and Recipient right under Agent, as described here, but Patient considerably farther down. This is very typical of descriptions of the thematic hierarchy. The reason is that these descriptions consider Patient (affected entity) and Theme (entity in motion) to be the same. However, as discussed in detail by Jackendoff (1987), Patient and Theme are distinct thematic roles. The Theme role is lower on the hierarchy, but Patient belongs high, along with the other undergoer roles. Also, as noted by Jackendoff (1990), descriptions of the thematic hierarchy which place Goal above Theme base this on the properties of possessional Goals, which are also Beneficiaries.

hierarchies vanish. For example, the thematic hierarchy that we are assuming here is reflected in the formalism for conceptual representations in theories like that of Jackendoff (1990). In Jackendoff's theory, conceptual representation consists of two tiers: the action tier, which represents Actor–Patient relations, and the thematic tier, which represents the abstract spatial aspects. Jackendoff's description of the thematic hierarchy is:

(6) Order the A-marked[3] arguments in the action tier from left to right, followed by the A-marked arguments in the main conceptual clause of the thematic tier, from least embedded to most deeply embedded.

In informal representations such as we are using here, the thematic hierarchy is reflected in the linear order of the thematic roles:

(7) *put*: Agent, Patient/Theme, Location

However, our interest here is in syntactic selection, or syntactic argumenthood, not thematic structure. While there is a relation between them, syntactic argumenthood cannot be identified with thematic argumenthood. Sometimes the mapping of arguments is not predictable from the semantics. Note the following contrast:

(8) a. The dinosaur went into the room.
 b. The dinosaur entered the room.
 c. **Hebrew**
    Ha- dinozaur nixnas l- a-   xeder.
    the- dinosaur enter.PST to- the- room
    'The dinosaur entered the room.'

In all three sentences, *the room* is the Goal of the action, but with the English verb *enter* (but not the synonymous Hebrew verb *nixnas*), this argument is realized idiosyncratically as OBJ. This is a syntactic fact, not a semantic/thematic one. Another difference between thematic and syntactic argumenthood is a consequence of the fact that verbs sometimes select arguments which are not part of the semantics: expletives (such as the SUBJ in the Norwegian sentence [3] above and in the English [9a]) and idiom chunks (such as the OBJ in the English [9b]).

(9) a. <u>It</u> seems that the dinosaur ate the students.
 b. We kept <u>tabs</u> on the dinosaur.

---

3 A-marking in Jackendoff's system is a diacritic in lexical conceptual structure indicating the syntactically realized arguments.

For these reasons, many theories (including LFG) posit a syntactic level of argument structure (or a-structure) in addition to the thematic level. The (semantic) thematic structure includes information about the thematic roles of the open arguments in the verb's semantics, while the (syntactic) a-structure includes all elements selected syntactically, including expletives and idiom chunks, and constrains their mapping to the syntax.

A-structure must therefore project the syntactically relevant aspects of thematic structure, while simultaneously giving expression to the purely syntactic aspects of argumenthood. The thematic structure is reflected primarily in the hierarchical ranking of the arguments: the thematic arguments are ranked in accordance with the conceptually based hierarchy of thematic roles, a ranking which is conventionally represented by the linear ordering of elements in the a-structure. Following standard terminology in LFG, we will refer to the highest ranked argument (represented graphically as the leftmost argument in the a-structure) as $\hat{\theta}$. At the same time, a-structure will include elements which are selected syntactically but not semantically, and will constrain the mapping of the arguments.

Expressing arguments of predicates is one of the functions that syntactic elements serve. For this reason, the framework within which we are working formalizes argument selection in terms of grammatical functions, not structural position. There is a clear distinction between two classes of argument-expressing grammatical functions: SUBJ and OBJ on the one hand, and the OBL_θ (in English, preposition-marked) functions on the other. The latter are little more than grammaticalizations of thematic roles, while the former are more strictly syntactic in nature. Following the terminology of Bresnan (2001), we will refer to the more syntactic grammatical functions as core functions, and the oblique functions as non-core functions.[4] Standardly, Agents, Patients, and Themes are mapped to core functions and other thematic roles to non-core functions, but (as illustrated above with *enter*) exceptions are possible. A-structure must therefore include the syntactic information of whether arguments are core or non-core.[5] For the purposes of this book, arguments are core unless otherwise specified.

---

4 Secondary objects (OBJ_θ) seem to be transitional between core and non-core. This is reflected in the LFG analysis (Bresnan 2001, Falk 2001) by treating the secondary object function as a core function but characterizing it as being thematically restricted like the oblique functions.
5 This is not to say that this is the only information in a-structure that constrains the mapping of arguments to syntax. The standard LFG theory of a-structure, Lexical Mapping Theory (LMT), is more fine-grained than this. However, this will suffice for our purposes.

(10)   a. *put*:   ⟨x, y, z_{non-core}⟩
       b. *enter*:   ⟨x, y⟩
       c. *nixnas* (Hebrew 'enter'):   ⟨x, y_{non-core}⟩

In each of these a-structures, the leftmost argument (arbitrarily designated x here) is the $\hat{\theta}$.

As noted above, non-thematic arguments, elements which are not part of the thematic structure, are represented in the a-structure. Their presence is either the result of the existence of an idiom or, in the case of expletives, licensed by lexical rules. A lexical rule will specify what position in the hierarchical arrangement of arguments an expletive occupies; they are very frequently introduced as $\hat{\theta}$. For example, the a-structure of the verb in the Norwegian existential (3) is:

(11)   *leke*: ⟨det, x⟩

Here, it is the expletive *det* which is the $\hat{\theta}$. Since a-structure includes such non-thematic arguments, the a-structure hierarchy is not strictly speaking identical with the thematic hierarchy, although it is derived from it. Despite this, we will retain the familiar term "thematic hierarchy" here. Similar remarks apply to the notation $\hat{\theta}$.

It has often been noted that grammatical functions representing arguments are related to each other in a hierarchy, a hierarchy which has been referred to variously as the accessibility hierarchy (Keenan and Comrie 1977), the obliqueness hierarchy (Pollard and Sag 1994), the functional hierarchy (Dalrymple 2001), and the relational hierarchy (Perlmutter 1983, Bresnan 2001).

(12)   SUBJ > OBJ > OBJ$_\theta$ > OBL$_\theta$

Unlike the thematic hierarchy, the relational hierarchy seems to be an arbitrary fact about syntax; presumably part of the characterization of the argument functions. The relational hierarchy is based partially on classes of grammatical functions: the core functions SUBJ and OBJ (and OBJ$_\theta$) outrank the non-core functions. However, even within these larger groupings the functions are ranked. In particular, SUBJ outranks OBJ. We can think of the function names SUBJ and OBJ as nothing more than shorthand for "first core argument on the relational hierarchy" and "second core argument on the relational hierarchy."

2.1.3   Most prominent argument

Given the thematic hierarchy and the relational hierarchy, we can characterize the nature of argument realization in syntax. In the unmarked case (for example, actives as opposed to passives), the hierarchical relations between the arguments at the functional level match the hierarchical relations at the argument level. If we treat the mapping of arguments as a hierarchy-to-hierarchy mapping (as in, inter alia, Jackendoff 1990), we can derive the correct mappings.

(13)   Argument mapping (informal)
       The highest available argument maps to the highest available grammatical function, the next argument to the next grammatical function, and so on, respecting the constraints on mapping which are expressed in the a-structure.

Limiting our attention to core arguments, we derive mappings such as the following:

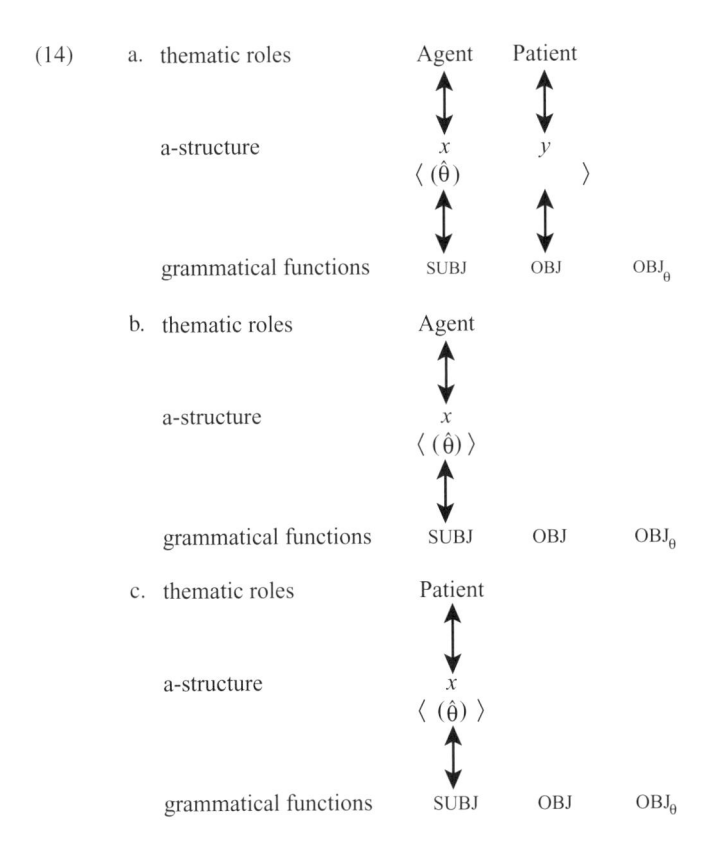

(14)   a. thematic roles   Agent   Patient

           a-structure x y
                                   $\langle\,(\hat{\theta})\quad\quad\quad\rangle$

           grammatical functions   SUBJ   OBJ OBJ_θ

       b. thematic roles   Agent

           a-structure x
                                   $\langle\,(\hat{\theta})\,\rangle$

           grammatical functions   SUBJ   OBJ OBJ_θ

       c. thematic roles   Patient

           a-structure x
                                   $\langle\,(\hat{\theta})\,\rangle$

           grammatical functions   SUBJ   OBJ OBJ_θ

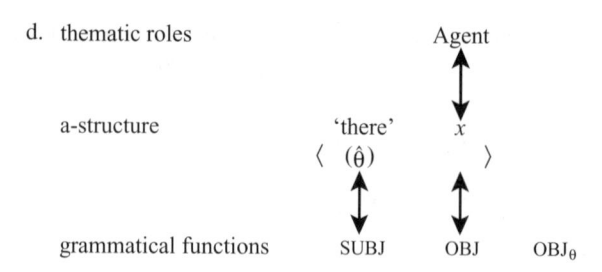

d. thematic roles   Agent
                                              ↕
a-structure   'there'   x
                              ⟨   (θ̂)   ⟩
                                   ↕   ↕
grammatical functions   SUBJ   OBJ   OBJ_θ

A hierarchy-to-hierarchy mapping of this kind is more principled than a one-to-one mapping of thematic roles and grammatical functions. As noted above, a one-to-one mapping of thematic roles and grammatical functions is unexplanatory: it simply stipulates an arbitrary relationship between a particular thematic role and a particular syntactic expression. On the other hand, research on linguistic hierarchies (particularly in Optimality Theory) shows that hierarchies align "harmonically" (Aissen 1999): different linguistic dimensions often reflect each other's hierarchical prominences. From a communicative perspective, this is a very useful design feature of language. The hierarchy-to-hierarchy mapping between thematic roles and grammatical functions is an example of harmonic alignment, and thus a principled and explanatory theory of argument mapping.

Given this hierarchy-to-hierarchy view of argument mapping, we can now improve our characterization of the argumenthood status of the subject.

(15)   The SUBJ is the element with the function of expressing the hierarchically most prominent core argument.

Unlike our first approximation, this correctly expresses the fact that SUBJ is not inherently linked to a particular thematic role. It does not stipulate an arbitrary relation between the syntactic concept of subjecthood and the thematic concept of agenthood. Instead, it explains the affinity between subjects and Agents: since Agent is (conceptually) the highest role on the thematic hierarchy and SUBJ is (by definition) the highest function on the relational hierarchy, a hierarchy-to-hierarchy mapping could do nothing other than map Agent to SUBJ in the case of a verb which takes an Agent argument and does not have a higher-ranked expletive argument.

Since, as we will show in the next chapter, the traditional notion of subject involves a second function, we will not use the name "SUBJ" for the most prominent argument function. Instead, we will extend the LFG notation and use the name "$\widehat{GF}$" for the relationally most prominent argument function, the traditional SUBJ. We therefore update our definition:

(16)   The $\widehat{GF}$ is the element with the function of expressing as a core argument the hierarchically most prominent argument.

2.1.4 Mismatches between argument structure and grammatical functions

The approach to argument mapping taken here posits two different argument-related hierarchies: the argument hierarchy at a-structure (the thematic hierarchy, in the sense that we are using the term here) and the hierarchy of grammatical functions at f-structure (the relational hierarchy). There are thus two ways in which an argument can be more prominent than other arguments: it can be the most prominent on the thematic hierarchy, the $\hat{\theta}$; or the most prominent on the relational hierarchy, the $\widehat{GF}$. Since argument expression in the syntax is the result of a hierarchy-to-hierarchy alignment, this leads one to expect that, under normal circumstances, the same argument will function as both $\hat{\theta}$ and $\widehat{GF}$. On the other hand, since parallel architecture leaves open the possibility of mismatches between levels, one might expect that situations would arise in which these two concepts of most prominent argument do not coincide. Furthermore, since rules of grammar can be expected to be able to refer to either the argument level or the functional level (or both), both of these types of prominence should be reflected in linguistic data. Constructions in which there is a mismatch in the two types of prominence would then be valuable in distinguishing $\hat{\theta}$ properties and $\widehat{GF}$ properties.

Mismatches of this kind do occur, and the ability to account for them is one of the strengths of a parallel-architecture theory. Theories which assume a non-parallel-architecture account for constructions in which such mismatches occur in a variety of ways. Typically, they consider both $\hat{\theta}$ properties and $\widehat{GF}$ properties to be "subject properties," and allow clauses to have multiple subjects, either through a derivational or multistratal architecture in which different elements are subjects at different strata, or through a process of clause union or incorporation under which a superficial clause is analyzed as biclausal (and thus containing two subjects, one for each clause).

The simplest, and most common, situation in which such a mismatch arises is when the $\hat{\theta}$ is not mapped to the syntax: the passive construction. This is exemplified in the following examples (drawn from Perlmutter and Postal 1983).

(17) a. **English**
That book (ĜF) was reviewed by Louise (θ̂).

b. **Turkish**
Bavul   Hasan   tarafından   aç-   ıl-   dı.
suitcase Hasan   by   open-   PASS-   PST
ĜF   θ̂
'The suitcase was opened by Hasan.'

c. **Latin**
Puerī   ā   magistr-   ō   laud-   antur.
boys.NOM   by   teacher-   ABL   praise-   PASS.3PL
ĜF   θ̂
'The boys are praised by the teacher.'

In multistratal frameworks this construction is analyzed as involving different subjects at different strata (Chomsky 1965, Perlmutter and Postal 1983). The standard lexically based analysis of passivization (Chomsky 1981, Bresnan 2001), which we will adopt here, is that the passive represents an alternative mapping of arguments to the syntax. In passivization, the θ̂ argument is suppressed: marked as not mapped to a grammatical function. If expressed at all, it is expressed as an adjunct (*by* phrase).[6]

(18) a. Active argument mapping

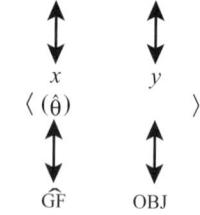

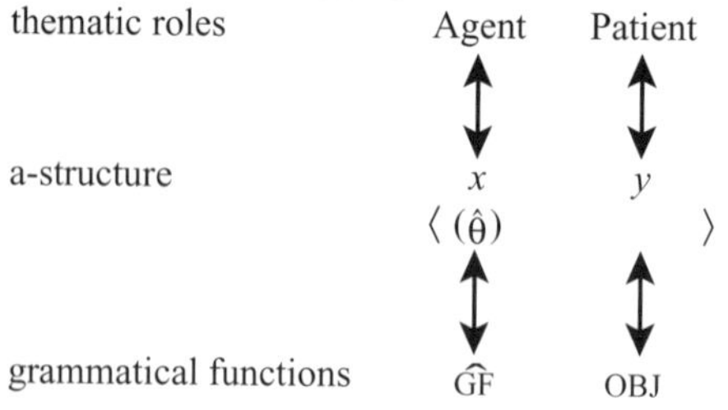

thematic roles   Agent   Patient
                         ↕   ↕
a-structure   x   y
                      ⟨ (θ̂)   ⟩
                         ↕   ↕
grammatical functions   ĜF   OBJ

b. Passive argument mapping

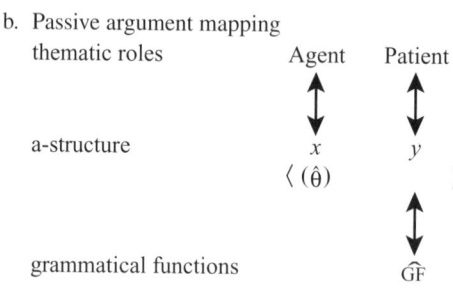

thematic roles   Agent   Patient
                         ↕   ↕
a-structure   x   y
                      ⟨ (θ̂)   ⟩
                                     ↕
grammatical functions   ĜF

---

6 An alternative analysis of the *by* phrase is that it is an oblique argument, as argued for Balinese by Arka (1998). This does not really change much in terms of the discussion here – there is still a mismatch between θ̂ and ĜF.

Thus in passive clauses argumenthood rank differs from functional rank, and θ̂ and ĜF are two distinct elements. Phenomena sensitive to argumenthood rank (the thematic hierarchy) will pick out the Agent as the most prominent argument, while those sensitive to functional rank (the relational hierarchy) will pick out the Patient.

Another type of construction in which θ̂ and ĜF can be distinguished is one in which two argument-taking predicates combine to form a single complex syntactic predicate. A very common complex predicate construction is the causative, discussed in LFG by Alsina (1992). In a causative, a single functional clause corresponds to two argument structures, one embedded in the other. Each argument structure has its own θ̂, but since there is only one array of grammatical functions expressing the arguments, only the outer θ̂ is mapped to ĜF. For example, the Chicheŵa sentences in (19) have the causative verb 'cause-cook'.

(19) a. Nǔngu   i-   na-   phík-   íts-   a
        (IX)porcupine IX.SUBJ-   PST-   cook-   CAUS-   VWL
        maûngu   kwá   kádzīdzi.
        (VI)pumpkins to   (Ia)owl
        'The porcupine had the pumpkins cooked by the owl.'

    b. Nǔngu   i-   na-   phík-   íts-   a   kadzidzi
        (IX)porcupine IX.SUBJ-   PST-   cook-   CAUS-   VWL   (Ia)owl
        maûngu
        (VI)pumpkins
        'The porcupine had the owl cook the pumpkins.'

Under Alsina's analysis, the basic a-structure of this verb is:

(20)   ⟨Agent$_{CAUS}$, Patient$_{CAUS}$ ⟨Agent$_{cook}$, Patient$_{cook}$⟩⟩

The causee argument (Patient of causation) is identified with one of the arguments of the base verb, reflecting whether the causation is exerted on the Agent or Patient of the subordinate predicate. Alsina and Joshi (1991) show that languages differ on which of these identifications is possible, some allowing only one, others allowing both, and still others allowing different identifications for different classes of verbs. Chicheŵa allows both identifications, and the result is the two mappings of arguments realized in the sentences in (19).

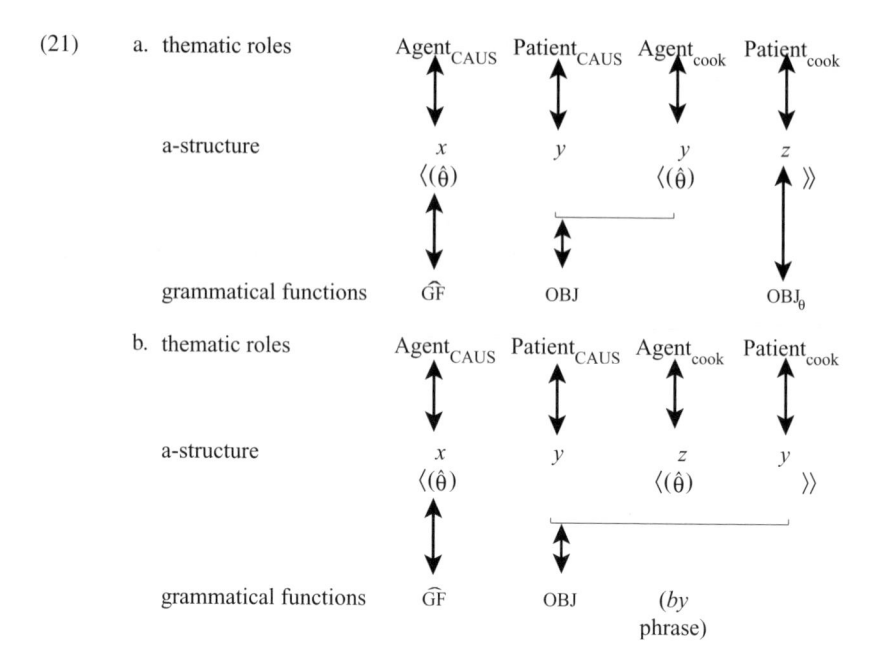

(21) a. thematic roles   Agent$_{CAUS}$ Patient$_{CAUS}$ Agent$_{cook}$ Patient$_{cook}$
           ↕   ↕   ↕   ↕
    a-structure x y y z
                      $\langle(\hat{\theta})$ $\langle(\hat{\theta})$ $\rangle\rangle$
                        ↕   ↕
    grammatical functions $\widehat{GF}$ OBJ   OBJ$_\theta$

b. thematic roles   Agent$_{CAUS}$ Patient$_{CAUS}$ Agent$_{cook}$ Patient$_{cook}$
           ↕   ↕   ↕   ↕
    a-structure x y z y
                      $\langle(\hat{\theta})$ $\langle(\hat{\theta})$ $\rangle\rangle$
                        ↕   ↕
    grammatical functions $\widehat{GF}$ OBJ   (by phrase)

Complex predicates thus have more than one $\hat{\theta}$ ('porcupine' and 'owl' in (19)), but only one $\widehat{GF}$ ('porcupine'). Other types of complex predicate constructions can also be found. For example, Manning (1996) discusses "double transitive affixes" in Inuit, where affixes meaning 'say', 'think', 'want', 'intend', and so on, can be added to the verb and add a layer of a-structure.

(22) a. Aani-   p   miiqqat   Juuna-   mut
         Aani- ERG   children   Juuna-   DAT

         $\hat{\theta}_{think}$ $\hat{\theta}_{understand}$
         $\widehat{GF}$

         paasi-   sur(i- v)-   a-   i.
         understand-   think- IND- TR-   3SG.3PL
         'Aani thinks that Juuna understands the children.'

      b. Aani-   p   miiqqat   qasu-   nirar- p-   a-   i.
         Aani- ERG children be.tired-   say-   IND- TR-   3SG.3PL

         $\hat{\theta}_{say}$ $\hat{\theta}_{be.tired}$
         $\widehat{GF}$
         'Aani said that the children were tired.'

Other frameworks often analyze complex predicate constructions as involving biclausal structure, in which each $\hat{\theta}$ is the subject of a distinct clause.

Finally, in some languages there are verbs (primarily experience verbs) in which the $\hat{\theta}$ is mapped to a lower grammatical function (and typically marked with dative Case), and a hierarchically lower argument (if there is one) is mapped to $\widehat{GF}$. In a recent insightful study of this construction, referred to in the Relational Grammar literature as Inversion (and analyzed with different subjects at different strata), Moore and Perlmutter (2000) contrast this construction in Russian with true dative $\widehat{GF}$. They show that in Russian both inversion and dative $\widehat{GF}$ constructions exist; the latter have full subject properties (Russian is a uniform-subject language), but the former only have a limited set of such properties by virtue of their $\hat{\theta}$ status, as we will see when we discuss anaphora. There are two cases of Inversion in Russian: the better-known example involves experience predicates and is illustrated in (23a,b): in both of these cases 'Boris' is the $\hat{\theta}$ but 'shirt(s)' is the $\widehat{GF}$. The other instance of Inversion is illustrated in (23c): it involves an unergative verb ('think' in this case) to which the "reflexive" suffix *sja* has been added. The addition of this suffix does not create a reflexive or unaccusative verb: semantically, it adds modality to the meaning (note the translation of the sentence), and syntactically it maps the $\hat{\theta}$ argument ('me' here) to a non-$\widehat{GF}$ function.

(23)   a. Borisu   nravjatsja takie   rubaški.
          Boris.DAT like.3PL   such   shirts.NOM
          'Boris likes such shirts.'

       b. Borisu   nužna   novaja rubaška.
          Boris.DAT need(ADJ).FSG   new   shirt(F)
          'Boris needs a new shirt.'

       c. Pri   takom šume mne   ne   dumaet-   sja.
          in.presence.of such   noise me.DAT not think.3SG- REFL
          'With such noise I can't think.'

With predicates of this kind, the mapping of arguments goes as follows (assuming, with Moore and Perlmutter [2000], that the Inversion nominal is an indirect object):

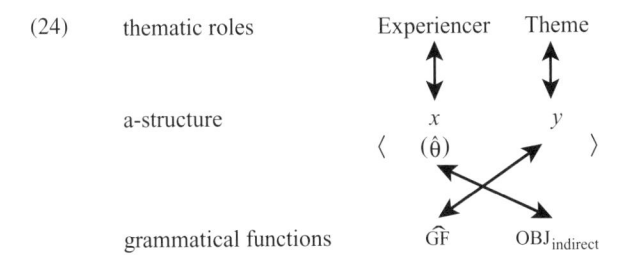

(24)   thematic roles   Experiencer   Theme
                                    ↕   ↕
       a-structure   x   y
                                ⟨ ($\hat{\theta}$)   ⟩

       grammatical functions $\widehat{GF}$ OBJ$_{indirect}$

Here the Experiencer is the highest in argumenthood rank ($\hat{\theta}$), but the Theme is the highest in functional relational rank ($\widehat{GF}$).

In all three of these types of constructions, the usual situation under which the same element serves as both $\hat{\theta}$ and $\widehat{GF}$ does not hold. Such constructions are therefore important for teasing apart properties of $\hat{\theta}$ and $\widehat{GF}$.

2.1.5 Mapping in mixed-subject languages

The approach to mapping adopted here makes an important prediction concerning mixed-subject languages. The heart of the mapping system is a universal alignment of the hierarchy of arguments (the thematic hierarchy) and the hierarchy of grammatical functions (the relational hierarchy). While some cross-linguistic variation is to be expected (this is discussed in the next section), and marked mappings such as Inversion apparently exist, the basic system should be universal. The essential claim is that syntactic (functional) prominence levels are anchored in conceptual/semantic prominence.

This approach contrasts sharply with an approach which has been taken in some of the literature on mixed-subject languages. As we observed in Chapter 1, studies of subject properties in mixed-subject languages show that they divide neatly into two classes, which we have dubbed Type 1 properties and Type 2 properties. The alternative view, dubbed "inverse mapping" by Manning (1996), takes the position that mixed-subject languages differ from uniform-subject languages in the nature of argument mapping. Specifically, it is claimed that the element with Type 2 properties is the grammatical subject: in a transitive clause in a syntactically ergative language, this means that the P argument is the subject and the A is the object. As Marantz (1984: 196) puts it, the familiar relationship between agenthood and subjecthood is an idiosyncrasy of English; there is no theoretical block to mapping Patient to subject in other languages. In an LFG-based analysis, Manning (1996) proposes that argument-structure prominence universally matches conceptual/semantic prominence, but syntactically ergative languages reverse the prominence in the mapping to grammatical functions.

(25) Argument mapping according to Manning
 a. Uniform subject languages

Thematic roles	Agent	Patient
	↕	↕
Argument structure	x	y
	($\hat{\theta}$; Manning's a-subject)	
	↕	↕
Grammatical functions	SUBJ	OBJ

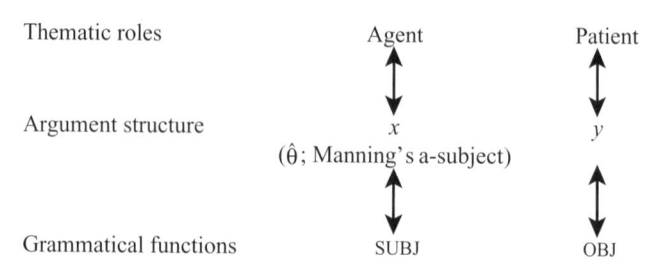

b. Syntactically ergative languages

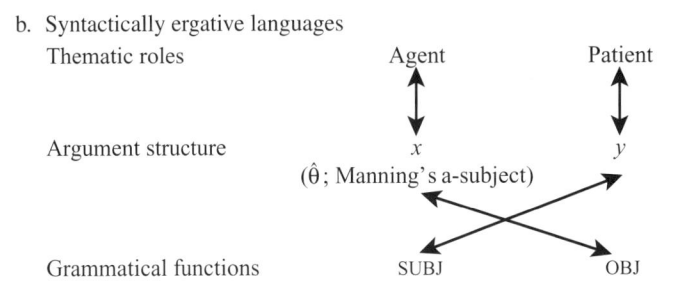

Thematic roles: Agent ↕, Patient ↕

Argument structure: x, y ($\hat{\theta}$; Manning's a-subject)

Grammatical functions: SUBJ, OBJ (with crossing mapping lines: Agent→OBJ, Patient→SUBJ)

Wechsler and Arka (1998) extend this to the Philippine-type language Balinese by defining the two types of mappings as both being available in the same language. In the formalism of HPSG, they define *acc-verb* and *erg-verb* as sorts of *active-verb*:

(26) Argument mapping according to Wechsler and Arka

a. $\textit{acc-verb} : \begin{bmatrix} \text{SUBJ} \langle \boxed{1} \rangle \\ \text{ARG-S} \langle \boxed{1}, \ldots \rangle \end{bmatrix}$

b. $\textit{erg-verb} : \begin{bmatrix} \text{SUBJ} & \langle \boxed{1} \rangle \\ \text{ARG-S} & \langle \boxed{1}, \ldots \rangle \\ \text{STEM} & \textit{intrans-stem} \end{bmatrix} \vee \begin{bmatrix} \text{SUBJ} & \langle \boxed{1} \rangle \\ \text{ARG-S} & \langle \boxed{}, \ldots \boxed{1}, \ldots \rangle \\ \text{STEM} & \textit{trans-stem} \end{bmatrix}$

That is to say, in a transitive ergative verb an argument other than the most prominent is realized as subject.

Under this approach, the Type 2 subject (P in syntactically ergative languages) is the highest-ranked element at the level of grammatical functions. Any situation where A has to be taken to outrank P (i.e., in Type 1 properties) must therefore be a consequence of the a-structure hierarchy. In other words, the universal "subject" identity of A is as the most prominent a-structure element; what we, following standard LFG terminology, have called $\hat{\theta}$.[7] This contrasts with the approach taken here, in which A (normally) has both argument-structure prominence and functional prominence, i.e., it is both $\hat{\theta}$ and $\widehat{\text{GF}}$.

The inverse-mapping theory thus conflates our $\hat{\theta}$ and $\widehat{\text{GF}}$. Our claim is that these two notions of most-prominent-argument, while closely related (by virtue of the hierarchy-alignment nature of argument mapping), need to be kept distinct. We have discussed this in the abstract in the previous section, where

---

7 Manning calls this the a-structure subject, or A-SBJ.

we saw three types of constructions in which θ̂ and ĜF can be distinguished. We will see concrete examples of the distinction in the discussion of anaphora in section 2.3.

We take this distinction between our approach and Manning's to be crucial. In the theory proposed here, Agents map to ĜF in all languages, regardless of typological classification. Our approach conforms to the idea that prominence hierarchies align harmonically; inverse mapping violates this.

2.1.6 Further thoughts on argument mapping

This discussion has not exhausted the question of the nature of argument mapping. Even within the bounds of what we have discussed, a theory of argument mapping must allow for differences between languages, and must be able to express differences between agentive ĜFs and non-agentive ones.

One potential problem that might be raised is the nature of mapping in "active" languages: languages in which non-agentive arguments of intransitive verbs are (apparently) not mapped as ĜF, but as OBJ. One such language is the Arawakan language Waurá, in which the ĜF is preverbal and triggers agreement on the verb, while the OBJ is postverbal and does not trigger agreement (Dixon 1994).

(27) a. Yanumaka inuka p- itsupalu.
         jaguar 3SG.kill 2SG.POSS- daughter
         'The jaguar killed your daughter.'

      b. Wekíhi katumala- pai.
         owner 3SG.work- STAT
         'The owner worked.'

      c. Usitya ikítsii.
         catch.fire thatch
         'The thatch caught fire.'

Minimally, such a language shows the need for a more sophisticated view of the mapping of arguments. As a first approximation, under the controversial (but, we believe, correct) assumption that reference to grammatical functions is relevant to these languages,[8] we can hypothesize that in such languages the statement of argument mapping is (28) rather than (13).

---

8 We return in Chapter 6 to the question of whether argument mapping in these languages, which fall under the umbrella of what we are calling non-subject languages, requires reference to grammatical functions at all. We will argue there that it does.

(28)   Argument mapping in "active" languages (informal)
         The highest argument role maps to the highest grammatical function, the next argument to the next grammatical function, and so on. Grammatical functions whose corresponding argument role is missing are skipped.

Such languages do not call into question the hierarchy-to-hierarchy nature of argument mapping; they simply require a different implementation. Similarly, in languages like English, where Agent arguments cannot appear as OBJ in existential constructions, a different implementation of hierarchy-to-hierarchy mapping will be used.

A theory of argument mapping such as the Lexical Mapping Theory of LFG (Bresnan 2001, Falk 2001, and references cited there) provides a better framework in which to address such questions. In Lexical Mapping Theory (LMT), argument-structure elements are underspecified grammatical functions based on thematic roles. LMT provides a framework within which language-specific differences in argument mapping can be formally expressed in terms of parametric differences in the mapping principles. LMT also (as observed by Bresnan and Zaenen 1990) allows one to capture differences between agentive and non-agentive arguments of intransitive verbs (the unergative/unaccusative distinction) in a monostratal non-derivational theory of syntax. However, at its core, LMT is a formalization of the hierarchy-to-hierarchy view of argument mapping. For the purposes of the present study, an informal hierarchy alignment will suffice.

2.2   Specification of argument properties

2.2.1   Introductory remarks

We conclude from the foregoing that, on one understanding, the subject is $\widehat{\text{GF}}$. It is the grammatical element which has the function of expressing the most prominent core argument of the verb. Given our characterization of grammatical functions as the basis of explanation, we should expect certain properties to follow from this concept of subject. We also expect such properties to be constant across languages: mixed-subject languages should not differ from uniform-subject languages.

Since the $\widehat{\text{GF}}$ function is characterized in terms of its hierarchical position relative to other argument-expressing functions, the kinds of properties we should expect $\widehat{\text{GF}}$ to have are ones relating to hierarchies of argumenthood. Properties of this kind can be said to be explained by the nature of the $\widehat{\text{GF}}$ function, while other types of arguments would be stipulations. We claim that ĜF properties, which correspond to what we have dubbed Type 1 properties, have precisely the character that we predict.

One way that an argument hierarchy might be relevant in the present context involves the alignment of the relational hierarchy with other prominence hierarchies. In fact, we have already seen one example of such a property: the fact that if a verb has an Agent argument, it will be mapped to the ĜF function in the syntax. The relation between the thematic role Agent and the grammatical function SUBJ (or, rather, ĜF) follows as a consequence of our characterization of the function, and need not be stipulated.

A less obvious hierarchy-alignment-related property of ĜF is the fact that it generally displays prominence at the discourse level; specifically, it is most commonly the discourse topic (Andrews 1985). This has been shown to be true in mixed-subject languages as well (as shown by Cooreman 1988 for Dyirbal, and Cooreman et al. 1988 for Tagalog). We propose that this is a consequence of the harmonic alignment of the relational hierarchy with a hierarchy of discourse prominence. Since topics are the most prominent elements from a discourse perspective, the harmonic alignment of the discourse hierarchy with the relational hierarchy will result in the topicality of ĜF.

The harmonic alignment of the functionally most prominent argument, ĜF, with most prominent elements on the thematic and discourse dimensions thus provides us with an explanation of two very frequently noted properties of subjects. One or the other of these is often taken, especially pedagogically, to be a definition of subject (Huddleston 1984).

A second way argument hierarchies can be involved in grammatical rules involves the licensing ability of heads. While LFG is less "head-driven" than some other theoretical frameworks, it is generally accepted that heads serve to determine much of the environment in which they occur. This includes selecting their arguments, but it also includes licensing some of the arguments' functional properties. This licensing of arguments' properties is what is known in traditional grammar as government. Taking the notion of a functionally based relational hierarchy, this licensing ought to be subject to the relative prominence expressed in the hierarchy. Thus, ĜF should be the argument most susceptible to such specification. As we will see in the remainder of section 2.2, this has interesting consequences.

The relation between argument hierarchies and anaphora is less clear initially, so we will defer discussion until section 2.3. However, as we will see, the anaphoric prominence of ĜF is also a consequence of its prominent-argument status.

2.2.2 Null arguments

One often-discussed property of languages is the ability of some, but not others, to leave certain arguments with no overt (audible) expression, interpreted as a kind of pronoun; a construction often called pro-drop. While the description of this property varies between theories, there does seem to be general agreement that this ability is licensed by a head; in a lexicalist framework like LFG, the licensing head must be the verb. The claim we will make here is that this licensing follows the relational hierarchy, resulting in the property that if a language allows any argument of the verb to be null, it allows the $\widehat{\text{GF}}$ to be null. We note in passing the initial plausibility of this claim by observing the frequent use of the term "null subject" to describe languages that allow this.

2.2.2.1 The nature of null pronouns

Before discussing the relational hierarchy and the licensing of null pronominal arguments, we need to establish the nature of the construction. In this section, we will discuss the basic analysis we will be assuming, and the boundaries of the construction.

A null pronominal argument is an argument which is understood as being present, with an interpretation we can refer to broadly as pronominal, but is not pronounced. Consider the following Hebrew sentence.[9]

(29)   Pnina sama al ha- šulxan.
       Pnina put on the- table
       'Pnina put it on the table.'

The object of the verb 'put' is not expressed in this sentence. Such a sentence is unacceptable as an out-of-the-blue utterance, but it is well-formed given an

---

9 It has been argued, e.g., by Huang (1984), that non-subject null arguments in some languages have the properties of *wh* traces, and that this fact is crucial for understanding their licensing. From the perspective of the present study, the *wh* trace properties would mean that the relevant null arguments are required to have syntactically relevant discourse prominence, expressed as a syntacticized discourse function such as FOCUS or TOPIC. The formal expression of such a requirement would involve an inside-out functional uncertainty expression (see Chapter 4), which would be subject to island constraints and the like. Such a requirement would constitute part of the pronominal properties specified for the null pronominal. This does not affect the discussion here, however. The null argument is anaphoric in nature, and must be licensed just like any null argument. The discourse-related requirement is not part of the licensing. It also does not distinguish between subject and non-subject null arguments; it does not appear to apply to null subjects because subjects are automatically associated with a discourse-like function (see Chapter 3); it thus actually applies vacuously. In conclusion, we take issues of discourse-topic "licensing" of null arguments to be a question not of licensing but of pronominal properties.

appropriate context (for instance, as an answer to the question 'Where is the toy?'). The missing object is understood as referring to something which has already been mentioned in the discourse. In a constituent-structure-based theory, such a sentence is generally analyzed as having an unpronounced pronoun in the canonical object position.[10]

(30)

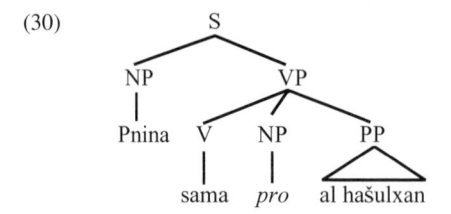

```
            S
           / \
          NP  VP
          |  /|\
        Pnina V NP  PP
              |  |  /\
            sama pro al hašulxan
```

An analysis with a null constituent is forced on a theory in which all syntactic information is expressed at constituent structure. On the other hand, LFG allows us to express the fact that the object is absent from the overt expression of the sentence, but is functionally a pronoun: it is represented as an f-structure pronoun which has no c-structure reflex.

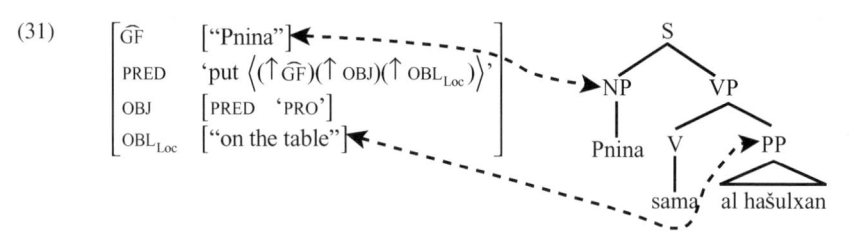

(31)

$$\begin{bmatrix} \widehat{GF} & [\text{"Pnina"}] \\ \text{PRED} & \text{'put} \langle (\uparrow \widehat{GF})(\uparrow \text{OBJ})(\uparrow \text{OBL}_{\text{Loc}}) \rangle \text{'} \\ \text{OBJ} & [\text{PRED} \quad \text{'PRO'}] \\ \text{OBL}_{\text{Loc}} & [\text{"on the table"}] \end{bmatrix}$$

```
            S
           / \
          NP  VP
          |  /|\
        Pnina V  PP
              |  /\
            sama al hašulxan
```

The object is a pronoun (an element with the special pronominal value 'PRO' for the PRED feature[11]) with no corresponding element in the c-structure.

As for the boundaries of the construction, there have been two sources of confusion: the distinction drawn in the GB/MP literature between two kinds of null pronouns, and the relationship between null pronouns and agreement.

In Chomsky (1982), a distinction is drawn between PRO (a null-pronoun-reflexive hybrid, or pronominal "anaphor"[12]) and *pro* (a null pronoun). The

---

10 The tree has been simplified in that the system of functional categories in the clausal structure has been omitted, and the verb is in V. Hebrew is a V-to-I language (the finite verb is located in I, not in V), but the question of functional categories is irrelevant to the point at hand.
11 See Chapter 1.
12 It is unfortunate that transformational work has departed from the otherwise accepted use of the word *anaphor* to refer to any pro-form, and has limited it to refer to reflexives and reciprocals. To prevent confusion, we will place the word in scare quotes when it is used with the narrower meaning.

justification for this distinction is theory-internal: technical problems with the licensing mechanism arise if all null pronominals are assumed to be PRO, as they were in Chomsky (1981). Distinguishing formally between empty pronouns in non-finite clauses and those in finite clauses resolves the licensing problems. However, it has long been known that this distinction is problematic. As observed by Mohanan (1983), the characterization of PRO as a pronominal "anaphor" is a stipulation not deducible from the observed properties of PRO. Most importantly (and contrary to what is often stated in the literature), unlike reflexives PRO can have discourse reference.[13] In a similar vein, Bouchard (1984) argues that PRO is either an "anaphor" (in obligatory control structures)[14] or a pronoun (in non-obligatory control), but not both simultaneously. In another GB analysis, Huang (1989) treats PRO and *pro* as essentially the same element, speaking of "one single pronominal empty category (of which *pro* and PRO are two variants) [Huang 1989: 192]". More recently, Hornstein (1999) has proposed a Minimalist analysis in which non-obligatory control involves *pro*.[15] PRO and *pro* can also not be distinguished in terms of referential potential. Both can have either specific or arbitrary reference. The following examples from Mohanan (1983) illustrate arbitrary *pro* in Malayalam, a language which has no overt arbitrary pronoun (like the English *one*).

(32) a. [Guṟuṇaaṭhan paraññaal] anusaṟikkaṇam.
         teacher.NOM   said.if   obey.must
         'If the teacher says (anything), (one) must obey (it).'
      b. Wakkiilanmaar caṭikkum.
         lawyers.NOM   cheat.FUT
         'Lawyers will cheat (one).'
      c. Wakkiilanmaar awane caṭikkum.
         lawyers.NOM   him   cheat.FUT
         'Lawyers will cheat him/*one.'

While distinctions do need to be drawn between different types of pronominal properties that null pronouns may have in a language, they are more complex than the simple binary PRO/*pro* approach. Rather, pronouns (null and overt) will

---

13 An interesting problem arises with the characterization of PRO as a pronominal "anaphor" within the government-based approach of standard GB. A pronominal is an element which obeys Binding Principle B, and an "anaphor" is one which obeys Binding Principle A. Since these principles are stated in terms of governing categories, an ungoverned element obeys neither principle. Since PRO only occurs in ungoverned positions, it obeys neither of the binding principles. In this sense it is neither a pronominal nor an "anaphor".
14 We disagree with this characterization of obligatory control constructions, but we postpone discussion until Chapter 6. See also the following footnote.
15 In Hornstein's analysis, as in LFG, obligatory control resembles Raising.

carry additional lexically defined properties, many of which are discussed by Dalrymple (1993). The PRO/*pro* distinction itself is completely superfluous – no more than a theoretical artifact. We will therefore not draw a distinction between PRO and *pro* in this study.

The rejection of a distinction between PRO and *pro* is not an innocuous decision. It has important consequences for the typology of null-subject languages. Consider English. English, since it requires overt subjects in finite clauses and thus lacks "*pro*", is considered by the received wisdom to be a non-pro-drop language. However, English does have "PRO", unexpressed pronominal subjects in non-finite clauses. Under our conception, contrary to the usual description, English is a language with null pronominal subjects, and thus enters into typological considerations of null subjects.

Another issue that needs to be addressed is the relationship between "rich" agreement and null pronominal arguments. The conventional wisdom is that the licensing of null pronominal arguments is achieved by agreement which contains enough features to recover the unexpressed argument.[16] This is the reason, so the story goes, that languages like Spanish and Greek, which have complex subject-agreement systems, allow null subjects, while languages like French and English, where agreement is much more impoverished, do not. It has even been observed that, within a language, when the tenses differ on the nature of agreement, the possibility of a null argument is correlated with the agreement facts. For example, in Hebrew the verb agrees with the subject in person in the past and future tenses but not in the present. A referential null subject is therefore possible in the past and future, but not the present.

(33)   a. Gidal-   t   ogrim.
               Raise.PST- 2FSG hamsters
               'You (f.) raised hamsters.'

        b. Te- gadl-   i   ogrim.
               2- raise.FUT- FSG hamsters
               'You (f.) will raise hamsters.'

        c. *Me- gadel- et ogrim.
               PRES- raise- F hamsters
               'You (f.) raise hamsters.'

---

16 An anonymous reader has suggested that this is not really the conventional wisdom anymore, because of the discovery of languages that lack agreement but have null subjects. Conventional wisdom or not, one still finds people referring to it as if it were acknowledged truth. For example, Radford (1997: 227) suggests that the reason that Early Modern English allowed null subjects in finite clauses while contemporary English does not is that agreement was richer in the former than it is in the latter. In addition, the Hebrew and Pashto facts show that agreement is at least sometimes involved.

           d. At   me-   gadel- et ogrim.
              You.F PRES- raise-   F hamsters
              'You (f.) raise hamsters.'

A striking example of this is Pashto (Huang 1984), where the present tense verb agrees with the subject and the past tense verb agrees with the object if it is transitive. Whatever the verb agrees with can be omitted.

(34)   a. Jān   ra-   z-   i.
           John DIR- come- 3MSG
           'John comes.'
        b. Zə maa   xwr- əm.
           I   apple eat- 1MSG
           'I eat the apple.'

(35)   a. Jān   ra-   ǧ-   ay
           John ASP- come- 3MSG
           'John came.'
        b. Ma maa   wə-   xwar- a.
           I   apple(F) PERF- eat-   3FSG
           'I ate the apple.'

(36)   a. Ra-   z-   i.
           DIR- come- 3MSG
           'He comes.'
        b. Maṇa xwr- əm.
           Apple eat- 1MSG
           'I eat an apple.'

(37)   a. Ra-   ǧ-   ay.
           ASP- come- 3MSG
           'He came.'
        b. Ma wə-   xwar- a.
           I   PERF- eat-   3FSG
           'I ate it[fem. sg.].'

(38)   a. *Zə xwr- əm.
           I   eat- 1MSG
           'I eat it.'
        b. *Maṇa wə-   xwar- a.
           apple(F) PERF- eat-   3FSG
           'I(or whoever) ate the apple.'

This relationship between agreement and pro-drop carries much intuitive appeal. Unfortunately, a closer look makes it seem less attractive. There are languages with no object agreement in which null objects are allowed; this is exemplified for Hebrew in (29) above and for Italian (Rizzi 1986) and Imbabura Quechua (Cole 1987) below.

(39) **Italian**
    a. Il bel tempo invoglia a restare.
       the nice weather induces to stay
       'The nice weather induces [one] to stay.'
    b. La buona musica riconcilia con se stessi.
       the good music reconciles with oneself
       'Good music reconciles [one] with oneself.'
    c. Di solito, Gianni fotografa seduti.
       in general Gianni photographs seated.PL
       'In general, Gianni photographs [people] seated.'

(40) **Imbabura Quechua**
    Juzi rikurka.
    José saw
    'José saw [him/her/it].'

In addition, the literature abounds with examples of languages with no agreement whatsoever, which nevertheless allow null pronominal arguments. These examples are drawn from Cole (1987):

(41)   a. **Mandarin**
       Zhangsan shuo kanjiale Lisi.
       Zhangsan says saw Lisi
       'Zhangsan says that [he] saw Lisi.'
    b. **Korean**
       John- un Bill- i cenhwaha- ess- ta- nun
       John- TOP Bill- NOM call- PST- DECL- ADNOM
       sasil- ul acik moru- n- ta.
       fact- ACC yet not.know- PRES- DECL
       'John doesn't know the fact that Bill called [him].'
    c. **Thai**
       Nit bɔɔk waa Nuan hen.
       Nit speak say Nuan see
       'Nit said that Nuan saw [him].'

Even in English, as discussed above, null pronoun subjects are allowed in forms where there is no agreement: non-finite forms (infinitives, gerunds). Such facts have led Jaeggli and Safir (1989) to reject the criterion of rich agreement, in favor of a system-wide notion of uniformity of agreement, an intuitively less attractive approach.

The approach that we will take is different. The characterization of null pronouns with agreement and those without are entirely different, inviting an analysis under which these are two different phenomena. From a purely observational perspective, this is plausible. In the case of null pronouns triggered by agreement, it is not really the case that the pronoun has no overt realization. The agreement on the verb is itself a realization of the pronominal argument, a kind of incorporated pronoun. Consider the Hebrew example (33a) above.

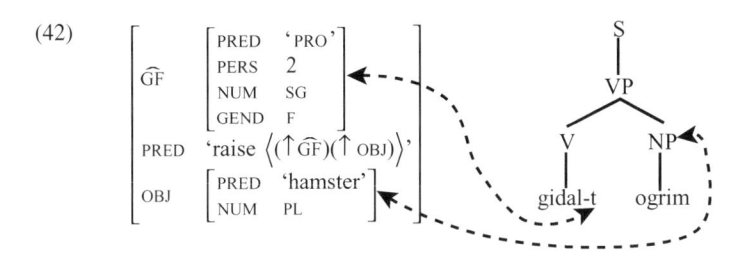

(42)
$$\begin{bmatrix} \widehat{GF} & \begin{bmatrix} \text{PRED} & \text{'PRO'} \\ \text{PERS} & 2 \\ \text{NUM} & \text{SG} \\ \text{GEND} & \text{F} \end{bmatrix} \\ \text{PRED} & \text{'raise} \langle(\uparrow \widehat{GF})(\uparrow \text{OBJ})\rangle\text{'} \\ \text{OBJ} & \begin{bmatrix} \text{PRED} & \text{'hamster'} \\ \text{NUM} & \text{PL} \end{bmatrix} \end{bmatrix}$$

S
|
VP
/ \
V   NP
gidal-t ogrim

The analysis of agreement as an incorporated pronoun has become the standard analysis in LFG following the arguments of Bresnan and Mchombo (1987). Formally, any verb with the agreement suffix *t* specifies that its $\widehat{GF}$ has the features of second person feminine singular, and optionally the pronominal PRED feature. Such lexical information is expressed formally in LFG by a series of constraints in the lexical entry of the verb, in the form of equations assigning values to f-structure attributes. (On the notation, see Chapter 1.)

(43)   *gidalt*: (↑ PRED) = 'raise ⟨(↑ $\widehat{GF}$)(↑ OBJ)⟩'
        (↑ $\widehat{GF}$ PERS) = 2
        (↑ $\widehat{GF}$ NUM) = SG
        (↑ $\widehat{GF}$ GEND) = F
        optional: (↑ $\widehat{GF}$ PRED) = 'PRO'

A similar idea has been formalized within the framework of the Minimalist Program by Vainikka and Levy (1999). The pronominal status of agreement is an area of cross-linguistic variation. In some languages (e.g., Italian) it is pronominal, and in others (e.g., English) it is not. Some languages (such as Hebrew) actually have a mixed system: first and second person agreement is pronominal, while third person and present tense agreement are not. The richness of the agreement system may be partially responsible for the ability of agreement to function as an incorporated pronoun, but the crucial point is that it is not a *null* pronoun. The only true null pronominal arguments are ones which are not referenced as agreement markers on the verb.

As in our rejection of the PRO/*pro* distinction, the treatment of agreement markers as incorporated pronouns has a significant effect on the typology of null pronouns. It is striking that much of the literature on null pronouns actually deals with agreement (incorporated pronouns), rather than truly null ones. Under our analysis, there is no difference between, say, English and Spanish in the ability of a subject to be a null pronoun: both allow it in non-finite clauses. In finite clauses, the verb agrees with the subject, so there is no possibility of a null pronominal subject: the potential pronominal status of the subject is a consequence of the lexical properties of agreement affixes in the languages: in Spanish the agreement morphemes carry optional pronominal features, while in English they do not.

2.2.2.2   Null pronouns and the relational hierarchy

Now that we have determined what null pronouns are, we can return to the question of the relationship between null pronouns and the grammatical function $\widehat{\text{GF}}$. True null pronouns, the ones not related to agreement triggers, must be licensed by something. The most natural licenser is the verb. Specifically, the verb will, according to the constraints of the language, optionally specify pronominal features for one or more arguments. This specification will include the pronominal PRED feature and other properties (referential, generic, etc.). For present purposes, we will represent the entire set of features informally as "pronominal properties." The lexical entry of the verb will thus include optional constraints of the following form, which can specify pronominal properties for non-agreement-triggering arguments:[17]

(44)   ($\uparrow$ GF) = "pronominal properties," where GF is chosen from a language-specific set Γ of argument functions.

Since this is a case of the head licensing properties of its arguments, we predict that this ability should follow the relational hierarchy. That is to say, for any

---

17 In this study, we will not discuss the formal description of pronominal properties in LFG. The reader is referred to Dalrymple (1993). In f-structures, we will represent pronouns with the pronominal semantic form, [PRED 'PRO'], and an INDEX feature representing its reference. The INDEX feature, like the "pronominal properties" notation, is a convenient shorthand: the reference of syntactic elements is properly represented as part of the correspondence between syntax and semantics/discourse.

given combination of pronominal properties ℘, a language may license ℘ only for ĜF or for both ĜF and OBJ, but not for just OBJ. In other words, if a language allows a particular kind of empty pronoun at all, it will allow it for ĜF.

This prediction is supported by the evidence. English, for example, allows both referential and arbitrary null pronouns as ĜF but not as OBJ. Hebrew allows referential null pronouns as both ĜF and OBJ, but it only allows ĜF to be an arbitrary pronoun. On the other hand, Italian (Rizzi 1986) allows arbitrary null pronouns as both ĜF and OBJ, but it limits referential ones to be ĜF. According to Huang (1984, 1989), Mandarin allows a null pronominal that refers to the discourse topic[18] to be either ĜF or OBJ, but one that is coreferential with an element in the higher clause is limited to ĜF. Many languages allow all kinds of null pronouns quite freely, vacuously conforming to the prediction. In no language does there appear to be any particular type of null pronoun which is available for OBJ but not ĜF. Nor does there appear to be any independent way to predict which pronoun types extend past ĜF.

We predict that mixed-subject languages should be no different from uniform-subject languages in the ability of arguments to be null pronouns: the most natural empty pronominals should be S/A. Here again, the prediction is supported. In Tagalog, arbitrary null pronouns are limited to ĜF (Kroeger 1993: 86–7).

(45) a. Mapanganib ang lumapit sa ahas.
       dangerous   NOM ACT.approach DAT snake
       'To go near a snake is dangerous.'

    b. Maaksaya -ng i-   tapon   ang damit na ito.
       wasteful LNK INS- throw.out NOM dress LNK this
       'To throw out this dress would be a waste.'

(They are also limited to control contexts. We will return to control in Tagalog in Chapter 5.) Kroeger also reports that his informants, while accepting both unexpressed referential ĜFs and unexpressed referential OBJs, dispreferred them as non-nominative OBJs.

(46) a. Huhugasan   ko   ang mga pinggan, at pupunasan
       FUT.wash.IO I.ERG NOM PL dish   and FUT.dry.IO
       mo.
       2SG.ERG
       'I will wash the dishes, and you dry (them).'
       [unexpressed nominative OBJ]

---

18 Recall that we are not taking the discourse-topichood to be a licensing factor, but rather one of the properties that an unexpressed pronoun may have.

b. Niluto   ni   Josie ang   pagkain at   hinugasan
   cook.DO ERG Josie NOM food   and wash.IO

   ang   mga pinggan.
   NOM PL   dish
   'The food was cooked by Josie and the dishes washed (by her).'
   [unexpressed non-nominative $\widehat{\text{GF}}$]

c. Nagnhuhuli   ang   ama   ko   ng   isda, at
   IMPERF.ACT.catch NOM father my   ACC fish   and

   nagtitinda.   ang   ina   ko   (nito).
   IMPERF.ACT.sell   NOM mother my   (this).
   'My father catches fish, and my mother sells them.'
   [optional but preferred pronoun non-nominative OBJ]

Unexpressed nominative arguments may be cases of the sharing of an argument across conjuncts; as will be seen in the next chapter, this involves nominative arguments in Tagalog. Unexpressed non-nominatives are most plausibly analyzed as null pronouns, and here there is a preference for $\widehat{\text{GF}}$. Similarly, Dyirbal freely allows $\widehat{\text{GF}}$ null pronouns, but not OBJ null pronouns, in transitive clauses (Dixon 1972).

(47)   a. Balan   jugumbil balga- n.
          II.ABS   woman   hit-   NFUT
          '[Someone] is hitting the woman.'

       b. Ḍayguna   balga- n.
          me.ACC   hit-   NFUT
          [Someone] is hitting me.

Another example is Chukchee (Comrie 1979), where S and A are the controlled arguments.[19]

(48)   a. Gəm-   nan   gət   tite   mə-   winret- gət
          me-   ERG   you.SG.ABS sometime 1SG- help-   2SG
          ermetwi-   k.
          grow.strong-   INF
          'Let me help you sometime to grow strong.'

       b. Morg- ənan   gət   mət- re-   winret- gət   riwl-   ək
          we-   ERG   you.SG.ABS 1PL- FUT- help-   2SG   move- INF
          əməl?o geče-   yo-   t.
          all.ABS   collect-   PSPRT- ABS.PL
          'We will help you to move all the collected items.'

As is the case for uniform-subject languages, many mixed-subject languages allow unexpressed pronouns freely.

19 But control is more complicated than this. See Chapter 5.

2.2.3 Imperative addressee

It is stressed in the typological literature (e.g., in Dixon 1994) that the addressee of an imperative (henceforth addressee) universally corresponds to the element which would be the addressee of the imperative in English, even in mixed-subject languages. That is to say, imperatives do not exhibit "ergative" behavior.

(49) **Tagalog** (Schachter 1976)
    a. Mag- bigay ka   sa   kaniya ng   kape.
        ACT- give   2SG.NOM DAT   him   ACC coffee
        'Give him some coffee.'
    b. Bigy- an mo   siya   ng   kape.
        Give- IO 2SG.ERG him.NOM ACC coffee
        'Give him some coffee.'
    c. I-   bigay mo   sa   kaniya ang   kape.
        INS- give   2SG.ERG DAT   him   NOM coffee
        'Give him the coffee.'

This is to be expected under the current theory. An imperative verb will specify that one of its arguments is a second person pronoun. Given the relational hierarchy, the most likely argument to be thus specified will be $\widehat{GF}$.

While the facts of imperatives are not in dispute, the need for a syntactic account is. For example, Dixon (1994) suggests that the identity of the addressee is the consequence of the semantics: someone can only be ordered to do something that they have control over. Therefore, only Agents can be addressees, and since Agents are invariably realized in the syntax as $\widehat{GF}$s, it follows that only $\widehat{GF}$ can be the addressee. This is correct as far as it goes. In fact, it provides us with an explanation of why addressees appear to differ from other null pronominals in not going farther down the relational hierarchy. In other words, given the cross-linguistic behavior of null pronominals, we might expect to find languages in which both $\widehat{GF}$ and OBJ are available as addressees. The semantic explanation correctly predicts that OBJs will never be addressees.

However, parallel architecture leaves open the possibility that the choice of addressee involves syntactic factors as well. Affirming the relevance of syntax does not entail a denial of the semantic aspect. We will provide two arguments, based on English, for the relevance of syntax.

In the first place, an imperative verb must license the syntactic properties of the construction. This will include the specification of an unexpressed pronominal second person subject ($\widehat{GF}$).

(50)   ($\uparrow \widehat{GF}$ PRED) = 'PRO'
         ($\uparrow \widehat{GF}$ PERS) = 2

Crucially, even English, in which finite inflection generally disallows null pronominals, has an unexpressed ĜF in the imperative construction. Furthermore, the distinction between null and overt pronominals is a syntactic fact, not a semantic one. There must therefore be a syntactic constraint licensing null addressees.

In the second place, non-agentive subjects can be the addressees of imperatives in some languages (including English), with a coerced agentive reading. (Dixon notes this as well, but does not draw the logical conclusion.)

(51)   a. Be happy!
        b. Be registered before the semester starts!

The coerced agentive reading[20] follows from the semantic aspect of imperatives: the addressee must be understood as an Agent. But it is curious that inherently non-agentive ĜFs should be available as imperative addressees; this is unexpected under a purely semantic account. Under a syntactic approach such as we are proposing, the availability of these ĜFs as addressees follows.

We concur with Dixon (1994) that apparent counterexamples to this universal generalization are not true counterexamples. He discusses cases where verbal agreement in imperatives operates on an ergative basis; for example, in Tsimshian the A agreement affix can be omitted from an imperative but the S affix cannot, while the reverse is true in Nadëb. Following Dixon, we take such facts to show that morphosyntactic systems, such as agreement, are subject to their own principles, which include the obligatoriness or optionality of cross-referencing particular arguments on the verb. As in the general case of null pronouns, the interaction between the syntax and the morphosyntax result in a complex combination of properties.

In conclusion, the choice of addressee is subject to both syntactic and semantic constraints. On the syntactic side, the imperative verb licenses the properties of the addressee. The limitation of addressees to ĜF is a consequence of the relational hierarchy.

2.3   Anaphora

2.3.1   *Anaphoric prominence*

One of the clearest places where argument status and hierarchies of arguments are implicated is anaphora. Various hierarchy effects, both relational and thematic, have been observed in the literature. We will explore these in this section.

---

20 Of course, in some of these cases a circumlocution is more natural.

It is not immediately clear why argument hierarchies should be relevant to anaphora. Unlike null pronouns and imperatives, anaphora does not involve a head specifying information about its arguments. Nevertheless, the observation that argument status is relevant to the operation of binding is not new. It is, for example, enshrined in the standard transformationalist view of anaphora (Chomsky 1981), under which Binding Theory is about A-binding, i.e., binding by an argument. Why this should be so is somewhat mysterious – one possible reason might be that, as suggested by Jackendoff (1990), anaphora is a grammaticalization of a relation in lexical conceptual structures where one entity has two "thematic roles." If this is correct, we would expect anaphora to be essentially a relation between arguments, and thus be sensitive to argumenthood.

The exact nature of the binding-theoretic prominence of subjects ($\widehat{\text{GF}}$ under the analysis proposed here) is more complicated than often thought. The central observation is that, in a transitive clause in which the two arguments have the same reference, it is the OBJ which is expressed as a reflexive pronoun, and the $\widehat{\text{GF}}$ is its antecedent:

(52)   a. Joan saw herself.
       b. *Herself saw Joan.

As has been noted in the literature on mixed-subject languages, it is the A in such cases that displays the subject-like behavior, the argument we are claiming is the $\widehat{\text{GF}}$. This can be illustrated with an example from the Philippine-type language Toba Batak (discussed by Manning 1996), which, like most Philippine-type languages outside of the Philippines, has no Case marking but has morphological marking on the verb indicating which argument is the distinguished element of the clause. In Toba Batak, *mang-* designates the $\widehat{\text{GF}}$ as this special element and *di-* designates the OBJ. (Neither of these is an agreement marker.) Manning argues that this morphologically designated element is outside the VP, while the other core argument (whether $\widehat{\text{GF}}$ or OBJ) is inside. Note the anaphoric pattern:

(53)   a. [$_{VP}$ Mang- ida diri- na] si   John.
            ACT- see self- his PROP John
            'John saw himself.'
      b. *[$_{VP}$ Mang- ida si   John] diri- na.
            ACT- see PROP John self- his
            'Himself saw John.'
      c. *[$_{VP}$ Di- ida diri- na] si   John.
            DO- see self- his PROP John
            'Himself saw John.'

d. [$_{VP}$ Di- ida si John] diri- na.
   DO- see PROP John self- his
   'John saw himself.'

The conventional structure-based account attributes this to the c-command relation: the reflexive must be c-commanded by its antecedent. However, the Toba Batak examples show that this cannot be maintained: the argument picked out by the "voice" morphology on the verb c-commands the other argument, regardless of which is the ĜF and which is the OBJ, yet the ĜF antecedes the OBJ.

The basic idea behind what the c-command condition is supposed to capture can be stated, somewhat vaguely, as follows:

(54)   The antecedent of an anaphor must be more prominent than the anaphor.

What this statement leaves open is the nature of the prominence involved. Viewed from this perspective, c-command is a popular hypothesis as to the nature of this prominence. It is, however, only a hypothesis. A cross-linguistic survey of anaphora, with facts such as those in Toba Batak, raise questions about its correctness. Work on anaphora in LFG (Dalrymple 1993, Bresnan 1995) suggests a more complex picture, under which prominence at three different dimensions of syntax is relevant: constituent structure (linear order), functional structure (the relational hierarchy), and argument structure (the thematic hierarchy). At the functional level, this results in the situation where ĜF binds OBJ, and not vice versa.

For some kinds of anaphors in some languages, the relative prominence constraint is strengthened:

(55)   The antecedent of an anaphor must be the most prominent element in its clause.

This prominence can be either in terms of functional status or argument status. In such languages, the antecedent of one type of anaphor must be either an element bearing the grammatical function ĜF or one with the argumenthood status of $\hat{\theta}$[21] It should be noted that, while these anaphors are often called reflexives, a terminological convention we will be following here, ĜF/$\hat{\theta}$ orientation is distinct from locality. For example, Dalrymple (1993) shows that the Norwegian anaphor *seg*[22] must be bound by a ĜF in the minimal finite clause that contains it, but may not be bound by a coargument.

---

21 I am not aware of any language in which the antecedent of some anaphor must be the first argument in its clause. Linear order seems to differ in this way from the relational and thematic hierarchies.

22 *Seg* also has non-anaphoric uses, in which it appears to be a coargument of its "antecedent."

(56)   a. non-coargument $\widehat{\text{GF}}$
Jon hørte oss snakke om   seg.
Jon heard us talk   about self
'Jon$_i$ heard us talking about him$_i$.'

   b. non-$\widehat{\text{GF}}$
*Jeg lovet   Jon å snakke pent   om   seg.
I   promised Jon to talk   nicely about self
'I promised Jon$_i$ to speak nicely about him(self)$_i$.'

   c. coargument $\widehat{\text{GF}}$
*Jon snakket om   seg.
Jon talked about self
'Jon$_i$ talked about himself$_i$.'

Teasing apart the effects of the relational hierarchy and the thematic hierarchy is not easy. Since argument mapping is essentially an alignment of the two hierarchies, in most cases it is impossible to tell which is relevant. As we have seen, though, there are constructions in which the most prominent argument at a-structure ($\hat{\theta}$) is not identical to the element bearing the most prominent argument function ($\widehat{\text{GF}}$): passivization, complex predicates, and inversion in particular. Such constructions provide an invaluable way to investigate the roles of the two hierarchies.

As we have seen, the argument structure of a complex predicate, such as a causative, is as follows, where the causative Patient is identical with one of the arguments of the base verb:

(57)   ⟨Agent$_{\text{CAUS}}$, Patient$_{\text{CAUS}}$ ⟨Agent$_{\text{base-verb}}$, Patient$_{\text{base-verb}}$⟩⟩

This argument structure contains two argument domains, and thus two $\hat{\theta}$s. In complex predicate constructions, many languages allow the $\hat{\theta}$ of either predicate to antecede the reflexive, as in the Japanese example (58);[23] a variant of this is only allowing the embedded $\hat{\theta}$ to antecede a reflexive corresponding to a lower argument of the embedded predicate, as in the Chimwiini examples (59).[24] (Both of these are from Baker 1988.)

(58)   John ga   Mary ni zibun no uti de hon o
John NOM Mary DAT self GEN house in book ACC
yom- ase- ta.
read- CAUS- PST
'John made Mary read the book in his/her own house.'

---

23 I am following the standard, though controversial, view that *zibun* is constrained syntactically.
24 In this kind of language, reflexive locality is determined by argument structure.

(59) a. Mi   m-   phik-   ish-   ize   ru:hu-y-a   cha:kuja.
        I   1SG- cook-   CAUS-   ASP   myself   food
        'I made myself cook food.'
    b. Mi   ni-   m-   big-   ish-   ize   mwa:na   ru:hu-y-e.
        I   1SG- OBJ-   hit-   CAUS- ASP   child   himself
        'I made the child hit himself.'
    c. *Mi   ni-   m-   big-   ish-   ize   Aɬ i   ru:hu-y-a.
        I   1SG-   OBJ-   hit-   CAUS-   ASP   Ali   myself
        'I made Ali hit myself.'

In such languages, it is clear that it is argument-structure prominence that is relevant, since the causee is θ̂ but not ĜF. Facts of this kind have often been taken, under non-parallel theoretical architectures, to be evidence for the biclausality of causatives. Since the antecedent of a reflexive must be a subject, so the argument goes, this is evidence for two subjects and thus two clauses. Under the parallel architecture we are assuming, there is no need for a biclausal analysis.

However, complex predicate constructions do not provide any conclusive evidence on whether reference to functional prominence is also necessary, since the ĜF is one of the θ̂s. More instructive are the constructions in which there is a dissociation between θ̂ and ĜF. One such construction is the passive: the Agent is θ̂ and the Patient is ĜF. Similarly, in the inversion construction the Experiencer is θ̂ and the Theme (if there is one) is ĜF. As observed by Manning (1996), there are languages which allow either of these elements to antecede a reflexive. Examples of this in Russian passives were given in Chapter 1; here are examples of passives from the uniform-subject language Sanskrit and the mixed-subject language Inuit,[25] and an example of θ̂ anteceding a reflexive in Russian inversion.

(60) **Sanskrit**
    a. Sarpas   tenātmanā   svālayaṃ   nītaḥ.
       snake.NOM   himself.INSTR   self.house.ACC   brought.PSPRT.NOM
       'The snake was brought by him$_i$ himself to self$_i$'s house.'
    b. Anṛtam   tu   vadan   daṇḍyaḥ
       untruth.NOM   but   telling.NOM   fine.GER.NOM
       svavittasyāṃśam.
       self.property.GEN.part.ACC
       'But a perjurer$_i$ is to be fined one eighth (lit. part) of self$_i$'s property.'

---

25 In the Inuit example, the reflexive (incorporated into the verb as a agreement marker) cannot be coreferential with the subject in its own clause because of a non-coargument condition (like that applying to Norwegian *seg*), which holds if the reflexive bears a core function, as discussed by Manning.

(61) **Inuit**
      Naja Tobiasi- mit   uqaluttuun- niqar- p-   u-   q
      Naja Tobias- ABL tell-   PASS- IND- INTR- 3SG
      taa- ssu- ma itigartis- sima- ga-   a- ni.
      DEM- SG- ERG turn.down- PERF- PART.TR- 3SG.ERG- REFL.ABS
      'Naja$_i$ was told by Tobias$_j$ that he$_k$ had turned self$_{i/j}$ down.'

(62) **Russian**
      Borisu   žal   sebja i   svoju sem'ju.
      Boris.DAT sorry self and self's family
      'Boris$_i$ feels sorry for himself$_i$ and his$_i$ family.'

For a language like Russian, Sanskrit, or Inuit, the antecedent of a reflexive can be either $\hat{\theta}$ or $\widehat{\text{GF}}$. In languages like these, the conflation of $\hat{\theta}$ and $\widehat{\text{GF}}$ in theories such as that of Manning (1996) appears justified. For the inverse mapping theory, where our $\widehat{\text{GF}}$ is simply a variety of $\hat{\theta}$, the antecedence of reflexives can simply be stated in terms of a-structure. In our framework, we need to say that any $\hat{x}$ can be the antecedent.

However, there are other languages which restrict reflexives to be anteceded only by $\widehat{\text{GF}}$ or only by $\hat{\theta}$. This is unexpected under the inverse mapping theory, since it has no way to distinguish between the two types of prominence. One example of this type of language is Malayalam (Mohanan 1982, Manning 1996), in which only the $\widehat{\text{GF}}$ can antecede the reflexive. This is shown in the following causative and passive examples:

(63) a. Amma   kuttiyekonta aanaye   swantam wittil
         mother.NOM child.INSTR elephant.ACC self's   house
         weccə nulliccu.
         at   pinch.CAUS.PST
         'Mother$_i$ made the child$_j$ pinch the elephant$_k$ at self's$_{i/*j/*k}$ house.'
      b. Jooniyaal   meeri   swantam wiittil   weccə nullappettu.
         John.INSTR Mary.NOM self's   house.LOC at   pinch.PASS.PST
         'Mary$_i$ was pinched by John$_j$ in self$_{i/*j}$'s house.'

On the other hand, in Marathi, the long-distance reflexive *aapan* can only take a $\hat{\theta}$ antecedent (Dalrymple 1993).[26]

(64) John laa   Bill kaduun aaplyaa   gharii   maarle gele.
      John ACC Bill by   self.GEN house.LOC hit   PASS
      'John$_i$ was hit by Bill$_j$ at self's$_{j/*i}$ house.'

---

[26] Dalrymple shows that the accusative-marked NP is the grammatical subject.

We thus see that languages that limit the antecedent of a reflexive to be the most prominent argument of its clause may allow it to be either ĜF or θ̂ or both.[27] The existence of languages that restrict antecedence to either ĜF or θ̂ provides an argument for a theory like ours, which does not conflate the two concepts of most prominent argument.

As we predict, even mixed-subject languages display this kind of behavior. For example, as we have seen above, Inuit requires the antecedent of a reflexive to be either θ̂ or ĜF (Manning 1996). Crucially, there appears to be no language in which the P argument outranks the A for the purposes of anaphora, as one might expect under an inverse mapping analysis. As Dixon (1994: 138–139) puts it,

> The important point is that, in reflexives [which use an anaphoric element], if one of the coreferential constituents is A or S then this will be the antecedent (maintaining its normal form), while the other constituent goes into the reflexive form ... In every ergative language, as in every accusative language, the 'antecedent', i.e. the controller of reflexivity is A (or S, where it is extended to intransitives).

2.3.2 Switch-reference

Some languages have a construction that has come to be known in the literature as switch-reference (sometimes called obviation, as in Cole 1983 and Hale 1992). In a switch-reference system, when clauses are combined there is some morphological marker indicating whether the clauses have the same "subject" or different "subjects." This is exemplified in the following Diyari sentences (Austin 1981), repeated from Chapter 1.

(65) a. Karna wapa- rna warrayi, jukudu nanda- lha.
       man   go-   PART AUX   kangaroo kill- IMPLIC.SAME
       'The man went to kill a kangaroo.'

   b. Karna- li   marda matha- rna   warrayi, thalara
      man-   ERG stone bite- PART AUX   rain
      kurda- rnanthu.
      fall- IMPLIC.DIFF
      'The man bit the stone so the rain would fall.'

---

27 A mismatch between θ̂ and ĜF in which the θ̂ is the antecedent also appears to be involved in cases discussed by Dixon (1994: 138 fn. 34), in which verbs referring to mental processes allow the ĜF to be the reflexive and the OBJ to be its antecedent. Dixon mentions such cases in Basque, Modern Greek, and Dargwa, and notes that the normal pattern for each of these languages is for the A (ĜF) to be the antecedent. While much remains mysterious about the nature of thematic roles in psych verbs, it is plausible that these are cases like the Inversion construction discussed earlier for Russian, and the Experiencer OBJ is the θ̂.

Similarly, note the following Mojave sentences (Langdon and Munro 1979).

(66) a. ʔinyeč   pap   ʔ- əkčoːr- k   ʔ-   salʸiː- k.
        me   potato   1- peel-   SAME   1-   fry-   TNS
        'After I peeled the potatoes, I fried them.'

  b. ʔinʸeč   pap   ʔ- əkčoːr- m   Judy- č   salʸiː- k.
     me   Potato   1- peel-   DIFF   Judy- SUBJ   fry-   TNS
     'After I peeled the potatoes, Judy fried them.'

Switch-reference marking can also appear in coordination structures, as in the following sentences from Maricopa (Gordon 1983) and Lenakel (Lynch 1983).

(67) **Maricopa**
  a. Nyaa   ʼ-   ashvar- k   ʼ-   iima-   k.
     me   1SUBJ-   sing-   SAME   1SUBJ-   dance- ASP
     'I sang and danced.'

  b. Bonnie- sh   ashvar- m   ʼ-   iima-   k.
     Bonnie- SUBJ   sing-   DIFF   1SUBJ-   dance- ASP
     'Bonnie sang and I danced.'

(68) **Lenakel**
  a. I-   im-   vɨn   (kani) m-   ɨm-   apul.
     1EXCL.SUBJ-   PST-   go   and   SAME-   PST-   sleep
     'I went and slept.'

  b. I-   im-   vɨn   (kani) r-   ɨm-   apul.
     1EXCL.SUBJ-   PST-   go   and   3SG.SUBJ- PST-   sleep
     'I went and he slept.'

Switch-reference bears some similarity to control/equi, to be discussed in Chapter 5, but it is a distinct construction. The differences are discussed by Hale (1992); the most important being that in switch-reference the identity of the antecedent is a property of the switch-reference morphology, while in control there is no overt marking of antecedent.

Following previous researchers (such as Finer 1985, Hale 1992, Déchaine and Wiltschko 2002), we analyze switch-reference as being essentially anaphoric in nature. There are several reasons to take such a view. In the first place, it often disambiguates what would be an ambiguous anaphoric construction in other languages.[28] In the following example from Mojave (Langdon and Munro 1979), for example, the English translation is ambiguous (which is why the annotation with referential indices is necessary) while the Mojave sentences are unambiguous.

---

28 This is not to say that the function of switch-reference is disambiguation. As Finer (1985) points out, if it were just a disambiguation mechanism one would not expect it to be required in situations that are unambiguous. It is an anaphoric mechanism.

(69) a. Nya- isvar- k iːma- k
when- sing- SAME dance- TNS
'When he$_{i,*j}$ sang, he$_i$ danced.'

b. Nya- isvar- m iːma- k
when- sing- DIFF dance- TNS
'When he$_{j,*i}$ sang, he$_i$ danced.'

Perhaps a more convincing argument is the possibility of same-reference marking when the subjects of the two clauses overlap in reference. This use of same-reference marking can be seen in the following Diyari examples (Austin 1981):

(70) a. Ngathu nganyja- yi, ngalda diyari yawada
I.ERG want- PRES we.DU.INCL.NOM Diyari language
yathayatha- lha.
speak- IMPLIC.SAME
'I want us to speak Diyari.'

b. Yula wapa- mayi, ngayana
you.DU.NOM go- IMP we.PL.INCL.NOM
nhayi- lha nhanha.
see- IMPLIC.SAME her.ACC
'You two go, and we'll all see her.'

Overlapping reference is also apparent in the following sentences from the Uto-Aztecan language Huichol (Comrie 1983).

(71) a. Taame te- haataʔazɨa- ka, nee ne- petɨa.
we 1PL- arrive- SAME I 1SG- leave
'When we arrived, I left.'

b. Nee ne- haataʔa- ka, tanaitɨ te- pekɨɨ.
I 1SG- arrive- SAME together 1PL- leave
'When I arrived, we left together.'

The use of same marking with overlapping reference is not obligatory in all languages, as shown in the following Mojave sentence (Langdon and Munro 1979):

(72) ʔ- ivaː- k / m John mat ʔ- kunav- m.
1- arrive- SAME / DIFF John RECIP 1- talk- TNS
'When I arrived, John and I talked together.'

In the Benue-Congo language Gokana (which marks same subject but not different subject), same-subject marking is optional if the (third-person) subordinate subject includes the matrix subject, and impossible if the matrix subject includes the subordinate subject.

(73) a. Aè kɔ baè dɔ- ɛ̀.
       he said they fell- SAME
       'He$_i$ said that they$_{i+j}$ fell.'

   b. Aè kɔ baè dɔ.
       he said they fell
       'He$_i$ said that they$_{i+j}$ fell.'

(74) a. Baè kɔ aè dɔ.
       they said he fell
       'They$_{j/i+j}$ said that he$_{i+j}$ fell.'

   b. *Baè kɔ aè dɔ- ɛ̀.
       they said he fell- SAME

Despite the different implementation in different languages, the possibility of same-reference marking for overlapping reference is a clearly anaphor-like property of switch-reference systems. Finally, the existence of markings for coreference and disjoint reference with an element which is structurally close is reminiscent of the reflexive/non-reflexive pronoun distinction in anaphoric binding.

Note that we are not claiming that the switch-reference morpheme is necessarily itself a kind of incorporated pronoun. In the different-reference sentences, it clearly is not a pronoun as there can be overt subjects in the subordinate clause. Even in same-reference clauses, while overt subjects are less common, they are attested, as in the Diyari examples in (71). Instead, switch-reference defines anaphoric possibilities for the subject, and is at best optionally pronominal itself. In this respect, switch-reference is similar to agreement, which can also be optionally pronominal. We thus agree with Haiman and Munro (1983), who suggest that switch-reference is an agreement-like construction.

The crucial question concerning switch-reference is what is meant by "subject." If switch-reference is a kind of anaphora, we would expect some combination of $\widehat{\text{GF}}$ and $\hat{\theta}$ to be the relevant concept. That switch-reference marking can involve $\hat{\theta}$ has been demonstrated by Farrell *et al.* (1991) in their discussion of switch-reference in the Hokan language Seri. They show that in passives, it is the *by* phrase which counts as subject, not the Patient argument. (In Seri, same reference is not overtly marked.)

(75) a. M-   yo-   aː?-   kašni kokašni šo
       2SG.SUBJ- DIST- PASS- bite   snake   a
       m-   t-   aʔo ma / *∅.
       2SG.SUBJ- REAL- see   DIFF
       'You were bitten, after you had seen a snake.'

b. ʔp-   po-   aː?-   kašni ta-   / *ø- χ
   1SG.SUBJ- IRR- PASS- bite DIFF-   TNS
   ʔp-   si-   oːʔa ʔa=   ʔa.
   1SG.SUBJ- IRR- cry   AUX= DECL
   'If I am bitten, I will cry.'

To be more precise, we predict that the antecedent, the element in the unmarked clause, will be G͡F or θ̂. We make no prediction about the anaphoric element in the marked clause. In most cases, it is also some combination of G͡F and θ̂; in fact, it is the same as the antecedent. This is plausibly a result of functional pressure for parallelism. However, if switch-reference marking is similar to agreement, we would expect other possibilities. One example of a system in which the element in the subordinate (marked) clause is not limited to x̂ is Gokana (Comrie 1983), in which the antecedent is limited to subject, but the element in the subordinate clause can have any function.

(76) a. Aè kɔ   aè dɔ-   è̀.
        he said he fell- SAME
        'He_i said that he_i fell.'
     b. Aè kɔ   oò div- èè   e.
        he said you hit- SAME him
        'He_i said that you hit him_i.'
     c. Aè kɔ   oò ziv- èè   a   gíá́.
        he said you stole- SAME his yams
        'He_i said that you stole his_i yams.'

In mixed-subject languages, we would expect the A of a transitive clause to be the antecedent "subject" for the purposes of switch-reference marking, not the P. The existence of switch-reference marking in mixed-subject languages is controversial, but one convincing case is the Dyirbal *ŋurra* construction. The suffix -*ŋurra*, which replaces tense inflection, goes on the verb in a clause if its S/P is identical to the A in the previous clause and if the action of the second clause is immediately after the action of the first clause. The suffix replaces tense inflection. The nominal in the second clause is optionally present; it is more commonly omitted (Dixon 1972: 77–8).

(77) a. Bala   yugu baŋgul yara- ŋgu mada- n   (bayi yara)
        IV   stick I.ERG man-   ERG throw- NFUT I   man
        wayn^yji- ŋurra.
        go.uphill- IMM.SAME
        'The man threw the stick and then he [immediately] went uphill.'

b. Balan jugumbil baŋgul yara-ŋgu balga- n (bayi yara)
   II   woman I.ERG man-ERG hit- NFUT I   man
   baŋgul gambaru biji- ŋurra.
   I.ERG rain.ERG punch- IMM.SAME
   'The man hit the woman until the rain started to fall on him.'

Dixon (1994: 167) resists the analysis of ŋurra as a switch-reference marker. He states that switch-reference systems have two markers: one for same-subject and one for different-subject, and that Dyirbal has no different-subject marker. However, as can be seen in the above examples, not all systems have two contrasting markers. He also argues that switch-reference marks sameness or difference of reference for the same element in both clauses, while with ŋurra it is the A of the first clause and the S/P of the second clause. Here again, Dixon's characterization of switch-reference appears to be too narrow. The fact that -ŋurra can optionally co-occur with an overt argument makes it look very much like a switch-reference construction, and it is not clear to us what alternative analysis it could be given. Crucially for the issue at hand, the antecedent of the -ŋurra construction is the A argument.[29] This is as we predict, and rather unusual for Dyirbal, where S/P relations predominate in cross-clausal phenomena. The rarity of switch-reference in mixed-subject languages is not problematic;[30] our discussion of switch-reference in Chapter 6 leads us to expect that there will be few mixed-subject (or uniform-subject) languages with switch-reference constructions. The limited evidence that exists agrees with the consensus in the typological literature that switch-reference operates along "accusative" rather than "ergative" lines; i.e., subject is S/A, not S/P (Palmer 1994, Dixon 1994).

The switch-reference construction behaves the way we would expect an anaphoric construction to behave. The targeted element is the "subject" in the sense of either $\widehat{\text{GF}}$ or $\hat{\theta}$.

---

29 The coreferential element in the -ŋurra-marked clause is S/P, not A, but, as we have observed, the theory proposed here does not predict that the element in the switch-reference clause must be A; see the discussion of Gokana above.

30 Another possible case is the Eskimo languages, which have a construction which is sometimes identified as switch-reference, e.g., by Finer (1985), the so-called fourth person affix. However, it differs from switch-reference in that it is not limited to adjacent clauses. (In addition, the subordinate position need not be a subject; as we have seen, however, this is not an absolute requirement for switch-reference.) A more plausible analysis, which we have followed above, is that the verbal affix in question is an incorporated reflexive (Manning 1996). In any case, the antecedent for the Eskimo fourth person is $\hat{x}$, not P, so if it is a switch-reference construction it conforms to our prediction.

2.4 Summary

In this chapter, we have explored the nature of subjecthood from the perspective of argumenthood. We have concluded that one aspect of subjecthood is the expression of the highest-ranked argument of the verb as a core argument. The "subject" grammatical function which is involved, which we have dubbed ĜF, displays properties relating to the hierarchical nature of argument realization. The properties of ĜF follow from the functional nature of ĜF: properties resulting from the alignment of the relational hierarchy with other hierarchies (Agents as ĜF; ĜF as default topic); properties based on a hierarchical effect of specification of argument properties (null pronouns; imperative addressee); and binding-theoretic properties (anaphoric prominence; switch-reference target).

In this respect, there is no difference between uniform-subject languages and mixed-subject languages. We thus reject the idea (Marantz 1984, Manning 1996) that there are languages with an inverse mapping system, in which the hierarchical relations between arguments are reversed in the a-structure – f-structure mapping. Such an inverse mapping is conceptually undesirable in any case, since the usual tendency in language is for prominences at different hierarchies to align with each other.

3 *Pivot*

3.1 The pivot function

3.1.1 The concept

In the previous chapter, we examined the concept of subject from the perspective of argumenthood, and concluded that the subject is the most prominent core argument of the verb, $\widehat{\text{GF}}$. We saw that some subject properties, specifically those that are shared by uniform-subject languages and mixed-subject languages (Type 1 properties), are explained by this view of subjecthood. These are properties which are based in one way or another on the relational hierarchy of argument functions: the alignment of the relational hierarchy with other hierarchies (agenthood, topichood), the specification of properties of arguments by the head verb (null pronominals, imperative addressee), and anaphora (anaphoric prominence, switch-reference).

However, we still need to account for the Type 2 properties, the ones that differ in uniform-subject and mixed-subject languages. These properties are the following.

(1)   a. Shared argument in coordinated clauses
Controlled argument (PRO) (in some languages)
Raising
Extraction properties
b. Obligatory element
Definiteness or wide scope
"External" structural position

These "subject properties" differ from the ones discussed in the previous chapter. The properties of $\widehat{\text{GF}}$ are the result of the status of $\widehat{\text{GF}}$ as an argument in hierarchical relation with other arguments; they are relative properties which are, in some languages, shared with other arguments. The properties in (1) are related neither to argumenthood nor to hierarchies. They have nothing to do with hierarchies because they are unique properties of a single distinguished element in the clause. They have nothing to do with argumenthood because they are not properties that relate the "subject" to a head that selects it. We therefore would not expect the ĜF function to result in these properties; they must be the consequence of a different grammatical function. The fact that these properties characterize a different element from the argument-related properties in ergative and Philippine-type languages reinforces the conclusion that these properties do not follow from the nature of the function ĜF.

We propose that the Type 2 properties are associated with a grammatical function which we call PIV (pivot), loosely following Foley and Van Valin (1984) and Dixon (1979, 1994). The familiar concept of subject in uniform-subject languages is thus an amalgam of two distinct grammatical functions: ĜF and PIV. The realization that there is more to subjecthood than argumenthood has led some researchers in LFG (such as Bresnan 2001) to cross-classify the SUBJ function as a grammaticized discourse function, but the Type 2 properties are no more discourse-related than they are argument-related. We therefore do not consider PIV to be a grammaticized discourse function. We need to take a closer look at the PIV-related properties to determine the nature of the PIV function.

We begin our discussion of the PIV function by considering the properties in (1a), which we take to be the core properties of PIV. These properties relate to the sharing of a single element by more than one clause. In the coordination construction in question, an argument is shared by the coordinate clauses. In control and raising constructions, the main clause and subordinate clause share an argument. Since extraction is often long-distance, cross-clausal sharing of an element is often a factor in extraction constructions as well. These properties are inherently non-local, and lead to the conclusion that the PIV function is the function of cross-clausal connections, or cross-clausal continuity.

(2)   The PIV is the element with the function of connecting its clause to other clauses in the sentence.

This function is unrelated to questions of argument realization. It thus contrasts sharply with the ĜF function discussed in the previous chapter, and is not inherently related to it.

We will have less to say about the properties in (1b), which we take to be secondary properties. Unlike the (1a) properties, these properties do not relate elements of different clauses. However, they are similar to those other PIV properties in that they are not related to argument hierarchies either. Instead, they seem to be based on the notion that the PIV is a distinguished element of the clause, with properties beyond being in a particular position on the relational hierarchy. There is also a topic-like quality to some of these properties – in particular, definiteness and wide scope. We will discuss these properties briefly later.

In order to understand the PIV function better, we begin by noting that the grammatical functions generally assumed in theories like LFG (as in, for example, Bresnan 2001) can be divided into three groups:

(3) a. Argument functions: local, selected by predicate
     $\widehat{GF}$
     OBJ
     OBJ_θ (or OBJ2 or $OBJ_{indirect}$)
     OBL_θ
     COMP, XCOMP, etc.
  b. Adjunct functions: local, not selected by predicate
     ADJ, XADJ, etc.
  c. Grammaticized discourse functions: not local, related to discourse
     TOPIC
     FOCUS
     etc.

Of these, the argument and adjunct functions are local in their scope – they function to express relations within their clause, and they are locally licensed. Argument functions are licensed by being selected, and adjuncts by modifying meaningful elements. The grammaticized discourse functions (FOCUS, TOPIC, etc.), on the other hand, relate otherwise-licensed elements to the larger discourse within which they are embedded. That is to say, all elements are locally licensed,[1] but an argument (or adjunct) can be assigned an additional, not locally relevant, function. This is reflected in LFG's Extended Coherence Condition (and in transformational notions such as D(eep) structure and Merge at θ position, which give argument "positions" a special status). This property of the grammaticized discourse functions is captured particularly well terminologically in RG, where these functions are referred to as overlay functions (or relations). We will follow the RG terminology here.

Something is missing from this set of relations expressed by grammatical functions. We have grammatical functions that are local to the clause in which they are located and grammatical functions that relate a clause to the larger discourse. What we seem not to have is a function expressing the relation between elements of a clause and the sentence (i.e. larger *syntactic* structure) of which it is a part. It is this gap that we propose to close with the function PIV. The

---

1 A possible exception to this can be found in a subset of what are sometimes known as topic-oriented languages. We will discuss this briefly in Chapter 6.

PIV is a kind of sentence-internal topic.[2] Just as a discourse topic (represented syntactically in many languages as the grammatical function TOPIC) identifies a single participant as the common thread running through a discourse, the PIV is the common thread running through clauses that make up a sentence. Every clause in a syntactic structure (sentence) will have a PIV.

As we conceive of it here, PIV is an overlay function, but crucially not a discourse function. There is nothing inherently discourse-related about the PIV. It relates exclusively to syntactic properties. In this sense it is sui generis, although (as an overlay function) it is related to the discourse functions.

3.1.2   Formalization: the Pivot Condition

In a formal theory like LFG, the idea that PIV is the function of syntactic cross-clausal continuity needs to be expressed in terms of the technical concepts of the framework. It is the role of the formalism to provide a precise expression of intuitions of linguistic analysis. This formal instantiation will play a major role in our understanding of the properties of PIV.

As we saw in Chapter 1, the major formal tool for expressing relations between elements in LFG is the functional constraint, annotated to phrase structure rules or encoded in the lexicon. It was noted in passing in Chapter 1 that these functional constraints designate paths through the f-structure. To take an example from the previous chapter, if a verb includes the information that its object is a (covert) pronoun (that is to say, the OBJ has the attribute PRED with the value 'PRO'), this is expressed formally through the following constraint in the verb's lexical entry.

(4)   ($\uparrow$ OBJ PRED)= 'PRO'

The parenthesized expression on the left side of this equation defines a path through the f-structure, where '$\uparrow$' represents the local f-structure where the path begins:

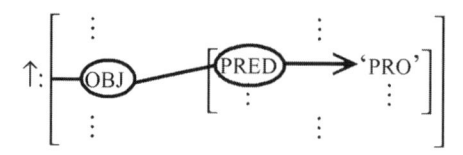

$$\uparrow: \begin{bmatrix} \vdots \\ \text{OBJ} \begin{bmatrix} \vdots \\ \text{PRED} \rightarrow \text{'PRO'} \\ \vdots \end{bmatrix} \\ \vdots \end{bmatrix}$$

---

[2] In class lectures on this material, I have anthropomorphized the concept and referred to the PIV as the clause's ambassador to the rest of the sentence. I think that this metaphor actually goes a long way towards explaining the concept and some of its consequences.

In early LFG (Kaplan and Bresnan 1982) it was proposed that such paths be limited to a length of 2, by what was called the Functional Locality Condition. This idea was subsequently abandoned with the advent of the formalism of functional uncertainty (Kaplan and Zaenen 1989) for licensing long-distance dependency constructions.[3] The abandonment of the Functional Locality Condition, justified though it was, has left LFG with no formal expression of the intuitive idea that arguments are beholden exclusively to the predicates of which they are arguments. The PIV function allows us to return to the intuition that the theory needs to express this.

The core of Kaplan and Bresnan's Functional Locality Condition is the idea that a functional expression should not be allowed to directly specify properties of an argument function in a lower or coordinate clause. As suggested in the previous paragraph, this follows from the nature of argumenthood. Arguments are selected by their local predicates. As we saw in Chapter 2, the properties of arguments can be determined by their local predicates. Arguments are strictly local in their scope. A formal theory based on grammatical functions should express this.

The PIV function is not an argument function, and therefore is not local in its scope. It is an overlay function, a second function assigned to a locally licensed element. Assigning the PIV function to an element which bears an argument function provides a formal escape hatch to the locality of arguments: it allows higher clauses to specify information about it. We propose to formally restrict functional designations in such a way that the only way to refer to a function in a lower or coordinate clause is through the function PIV. We refer to this as the Pivot Condition.

The Pivot Condition needs to constrain two types of paths: the path inward from a superordinate argument domain to a subordinate one (argument or adjunct), and the path from one conjunct of a coordinate structure to the other. The former case can be shown schematically as follows:

(5) $$f : \begin{bmatrix} \vdots \\ g : \begin{bmatrix} \text{PRED } \text{`P} \langle \ldots \rangle \text{'} \end{bmatrix} \end{bmatrix}$$

A functional constraint associated with f cannot refer to a non-PIV function inside g: it cannot assert its identity to an element in f or specify any features for it. It is crucial that g be a distinct predicate-argument domain; we do not want

---

3 We will discuss long-distance dependencies in Chapter 4.

78 Subjects and their properties

to rule out reference to, say, the object of a non-predicative "Case-marking" preposition by a designator such as (↑ OBL$_\theta$ OBJ). The formal statement will therefore have to distinguish argument-taking PREDs. The second kind of path is illustrated by the following f-structure and corresponding c-structure:

(6) $\left[\begin{array}{l}\left[h:\left[\quad\right]\right]\\\left\{i:\left[\quad\right]\right\}\end{array}\right]$
$\begin{array}{c}S\\/\quad\backslash\\S_h\quad S_i\end{array}$

Here, the restriction will be against a constraint associated with h referencing a non-PIV element of i, and against a constraint associated with i referencing a non-PIV element of h. We can think of a path from h into i or from i into h informally as a sideways path.[4] Formally, we want to restrict the form of a path stated in terms of "f-structure element corresponding to the right sister" – $\phi(*>)$ – or "f-structure element corresponding to the left sister"– $\phi(<*)$. We include both an informal version of the Pivot Condition and a formal version.

(7)   *The Pivot Condition*

Informal statement
A path inward through f-structure into another predicate-argument domain or sideways into a coordinate f-structure must terminate in the function PIV.

Formal statement[5]
In a functional designation of the form (↑ ... α ... β γ) where
    α   or ($\phi(<*$ ... β γ)) or ($\phi(*>$ ... β γ)), if β is a
(→ PRED ARG1)'
grammatical function and either γ = ∅ or γ is a feature, β = PIV.

The Pivot Condition is the formal statement of the functional role of PIV. It plays a major role in pivot properties, because it restricts reference from one clause to a lower (or coordinate) clause to the PIV of the lower clause.

3.2   Uniform subjects and mixed subjects

The foregoing says nothing about which element of the clause is the PIV. Unlike the ĜF function, PIV is not part of a hierarchical system which is associated

---

4 The term "sideways" is perhaps not the most felicitous, as it fits the visual orientation of c-structure rather than f-structure.
5 The off-path constraint checks for argument-taking PREDs only. The notation comes from Kaplan and Maxwell (1996), and checks for the presence of a first argument in the value of the PRED feature.

with another hierarchical system. Since PIV is an overlay function, and thus subject to LFG's Extended Coherence Condition, it must be an element which is also locally licensed. But nothing else follows. We are thus led to expect that different languages will make different choices about which element is the PIV. We already know that this is true, since PIV properties (Type 2 subject properties) are associated with different elements in different languages. This is what differentiates uniform-subject languages from mixed-subject languages.

One very common assignment of the PIV function is to identify it with the $\widehat{\text{GF}}$. In languages which make this identification, every verb will have the following predictable lexical specification:

(8) $(\uparrow \text{PIV}) = (\uparrow \widehat{\text{GF}})$

This is the assignment which defines what we have been referring to as uniform-subject languages. It appears to be the unmarked assignment, perhaps because it enhances the high prominence of the $\widehat{\text{GF}}$ argument by assigning it a different kind (albeit not hierarchical) of prominence.[6] It results in a single element, the "subject," which has both the function of $\widehat{\text{GF}}$ and the function of PIV, and thus one element with "subject properties." Because this is the PIV identification in familiar European languages, it has led to the illusion that subject is a universal of language.

However, nothing requires the identification of PIV with $\widehat{\text{GF}}$. Since PIV is not part of a hierarchy, there is no hierarchy alignment involved here as there is in the topicality and agentivity of $\widehat{\text{GF}}$. If a different element is assigned the PIV function, the result is what we have been calling a mixed-subject language. In such a language, there is no single element which can be referred to as subject in the traditional sense, since the traditional concept of subject is an entity which is both $\widehat{\text{GF}}$ and PIV. One type of mixed-subject language is the syntactically ergative language; in such a language, the PIV is the OBJ if there is one.[7]

(9) $(\uparrow \text{OBJ}) \Rightarrow (\uparrow \text{PIV}) = (\uparrow \text{OBJ})$

This is what results in the mixed character of the subject properties in syntactic ergative languages: in a transitive clause those properties which are a consequence of the $\widehat{\text{GF}}$ function will be properties of the A argument ($\widehat{\text{GF}}$), while

---

6 I'd like to thank Chris Manning (personal communication) for suggesting this to me.
7 Otherwise, it is the $\widehat{\text{GF}}$. I assume this is a result of the need for the PIV to be identified with something, and the $\widehat{\text{GF}}$ being the only available element. The double-shanked arrow here is a conditional: "if $(\uparrow \text{OBJ})$ exists, then ..."

those which are a consequence of the PIV function will be properties of the P argument (OBJ).

The difference between uniform-subject languages and mixed-subject languages can be illustrated with f-structures of corresponding sentences in the two types of languages. We showed in Chapter 1 that Inuit is a mixed-subject (syntactically ergative) language, with the P argument displaying Type 2 subject properties (extractability and wide scope). We present here the f-structure of an Inuit sentence (from Marantz 1984) and its translation into English, a uniform-subject (nominative-accusative) language.

(10) **Inuit**
a. Anut- ip   arnaq   taku- vaa.
   man- ERG   woman see- IND.3SG.3SG
   'The man saw the woman.'

$$\begin{bmatrix} \widehat{GF} & [\text{"man"}] \\ OBJ & [\text{"woman"}] \\ TENSE & PAST \\ PRED & \text{'see} \langle (\uparrow \widehat{GF})(\uparrow OBJ) \rangle \text{'} \\ PIV & \end{bmatrix}$$

(11) **English**
a. The man saw the woman.

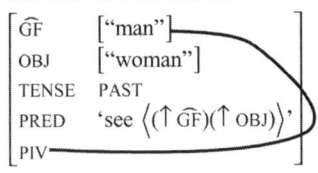

$$\begin{bmatrix} \widehat{GF} & [\text{"man"}] \\ OBJ & [\text{"woman"}] \\ TENSE & PAST \\ PRED & \text{'see} \langle (\uparrow \widehat{GF})(\uparrow OBJ) \rangle \text{'} \\ PIV & \end{bmatrix}$$

The arguments map to the same grammatical functions in the two languages: the Agent is $\widehat{GF}$ and the Patient is OBJ. The only difference is the identity of the PIV.

In Philippine-type languages, the lexical marking on the verb is governed by the "voice" morphology. As we showed in Chapter 1, the nominative nominal is the element with Type 2 subject properties (such as extractability and accessibility to raising), and thus it is the PIV.

(12)   with "Active voice" morphology: $(\uparrow PIV) = (\uparrow \widehat{GF})$
       with "Direct object voice" morphology: $(\uparrow PIV) = (\uparrow OBJ)$
       with "Indirect object/locative voice": $(\uparrow PIV) = (\uparrow OBJ_{Indirect})$
       with "Instrumental voice" morphology: $(\uparrow PIV) = (\uparrow OBL_{Instr})$
       etc.

Consider the following sentences from Schachter (1987: 941):

(13) a. Mag-   aalis   ang   tindero   ng   bigas
         ACT-   CNTMP.take.out NOM   storekeeper   ACC   rice
         sa   sako   para sa   babae.
         DAT   sack   for   DAT   woman
         'The storekeeper will take some rice out of a/the sack for a/the woman.'

      b. Aalis-   in   ng   tindero   ang   bigas
         CNTMP.take.out- DO   ERG   storekeeper   NOM   rice
         sa   sako   para sa   babae.
         DAT   sack   for   DAT   woman
         'A/The storekeeper will take the rice out of a/the sack for a/the woman.'

      c. Aalis-   an   ng   tindero   ng   bigas
         CNTMP.take.out- IO   ERG   storekeeper   ACC   rice
         ang   sako   para sa   babae.
         NOM   sack   for   DAT   woman
         'A/The storekeeper will take some rice out of the sack for a/the woman.'

      d. Ipag-   aalis   ng   tindero   ng   bigas
         BEN- CNTMP.take.out ERG   storekepper   ACC   rice
         sa   sako   ang   babae.
         DAT   sack   NOM   woman
         'A/The storekeeper will take some rice out of a/the sack for the woman.'

For each of these sentences, the lexical entry of the verb and the full f-structure are as follows.

(14) a. *magaalis*: ($\uparrow$ PRED) = 'take-out $\langle(\uparrow \widehat{\text{GF}})(\uparrow \text{OBJ})(\uparrow \text{OBJ}_{\text{Source}})(\uparrow \text{OBL}_{\text{Ben}})\rangle$'
         ($\uparrow$ TENSE) = CONTEMP
         ($\uparrow$ PIV) = ($\uparrow \widehat{\text{GF}}$)

$$\begin{bmatrix} \text{PRED} & \text{'take-out } \langle(\uparrow \widehat{\text{GF}})(\uparrow \text{OBJ})(\uparrow \text{OBJ}_{\text{Source}})(\uparrow \text{OBL}_{\text{Ben}})\rangle\text{'} \\ \text{TENSE} & \text{CONTEMP} \\ \text{PIV} & [\text{"storekeeper"}] \\ \widehat{\text{GF}} & \\ \text{OBJ} & [\text{"rice"}] \\ \text{OBJ}_{\text{Source}} & [\text{"sack"}] \\ \text{OBL}_{\text{Ben}} & [\text{"woman"}] \end{bmatrix}$$

b. *aalisin:* (↑ PRED) = 'take-out ⟨(↑ ĜF)(↑ OBJ)(↑ OBJ$_{Source}$)(↑ OBL$_{Ben}$)⟩'
   (↑ TENSE) = CONTEMP
   (↑ PIV) = (↑ OBJ)

$$\begin{bmatrix} \text{PRED} & \text{'take-out } \langle(\uparrow \widehat{\text{GF}})(\uparrow \text{OBJ})(\uparrow \text{OBJ}_{\text{Source}})(\uparrow \text{OBL}_{\text{Ben}})\rangle\text{'} \\ \text{TENSE} & \text{CONTEMP} \\ \text{PIV} & [\text{"rice"}] \\ \widehat{\text{GF}} & [\text{"storekeeper"}] \\ \text{OBJ} & \\ \text{OBJ}_{\text{Source}} & [\text{"sack"}] \\ \text{OBL}_{\text{Ben}} & [\text{"woman"}] \end{bmatrix}$$

c. *aalisan:* (↑ PRED) = 'take-out ⟨(↑ ĜF)(↑ OBJ)(↑ OBJ$_{Source}$)(↑ OBL$_{Ben}$)⟩'
   (↑ TENSE) CONTEMP
   (↑ PIV) = (↑ OBJ$_\theta$)

$$\begin{bmatrix} \text{PRED} & \text{'take-out } \langle(\uparrow \widehat{\text{GF}})(\uparrow \text{OBJ})(\uparrow \text{OBJ}_{\text{Source}})(\uparrow \text{OBL}_{\text{Ben}})\rangle\text{'} \\ \text{TENSE} & \text{CONTEMP} \\ \text{PIV} & [\text{"sack"}] \\ \widehat{\text{GF}} & [\text{"storekeeper"}] \\ \text{OBJ} & [\text{"rice"}] \\ \text{OBJ}_{\text{Source}} & \\ \text{OBL}_{\text{Ben}} & [\text{"woman"}] \end{bmatrix}$$

d. *ipagaalis:* (↑ PRED) = 'take-out ⟨(↑ ĜF)(↑ OBJ)(↑ OBJ$_{Source}$)(↑ OBL$_{Ben}$)⟩'
   (↑ TENSE) = CONTEMP
   (↑ PIV) = (↑ OBL$_{Ben}$)

$$\begin{bmatrix} \text{PRED} & \text{'take-out } \langle(\uparrow \widehat{\text{GF}})(\uparrow \text{OBJ})(\uparrow \text{OBJ}_{\text{Source}})(\uparrow \text{OBL}_{\text{Ben}})\rangle\text{'} \\ \text{TENSE} & \text{CONTEMP} \\ \text{PIV} & [\text{"woman"}] \\ \widehat{\text{GF}} & [\text{"storekeeper"}] \\ \text{OBJ} & [\text{"rice"}] \\ \text{OBJ}_{\text{Source}} & [\text{"sack"}] \\ \text{OBL}_{\text{Ben}} & \end{bmatrix}$$

Under the theory proposed here, then, there is a natural account of the typological distinction between the uniform-subject languages and the different types of mixed-subject languages. The difference is not, as in inverse mapping theories, in the mapping of the arguments, but rather in the assignment of the PIV function to an argument. The unity of "subject" seen in uniform-subject languages is something of an illusion – a consequence of the identification of PIV with ĜF. ĜF and PIV are not types of subjects, or subclasses of the larger class of subjects. The split of subject properties in mixed-subject languages is more revealing of the nature of the properties and the functions from which they derive: local, hierarchical, argumenthood properties are properties of ĜF, while cross-clausal properties are properties of PIV.

3.3 Pivothood and constructions

3.3.1 Types of constructions

The concept of pivothood which we have developed here owes much to previous work in the typological and functionalist literature, especially Dixon (1994). However, our PIV differs in one crucial respect from the pivot of these other researchers. Under our conception, the choice of PIV is determined by the grammar of the language: pivothood is a language-wide concept. In this respect, PIV is no different from any other grammatical function. However, the typological and functionalist literature often takes pivothood to depend on the construction involved, with different constructions using different pivots. For example, Dixon (1994: 175) states that "[s]ome languages combine S/A pivots and S/O pivots" and refers to these as mixed-pivot languages. Van Valin and LaPolla (1997: 275–278) are very emphatic about this.

> A very important feature of the concepts of controller and pivot is that they exist only with reference to specific morphosyntactic phenomena, and each grammatical phenomenon may define one controller and/or one pivot. . . . Pivots are construction-specific . . .
>
> Moreover, as we said above, controller and pivot are *construction-specific* [emphasis in the original]. The usual notion of subject in syntactic theory, on the other hand, is not construction-specific but rather is a feature of the grammatical system as a whole. For this reason one does not talk about "the subject of finite verb agreement" or "the subject of the matrix-coding construction", since subject is not a construction-specific notion; rather, one can talk about "subject in English" or "subject in Malagasy", etc. Conversely, one does not speak of, for example, "the pivot of English" or "the controller of English", as there is no such concept. We can only speak in terms of the controllers and pivots of specific phenomena or constructions, such as "the controller of finite verb agreement" and "the pivot of the matrix coding-construction" in English.

In contrast to the position expressed by Van Valin and LaPolla, we claim that there is such a thing as the pivot of English/Dyirbal/etc. The grammar of English identifies the PIV as being a second function borne by the ĜF, the grammar of Dyirbal identifies PIV with OBJ, and the grammars of some languages supply a tool (such as verbal morphology in the Philippine-type languages) to assign the PIV function. We address the issue of alleged multiple pivots in this section.

We believe that the typological/functionalist approach is based on a misunderstanding of the concept of construction in cross-linguistic study.[8] Our approach is based on a mixed formalist/functionalist perspective combined with the parallel architecture of the formal system we are assuming. From the functionalist perspective, we can identify a construction with the effect one wants it to have. We can call this a notional construction. For example, every language needs some way to distinguish the two major participants in a transitive clause. However, the formal linguistic system provides different ways to achieve this effect: Case marking, word order, verbal agreement markers, relative animacy, and so on. Formally, these are distinct devices which have little or nothing in common with each other. We can refer to a formal device as a formal construction.

It should not be controversial that notional constructions and formal constructions are distinct. The case discussed briefly in the previous paragraph is a relatively straightforward case.[9] We will discuss one more example before returning to issues of pivothood. Suppose one wishes to express a transitive sentence with a generic (or arbitrary) Agent. "Transitive sentence with a generic Agent" is a notional construction. Different languages use different formal tools (i.e., different formal constructions) to express this. For example, in English one would use the passive, in Spanish the reflexive, in French a generic subject pronoun, and in Hebrew (a language in which subjects must be overt in the present tense, and generally in the third person in all tenses) a (third person) plural verb form with no overt subject.

(15)   a. **English**
English is spoken in America.
      b. **Spanish**
Se   habla   español en México.
REFL speak.PRES.3SG Spanish in Mexico
'Spanish is spoken (literally: 'speaks itself') in Mexico.'
      c. **French**
On parle   français à   Paris.
one speak.PRES.3SG French at Paris
'French is spoken (literally: 'one speaks French') in Paris.'
      d. **Hebrew**
Medabrim   ivrit   be Yisrael.
speak.PRES.MPL Hebrew in Israel
'Hebrew is spoken (literally: '[they] speak Hebrew') in Israel.'

---

8 This misunderstanding is not limited to researchers in the typological and functionalist traditions; one also finds it in much work in formalist frameworks. See footnote 9 for an example.

9 In some formal theories of syntax, particularly those in the GB/MP tradition, many of the methods used to distinguish the major participants in a transitive clause are subsumed under "Case marking." This is an example of formalist conflation of notional and formal constructions.

These four languages exhibit four different formal constructions for the same notional construction.

This distinction between notional and formal constructions is also relevant, we claim, for constructions that are potentially pivot-related. The PIV function is part of the formal syntactic system; more specifically, the Pivot Condition is a restriction on the form of formal syntactic constraints. Sensitivity to pivothood is therefore a property of formal constructions. It is inappropriate to define constructions notionally for the purpose of identifying pivots, as is often done in the functionalist and typological literature. In the coming chapters, we will take a detailed look at long-distance dependency constructions and especially control constructions, where the availability of more than one formal construction obscures the basic facts about subject properties. At this point, we will take a look at shared elements in coordination. Consider the following contrasting sentences in English and Dyirbal (Dixon 1994: 15).

(16) a. **English**
You saw us and returned.
= 'You saw us and you returned.'
b. **Dyirbal**
N^{y}urra   ŋana- na   bura- n   banaga- n^{y}u.
you.all.NOM   we.all- ACC   see- NFUT   return- NFUT
= 'You saw us and we returned.'

This contrast has often been cited (e.g., Comrie 1989, Dixon 1994, Palmer 1994) as evidence that English has an S/A (uniform-subject) pivot while Dyirbal has an S/P (mixed-subject syntactically ergative) pivot. However, a closer look reveals that the situation is more complicated. Give the formal tools of LFG, there are at least three formal ways for conjoined clauses to appear to share an element. Of these three formal constructions, only one is sensitive to pivothood. We will illustrate the three possibilities using the English sentence, and then return to the question of the correct analysis in English and Dyirbal.

One possible formal construction is subclausal constituent coordination, such as VP coordination.[10]

---

[10] Following some analyses in LFG, we assume here, and throughout, that English sentences without auxiliaries (or with inverted auxiliaries in C) are S rather than IP. Readers who would prefer to see IP in the tree are welcome to make the appropriate substitutions. For some conceptions of constituent structure, the sentence in question might be better analyzed as I′ coordination rather than VP coordination.

(17)

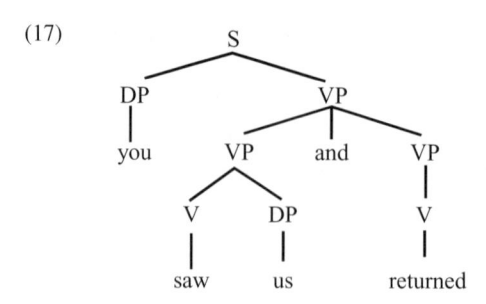

```
             S
          /     \
        DP       VP
        |      / | \
       you   VP and VP
             /\      |
            V  DP    V
            |  |     |
           saw us  returned
```

Under the LFG theory of coordination (Sadler 1999, Dalrymple and Kaplan 2000, Dalrymple 2001), coordinate structures are functionally sets. Some attributes which belong to the whole coordinate structures (including grammatical functions) are distributed over the conjuncts (that is to say, they are parts of both elements of the set). The constituent $[_{DP}you]$, which happens to bear the grammatical function PIV, is distributed over the two conjuncts. The two clauses thus share the PIV, but not because of any functional properties of the PIV. VP coordination is the result of c-structural properties – the ability of VP to be coordinated – as licensed by a phrase structure rule such as the following.

(18)   VP →   VP   CONJ   VP
                ↓∈↑   ↓∈↑

The function-sharing between the two clauses is merely a consequence of the c-structure properties of the language. Since, in English (and many other languages, but not universally) pivots have an external structural position, it is possible to coordinate constituents in such a way that the pivot will be shared. But pivothood (in our sense) is not directly implicated in constituent coordination. In fact, a topicalized OBJ can also be shared:

(19)   This kind of salad, I like and you hate.

This formal construction, as a structural (not functional) construction, is thus not pivot-sensitive.

   A second possible formal method of achieving the result of not having to repeat a shared element in both conjuncts is to use some anaphoric device, such as a null pronoun or an incorporated-pronoun agreement form (for the distinction between these, which are normally both called pro-drop, see Chapter 2). Under such an analysis, the non-initial conjuncts have a pronoun which is coreferential with an element in the first conjunct; however, this pronoun is not an overt pronounced element. This can be represented in the framework assumed here as the c-structure–f-structure pair (20), or in conventional c-structure-centric theories as (21).

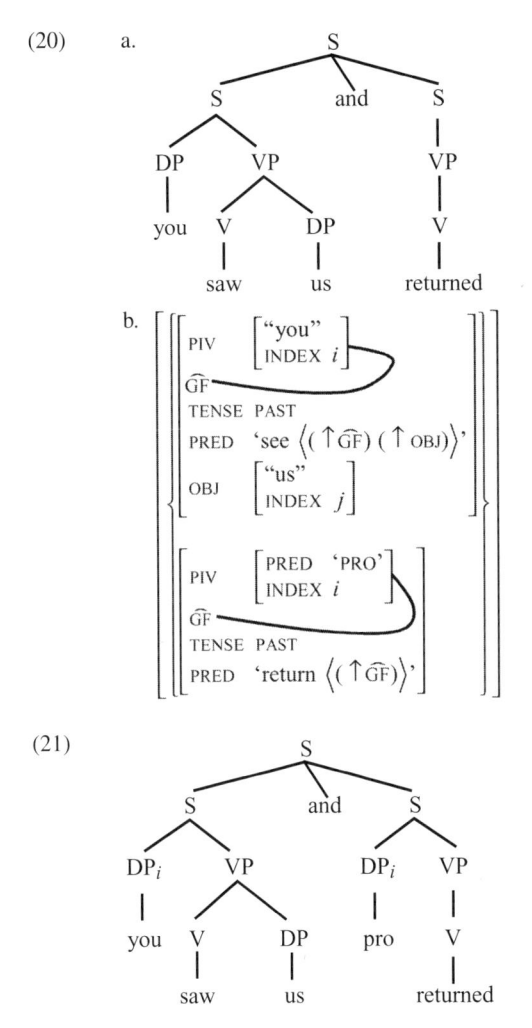

(20) a.

```
            S
          /   \
         S   and  S
        / \       |
       DP  VP     VP
       |   / \    |
      you V   DP  V
          |   |   |
         saw  us returned
```

b.

$$\left\{ \begin{bmatrix} \begin{bmatrix} \text{PIV} & \begin{bmatrix} \text{``you''} \\ \text{INDEX } i \end{bmatrix} \end{bmatrix} \\ \widehat{\text{GF}} \\ \text{TENSE PAST} \\ \text{PRED 'see} \langle (\uparrow \widehat{\text{GF}})(\uparrow \text{OBJ}) \rangle' \\ \text{OBJ} \begin{bmatrix} \text{``us''} \\ \text{INDEX } j \end{bmatrix} \end{bmatrix}, \begin{bmatrix} \text{PIV} & \begin{bmatrix} \text{PRED 'PRO'} \\ \text{INDEX } i \end{bmatrix} \\ \widehat{\text{GF}} \\ \text{TENSE PAST} \\ \text{PRED 'return} \langle (\uparrow \widehat{\text{GF}}) \rangle' \end{bmatrix} \right\}$$

(21)

```
                S
              /   \
             S   and  S
            / \       / \
          DP_i VP    DP_i VP
           |   / \    |    |
          you V   DP pro   V
              |   |        |
             saw  us    returned
```

In an anaphoric construction like this, there is no actual sharing of elements in the syntax; the elements in the conjuncts are merely coreferential, and the sharing is thus semantic rather than syntactic. From the perspective of the notional construction, the distinction between syntactic sharing and coreference is irrelevant, but formally the properties are very different. Pivothood is completely irrelevant here. As discussed in Chapter 2, the possibility of a true null pronoun is governed by the relational hierarchy and the availability of incorporated pronouns is based on the language's agreement system. This is therefore a second way to achieve the result of only naming a shared element once without using a pivot-related construction.

On the other hand, it is also possible to achieve the shared-argument notional construction through a constraint directly licensing a single syntactic element as having grammatical functions in more than one clause. Essentially following Dixon, we will refer to this kind of multifunctionality of a single syntactic element in coordination as chaining. Schematically, this would involve a phrase structure rule such as the following, where, as in the formal statement of the Pivot Condition, '$\phi(<*)$' means 'the f-structure corresponding to the left sister' and '$\phi(*>)$' means 'the f-structure corresponding to the right sister.'

(22) $\quad$ S $\rightarrow \quad$ S $\quad\quad\quad$ CONJ $\quad\quad\quad$ S
$\quad\quad\quad\quad\quad \downarrow \in \uparrow (\phi(<*)\text{GF}) = (\phi(*>)\text{GF} \quad \downarrow \in \uparrow$

The two functional designations in the constraint associated with the conjunction are subject to the Pivot Condition. Only the PIV function may be specified at the end of a path in a subordinate or coordinate clause. (22) thus reduces to (23).

(23) $\quad$ S $\rightarrow \quad$ S $\quad\quad\quad$ CONJ $\quad\quad\quad$ S
$\quad\quad\quad\quad\quad \downarrow \in \uparrow (\phi(<*)\text{PIV}) = (\phi(*>)\text{PIV}) \quad \downarrow \in \uparrow$

This licenses sentences with c-structures and f-structures that look like the following:

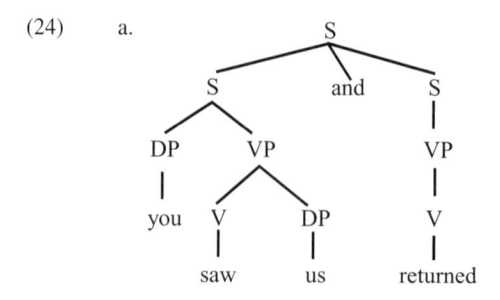

(24) a.

```
              S
        ┌─────┴─────┐
        S          and    S
      ┌─┴─┐               │
     DP   VP              VP
      │  ┌─┴─┐             │
    you  V   DP            V
         │   │             │
        saw  us         returned
```

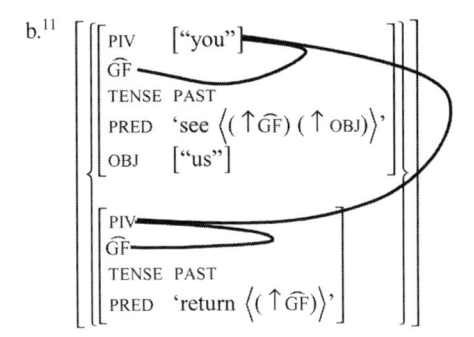

b.[11]
$$\begin{bmatrix} \begin{bmatrix} \text{PIV} & [\text{``you''}] \\ \widehat{\text{GF}} & \\ \text{TENSE} & \text{PAST} \\ \text{PRED} & \text{`see} \langle (\uparrow \widehat{\text{GF}})(\uparrow \text{OBJ}) \rangle \text{'} \\ \text{OBJ} & [\text{``us''}] \end{bmatrix} \\ \begin{bmatrix} \text{PIV} \\ \widehat{\text{GF}} \\ \text{TENSE} & \text{PAST} \\ \text{PRED} & \text{`return} \langle (\uparrow \widehat{\text{GF}}) \rangle \text{'} \end{bmatrix} \end{bmatrix}$$

In a language which uses the chaining construction, unlike the other two constructions, elements shared across coordination will be pivots.

3.3.2 Distinguishing formal constructions

Given the distinction between formal constructions and notional constructions, we can now turn to constructional properties. The properties of a construction in a particular language are a consequence of both the notional identity of the construction and its formal identity. It is often easier to determine the notional construction than the formal construction, because the notionally related properties are generally easier to identify, but a proper consideration of the question of multiple pivothood requires us to distinguish between formal constructions.

A closer look at some of the other characteristics of the language often helps tease them apart. Consider our example of the different formal constructions which can be used to realize sharing across coordination. In the case of English, a VP coordination analysis appears to be the right one. The anaphoric analysis is clearly wrong for English: subject agreement in English is anti-pronominal. Coordination is very free in English: *any* constituent can be coordinated. The grammar of English includes a rule of the form:

(25) $X^n \rightarrow X^n$ CONJ X^n
                $\downarrow \in \uparrow$ $\downarrow \in \uparrow$

Given the ease with which constituents of any category can coordinate in English, it would be very surprising if VPs were unable to coordinate, rendering the VP coordination analysis more plausible than the chaining analysis. But if this is true, sharing of elements across coordination in English does not constitute evidence for pivothood, contra Dixon (1994). In Dyirbal, on the other

---

11 Note the curved lines in the f-structure: the f-structure element corresponding to "you" has four different functions.

hand, a pivot-restricted chaining analysis appears to be correct. Coordination of VPs (or any other subclausal constituent) is not a possible analysis, given the order of elements: the unshared 'you' is farther from the verb than the shared 'us', so the shared element cannot be structurally higher.[12] That is to say, there is no constituent that could be coordinated. In addition, Dyirbal does not allow free subclausal coordination the way English does (Dixon 1972). An analysis in terms of null pronouns is also untenable for Dyirbal. Dyirbal allows null pronouns only for transitive $\widehat{GF}$ (A), not for OBJ or intransitive $\widehat{GF}$ (S) (Dixon 1979), so a sentence like (16b) cannot involve a null pronoun. Unlike English, then, argument sharing in coordination does seem to be pivot-based in Dyirbal.

We can illustrate the kinds of properties that formal constructions have by comparing multifunctionality constructions (like chaining) and null/incorporated pronoun constructions: two of the three formal constructions that can be used for the notional construction of sharing across coordination. As we will see in Chapter 5, these two formal constructions are also involved in (at least some types of) control constructions. It is easy to see why these two formal constructions should be in competition to express the same notional constructions. Both constructions provide a way to avoid using an extra nominal phrase to mention an element overtly, resulting in a more economical expression. Both constructions involve the sharing of an element: in the case of multifunctionality directly in the syntax; and in the case of null/incorporated pronouns at a semantic/pragmatic level incorporating a representation of reference. However, despite their notional similarity, the two constructions are formally different. The difference results from the fact that multifunctionality is a purely syntactic construction, while anaphora (overt or covert) involves the interaction of several components of the grammar: reference (semantics/discourse), information structure, and thematic roles, as well as syntax. In fact, one can argue that the role of syntax in anaphora is relatively small. One of the characteristics of syntax is that it tends to be more rigid in its requirements than other components of language. The pure syntactic nature of sharing as opposed to the largely non-syntactic nature of anaphora therefore means that one would expect sharing to be stricter in its requirements than null/incorporated anaphora.

The flexibility of anaphoric constructions is easy to demonstrate. It is well known, for example, that anaphoric constructions do not always involve strict

---

12 The word order here corresponds to the most frequent word order in Dyirbal, but Dixon (1972) emphasizes that word order is very free in Dyirbal.

coreference. For example, (26a) involves overlapping reference (given the relevant pragmatic context) and (26b) demonstrates a split antecedent.

(26) a. Bill said that they enjoyed dinner with us last night. (*they* = Bill + others)
b. Bill persuaded Jane that they should see the new *Star Trek* movie. (*they* = Bill + Jane)

Another type of flexibility involves pragmatically determined preferences in interpreting a pronoun. For example, in English, if there is a pronoun in a subordinate clause and a single possible antecedent in a higher clause, the usual preferred reading is for the pronoun to be coreferential with the higher nominal. However, given an appropriate discourse context, another reading may become more salient.

(27) a. Sara said that she wants to major in generative basketweaving. (preferred reading: *she* = Sara)
b. A lot of people told me that Miriam is going to study nuclear physics in college. However, Sara said that she wants to major in generative basketweaving. (preferred reading: *she* = Miriam)

While not all anaphoric constructions are equally flexible, some degree of flexibility is to be expected from a null/incorporated pronoun construction. A multifunctionality construction, on the other hand, should display none of these properties. The requirement that a certain element must be PIV, as a formal condition on the licensing constraint, should be absolute. Since a single syntactic element is literally being shared by two clauses, there should be no departures from strict identity.

In this context, it is useful to consider coordination sharing in Yidin^y. As noted in much of the literature (such as Comrie 1989 and Dixon 1994), argument sharing across coordination in Yidin^y differs from the Dyirbal construction: the shared elements bear unmarked Case. Since Yidin^y has a split-ergative Case-marking system, this means P (OBJ) for lexical NPs and A ($\widehat{\text{GF}}$) for pronouns. This is very much unlike the Dyirbal situation, where (in transitive clauses) the shared element is invariably P (OBJ) – the PIV in Dyirbal. The Yidin^y situation cannot be expressed in terms of pivothood, since the PIV in a transitive clause cannot be based on whether the argument in question is a lexical noun or a pronoun. For other constructions (such as extractability in relativization), as Dixon observes, Yidin^y has a clear S/P pivot. From the perspective of the theory being developed here, we would want to claim that the Yidin^y PIV is S/P (as in Dyirbal). We therefore hypothesize that the coordination structure is not true pivot-based chaining. In addition, as in Dyirbal, the Yidin^y word order facts make it unlikely to be a case of subclausal coordination. We therefore analyze argument sharing in Yidin^y as a null-pronoun construction. Critically, this theoretically driven analysis receives clear empirical support, based on the difference in properties between null-pronoun constructions and multifunctional constructions. For instance, while the preference for unmarked Case elements in Yidin^y is apparently very strong, it is only a preference, one which can be overridden by pragmatic considerations. This is illustrated by the following sentences (Dixon 1977).

(28)   a. Ŋayu   buɲa   wawa:l   yarŋga:n^y.
          I.NOM   woman   see.PST   be.frightened.PST
          'I saw the woman and she was frightened.'
          *'I saw the woman and I was frightened.'

       b. Ŋan^yan^y   buɲa   :ŋ   wawa:l   yarŋga:n^y.
          I.ACC   woman-   ERG   see.PST   be.frightened.PST
          'The woman saw me and she was frightened.'
          *'The woman saw me and I was frightened.'

This is not the behavior one expects from a syntactically conditioned pivot-based chaining construction, in which the restriction to a particular element is a result of the formal nature of the construction. Instead, this is a null-pronoun construction in which there is a strong preference for the pronoun and its antecedent to be null-Case elements. Other facts about the language also support this analysis: unlike Dyirbal, Yidin^y freely allows OBJs as well as GFs to be null pronouns (Dixon 1977).

The differences between formal constructions are relatively subtle, and published language descriptions do not always include all the relevant information. In some cases, we must propose an analysis on the basis of the incomplete information available. Such an analysis, however, always makes predictions about other properties of the construction and the language.

3.3.3 Multiple pivots

The Yidin^y coordination-sharing facts bring us back to the question of multiple pivots. Dixon (1994) cites these facts as an example of multiple pivots in a language, with Yidin^y having an S/P pivot for relativization and some cases of coordination, and S/A for other cases of coordination. Our analysis, for which we have presented independent evidence, is a counterargument to Dixon's analysis. Dixon's claim that Yidin^y has multiple pivots for coordination is odd in light of his rejection of a similar claim for Dyirbal by Heath (1979). Heath notes that Dixon (1972) cites sequences of clauses in which there appear to be shared A arguments. Dixon cites sequences such as the following:

(29) a. Bala yugu baŋgul yara- ŋgu nudi- n.   Bayi n^{y}alŋga
        IV   tree I.ERG man- ERG cut- NFUT I   child
        bunju- n.
        spank- NFUT
        'The man cut the tree. [He] spanked the child.'
    b. Ŋaja bala yugu yuba-   n.   Balan jugumbil jilwa- n.
        me   IV   stick put.down- NFUT II   woman   kick- NFUT
        'I put down the stick; [and] kicked the woman.'

Sequences like (29a), with a full NP, are relatively rare; those like (29b), with a pronoun, are more common. Both of these are apparent counterexamples to the claim that sharing across coordination always involves S/P, and Heath argues that there is no S/P condition or, in more current terms, that there is no uniform S/P pivot. However, Dixon (1979) rejects this conclusion and notes that, since $\widehat{GF}$ can pro-drop freely, (29) could (and should) be analyzed as involving a null pronoun.[13] This is what we have argued for in the case of Yidin^y. Yidin^y is thus not a case of a language with different pivots for coordination and for relativization: it is a language with an S/P pivot (a mixed-subject language of the syntactically ergative type) in which the coordination construction is not pivot-dependent.

Our view is that all the cases that have been cited in the literature for constructions with different pivots in the same language will turn out, on closer inspection, to involve at least some formal constructions which are not pivot-restricted. We cannot discuss every such case here, but the basic approach that we used for Yidin^y needs to be applied to other alleged multiple-pivot languages. As one final example, consider the case of the Mayan language Jakaltek, which Van Valin and LaPolla (1997) claim has multiple pivots. The following are the constructions that they mention.

(30)   **Jakaltek** (Van Valin and LaPolla 1997)
        Control constructions
            subject-triggered equi: controllee must be S of intransitive
            object-triggered equi: controllee either S of intransitive or derived passive
                S (←P)
            raising: either of the above, depending on dialect

---

13 Dixon also notes that the Dyirbal sequences in (29) do not have the intonation of single syntactic units, but rather appear to be sequences of separate sentences in discourse. This is reflected in the way we have presented the sequences.

Long-distance dependencies
 relatives: S or P (or derived S (←A) of antipassive)
 wh-questions: S or P (or derived S (←A) of antipassive)
 clefting: S or P (or derived S (←A) of antipassive)
Coordination
 preference for sharing S, passive S, A

Even a superficial survey of this list reveals that different formal constructions are involved. The coordination case looks like an incorporated pronoun and a preference for $\widehat{\text{GF}}$ to be interpreted as the shared element, presumably because it is the most natural discourse topic. The limitation to S/A is only a preference, not an absolute requirement, and therefore displays the flexibility that one would expect from an anaphoric construction. In addition, agreement in the Mayan languages is pronominal, so the overall structure of the language supports an incorporated-pronoun analysis. Coordination thus does not involve pivots in Jakaltek. The long-distance dependency constructions seem to have a clear "ergative" pivot, like Dyirbal. In control and raising constructions, there may be a combination of a pivot-based construction with a semantic constraint ruling out P as controllee. In Chapter 5 we will propose such a semantic constraint. If this is correct, Jakaltek does not have different PIVs for different constructions. It has one PIV: an ergative S/P PIV.

The concept of different pivots for different constructions is inherently less interesting and less explanatory than the approach we are taking here. Stipulating that different constructions have different pivots does not explain why the constructions in question differ in this way. Under our approach, we can utilize the non-one-to-one relationship between notional constructions and formal constructions to explain why different constructions target different elements of the clause.

It is also important to realize that the distinction that we are drawing between notional and formal constructions is necessary in any case. The LFG formalism allows for all three methods of sharing elements between coordinated clauses that we have discussed. Nothing needs to be added to the framework to allow for these options: in fact, the theory would have to be complicated to prevent these three methods from all being available.

In conclusion, a formal multidimensional approach allows us to see past the appearance of multiple pivots. We do not believe that the difference between our approach and those of researchers in the typological/functionalist tradition is primarily a difference in the understanding of the concept of pivot, but rather a difference in the understanding of constructions. By recognizing the existence of distinct formal constructions that can be used to express notional constructions, we can come to a clearer understanding of the constraints governing various constructions.

3.4 Clause-internal PIV properties

We turn now to a brief discussion of properties of PIV which are not cross-clausal, the properties mentioned in (1b). We view these properties as less central than the cross-clausal properties.

3.4.1 *External position*

Perhaps the most interesting of these properties is the external position which PIVs occupy in configurational languages. In c-structure-centric theories, this external position is taken to be a property which defines the subject, and thus is a stipulated property. Specifically, it is stipulated as an argumenthood property (the subject is often called the "external argument"): the Agent argument is said to be projected into the syntax externally.

There are several serious deficiencies in this relatively standard view of the external position of subjects. In the first place, the notion of Agent as external argument is entirely stipulative. Second, though it is generally thought to be true universally, it has been shown by Nordlinger (1998) and others that non-configurational languages do not have the same type of structure, and in particular do not have the subject in an external position.[14] Third, the evidence suggests that in mixed-subject languages, if one element of the sentence is external, it is the PIV, not the $\widehat{\text{GF}}$. This is suggested by constituent order facts from ergative languages discussed by Dixon (1994), which appear to show that the PIV has a unique position in c-structure. Dixon mentions, without examples, the Maku language Nadëb, in which the S can either precede or follow the verb, and P can either precede or follow the sequence A–V. This suggests a structure in which A–V forms a verb-final constituent, with a higher structural position for S/P (which has free ordering relative to the A–V constituent). This is entirely parallel to the gross structure of configurational languages like English, but with A and P reversed.

---

14 Arguments to the contrary that appear in the literature are circular, as they generally are based on showing that the language exhibits subject–object asymmetries. An argument of this kind only holds if one takes it as given that such asymmetries are to be explained on the grounds of asymmetrical constituent structure.

(31) a. **English**

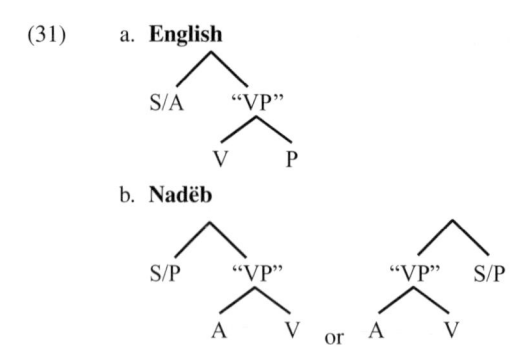

```
    S/A   "VP"
         V    P
```

b. **Nadëb**

```
   S/P   "VP"        "VP"   S/P
         A   V   or   A   V
```

Such a structure makes no sense under the view that subjects have an external position because A is an external argument. Dixon (1994: 178) notes that argument sharing in coordination in Nadëb involves S and P arguments, but not A; if this is a true PIV-based chaining construction, as in Dyirbal, Nadëb is demonstrably a syntactically ergative language (i.e., a mixed-subject language in which the PIV in a transitive clause is the OBJ), and the external position occupied by S/P is the structural position of the PIV.[15] Another language mentioned in this context by Dixon is the Western Nilotic language Päri, which has S/P–V(–A) order.

(32) a. Ùbúr á-   túuk`.
        Ubur COMPL- play
        PIV / ĜF
        'Ubur played.'

  b. Jòobì   á-   kèel   ùbúrr i.
     buffalo COMPL- shoot   Ubur- ERG
     PIV / OBJ   ĜF
     'Ubur shot the buffalo.'

Andersen (1988) takes the common structural position for S and P to be evidence of ergativity in Päri. Specifically, it appears that Päri is syntactically ergative: in transitive clauses the OBJ is the PIV, and the preverbal position is the pivot position. The VP would then be verb-initial, but would follow the PIV (as in English). Further suggestive evidence that preverbal position is outside of the VP comes from the fact that if A is topicalized it also precedes the verb (and the P). Unfortunately, Andersen does not present any evidence from cross-clausal constructions for the ergativity of Päri (for example, the controlled element

---

15 Dixon does not provide any further information, so the analysis is not certain. Dixon himself concurs with the analysis that S/P is the pivot, as does Manning (1996).

is S/A, which is allowed since being controllee is a Type 1 property in some languages, and anything can be focused or clefted), but the facts are certainly suggestive.

From the perspective of a multidimensional approach to syntax, the question of constituent structure position takes on a different complexion. Constituent structure is the overt expression of syntactic elements, and thus can be expected to reflect information about other dimensions. This leads to a problem, since different dimensions have different kinds of information and relations between elements, and it is impossible for constituent structure to express all of them simultaneously. The existence of different constituent structure patterns in different languages is expected under a parallel multidimensional approach to language: it is the consequence of differences in which dimensions of linguistic information are reflected in constituent structure. In many languages, for example, there is a flat structure with relatively free ordering, and the actual order reflects degrees of discourse prominence. In such languages, constituent structure primarily expresses aspects of information structure. Configurational languages, on the other hand, appear to design constituent structure in such a way that it is an iconic representation of grammatical functions.

The PIV is an element of a clause which is distinguished by being singled out as the element of cross-clausal continuity in a sentence. As noted earlier, this makes it similar to TOPIC, which is the function of cross-sentence continuity in a discourse. However, PIV is purely syntactic in its scope, not relating to discourse. It is thus intermediate in its scope between the local argument and adjunct functions on the one hand and the discourse-related functions on the other. The structural position of PIV reflects this intermediate status. The structural position for arguments in configurational languages is as sister to the lexical heads of which they are arguments, the closest possible structural position to the head. Adjuncts are typically adjoined to a higher node, farther away from the head. Elements bearing discourse functions are farther still, either adjoined to IP or in [SPEC, CP]. The structural position typically associated with PIV, [SPEC, IP], is closer to the lexical head than the place of discourse functions but farther than most adjuncts. The general picture that emerges is that configurational languages represent grammatical functions iconically in the c-structure, and the external position of the PIV is part of this iconicity. To put it slightly differently, while c-structure-centric theories take the position that structure determines function, our view is that (in configurational languages) function determines structure.

(33) Clause structure in configurational languages

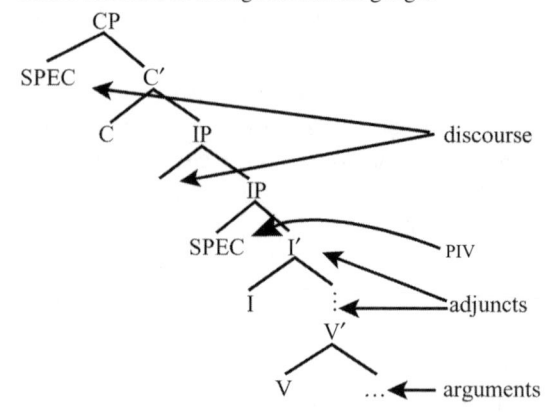

```
            CP
           /  \
        SPEC   C'
              /  \
             C    IP  ──────────→ discourse
                  /\
                 IP
                /  \
             SPEC   I'  ←──── PIV
                   /  \
                  I    : ←──── adjuncts
                       V'
                      /  \
                     V   ... ←── arguments
```

This approach thus provides an explanation for what in purely c-structural theories is a stipulated property of subjects: the "external" structural position.

3.4.2 Other clause-internal properties

The external position of pivot in configurational languages is an example of the clause-internal properties that pivots often have. From the perspective of the theory proposed here, these can be thought of as secondary properties. Other examples are obligatoriness, wide scope, definiteness, and inflectional properties of Case marking and agreement. These properties are secondary because they are not a direct result of the cross-clausal continuity function of the pivot. Instead, by virtue of being singled out as the element of cross-clausal continuity, the pivot has a certain functional prominence relative to the other elements of the clause. The secondary properties build on, or enhance, this functional prominence. We will briefly discuss obligatoriness, wide scope, and definiteness in this section, and then turn to a more lengthy discussion of morphological properties in the following section.

Since it establishes a relation between a clause and the larger sentence in which it is embedded, many languages require every clause to have a PIV.[16] The idea that every clause must have a "subject" is a well-known stipulated principle of many theories (such as the Extended Projection Principle of modern transformational theory, the Final 1 Law of Relational Grammar, the Subject Condition of LFG). Mixed-subject languages show that it is the PIV that is required. For example, Mosel and Hovdhaugen (1992) observe that in the ergative Polynesian language Samoan the A argument of a transitive clause

---

16 The "ambassador" metaphor mentioned in footnote 2 is appropriate here.

is optional, and when omitted it is interpreted existentially (similarly to a passive agent), but the P argument (the PIV) is only omissible if derivable from context (i.e., interpreted referentially and anaphorically). That is to say, the PIV is present, even if as a null pronoun, while the non-PIV ĜF is not.

It has been claimed that pivots take wide scope over other elements in the sentence (Bittner 1994), or must be interpreted as definite (Schachter 1976 on Tagalog). Compare the following Inuit (from Bittner 1994) and English sentences; the transitive ĜF and OBJ have opposite scopal properties in the two languages, but one can describe both by saying that the PIV must take wide scope over VP operators.

(34)   a. Aatuartu- p ataasi- p Juuna uqaluqatigi- sima-
student- ERG one- ERG Juuna talk.to- PERF-
nngi- la- a.
NEG- IND- 3SG.3SG
(i) 'No student has talked to Juuna (yet).'
(ii) 'One student hasn't talked to Juuna (yet).'
either 'one student' (ĜF) or '¬' can take wide scope

b. Atuagaq ataasiq tikis- sima- nngi- la- q.
book one come- PERF- NEG- IND- 3SG
'One book hasn't come (yet).'
'one book' (ĜF/PIV) has wide scope

c. Juuna- p atuagaq ataasiq tigu- sima- nngi- la- a.
Juuna- ERG book one get- PERF- NEG- IND- 3SG.3SG
'There is a book which Juuna hasn't got (yet).'
'one book' (OBJ/PIV) has wide scope

(35)   a. One student has not talked to Juuna yet.
'one student' (ĜF/PIV) has wide scope
b. One book hasn't come yet.
'one book' (ĜF/PIV) has wide scope
c. Juuna hasn't gotten one book yet.
either 'one book' (OBJ) or '¬' can take wide scope

Manning (1996) discusses these data and points to the difficulty in distinguishing between descriptions in terms of scope and definiteness. Whatever the correct description, though, this appears to be another property of PIVs. Such properties may also be due to the distinguished element status of the PIV, a way of enhancing its prominence. They also may be a consequence of the overlay status of the PIV function: a pairing of the purely syntactic status of PIV with semantic/discourse properties more commonly associated with topics.

The syntactic and semantic secondary pivot properties are less central to the theory of pivothood and, as mentioned above, only indirectly related to the

100 *Subjects and their properties*

function of the pivot. Their distribution cross-linguistically is less clear, as they have been less studied in the typological literature. Nevertheless, they provide an interesting insight into the architecture of syntax, in that they show that prominence at different dimensions are often related.

3.5 Some morphology

We turn now to a consideration of the morphological properties of subjects. The conventional wisdom is that the PIV is unmarked for Case (nominative/absolutive) and triggers agreement. While the conventional wisdom is right up to a point, it glosses over many details. To the extent that it is correct, it is another instance of non-syntactic enhancement of the syntactic prominence of pivots.

In the first place, the relation between unmarked Case and the triggering of agreement needs to be clarified. Case and agreement are both formal morphological devices, and they serve essentially the same function: distinguishing the core arguments of a predicate from each other. The morphological marking can be directly on the arguments, in which case we can speak of dependent marking, or Case. Alternatively, the marking can be on the verb (or on an auxiliary), in which case what is involved is head marking, cross-referencing, or agreement. Some languages use only Case, others use only agreement, while others use both. (Of course, there are also languages that use neither.)

The interesting case is languages which are primarily dependent-marking (i.e., Case languages), but in which the head is marked with agreement cross-referencing one of the elements of the clause. In such languages, the element cross-referenced on the verb is generally the element with unmarked Case. This is quite striking in Hindi-Urdu (Butt 1993): the SUBJ (ĜF and PIV) can be either marked with ergative Case or unmarked and the OBJ can be either marked with accusative Case or unmarked. The verb agrees with the highest-ranked unmarked nominal, whether it is the SUBJ or OBJ. If there is no unmarked nominal, the verb displays default (masculine) agreement. (The agreement trigger and agreement features on the verb are bolded in the word-by-word gloss.)

(36)   a. Naadyaa   xat   lik^h-   tii   hai.
           Nadya(**F**) letter(M) write- IMPERF.**F**.SG be.PRES.3SG
           'Nadya writes a letter.'

       b. Naadyaa   ne   xat   lik^h-   aa   hai.
           Nadya(F) ERG letter(**M**) write- PERF.**M**.SG be.PRES.3SG
           'Nadya has written a letter.'

c. Naadyaa   ne   citʰii   likʰ-   ii   hai.
      Nadya(F) ERG note(F) write- PERF.F.SG be.PRES.3SG
      'Nadya has written a note.'
   d. Naadyaa   ne   citʰii   ko   likʰ-   aa   hai.
      Nadya(F) ERG note(F) ACC write- PERF.M.SG be.PRES.3SG
      'Nadya has written a (particular) note.'

It should be noted that the correlation is one-way: Caselessness triggers agreement, but agreement is not the trigger for Caselessness. This is clear because of the existence of sentences in which both the ĜF and the OBJ are unmarked; the verb only agrees with the ĜF in such a situation. Agreement with an unmarked argument makes good functional sense: since Case marking serves to make it easier for the hearer to match overt elements to argument positions, it is reasonable to have an alternative identification system available for something that is not so marked.

Similar effects are discernible in other languages, although not generally described in these terms. Consider the English existential construction.

(37)   a. There is/*are a hamster in the cage.
       b. There are/*is three hamsters in the cage.[17]

When marked with Case, the postverbal position in existentials in Modern English is accusative, not nominative.

(38)   a. There is him.
       b. *There is he. [* on the existential reading; ?? as locative inversion]

In English, pronouns (aside from *you* and *it*) exhibit a distinction between nominative and accusative forms; lexical nouns do not. Suppose that lexical nouns are never accusative. This would follow the usual pattern for Case split: lexical

---

17 Of course, (i) is grammatical.

   (i)   There's three hamsters in the cage.

   This seems to be a matter of register; neutral third person singular agreement seems to be possible only in less formal styles of English. Since the discussion here is going to focus on whether *are* is grammatical, the treatment of sentences like (i) is irrelevant. An anonymous reader of this book states that, in his/her idiolect, sentences like *There is me* are only grammatical in the same informal register that allows (i). While this does not match my intuitions (or the lack of obligatory reduction of *is*), I do not think it is relevant to the point being made here. For all native speakers of English I have asked, it is impossible to get the agreeing form **There am me* on the existential reading in any register. (*There am I* may be grammatical for some as a locative construction, but that is a different sentence.) Since my claim is that agreement is impossible with a Case-marked (i.e., pronominal) postverbal element in English existential constructions, register limitations on *There is me* are beside the point.

nouns are less likely to be marked accusative than pronouns. A consequence would be that, if agreement is with the nominative, we should expect to find agreement with a postverbal lexical noun but not with a postverbal pronoun. This prediction is borne out. (Since the postverbal nominal in these examples is definite, these are grammatical only on a list reading.)

(39)   a. There are the linguists.
        b. There is/*are us.
        c. There is/*am me.
        d. There is/*are them.

This is an otherwise strange distribution of agreement. It would not work to say that the postverbal nominal agrees in number but not person, because the verb form is singular in all these examples. However, it follows from what seem to be principles of UG if nominals superficially unmarked for Case really are unmarked, and Caselessness triggers agreement.[18]

One final example is Modern Hebrew, which seems to display a similar array of facts, although some of the details are murky. Like English, Hebrew does not have the usual kinds of constructions that allow one to tease apart nominative Case and subjecthood as the trigger for agreement. However, evidence can be gleaned from possessive sentences. Possessive sentences in Hebrew have the structure: 'be' – possessor (in the dative) – possessed.

(40)   a. Haya   le-   rina sefer.
          be.PST.3MSG DAT- Rina book
          'Rina had a book.'
        b. Haya   li   keev roš.
          be.PST.3MSG DAT.1SG ache head
          'I had a headache.'

Historically, the possessed nominal was the subject. It thus was unmarked for Case and triggered agreement on the verb. Such usage is still considered

---

18 An interesting residual problem with the English is the status of *it* and *you*. The question is whether they, like lexical nouns, are never accusative, or whether these are simply cases of morphological syncretism, with the nominative and accusative forms coincidentally looking the same. I don't know of any way to test for the status of *it*, although its being always Caseless (nominative) would be consistent with the animacy hierarchy. On the other hand, the existential construction suggests that *you* can be accusative:

    (i)   There is/*are you.

This is what one would expect, given the animacy hierarchy. I would like to thank Cindy Allen (personal communication) for first suggesting to me that *you* may be a coincidence unrelated to the animacy hierarchy.

normative. However, in actual spoken Hebrew, the possessed nominal appears to have been reinterpreted as an object. This means that it is marked with accusative Case; in Hebrew, accusative Case only surfaces on definite nominals.

(41)   Haya   le-   rina et   ha- sefer.
       be.PST.3MSG   DAT- Rina ACC the- book
       'Rina had the book.'

As observed by Ziv (1976), the presence or absence of accusative Case is correlated with the absence or presence of agreement (Ziv's [11] and [17]).

(42) a. Hayta   li   mexonit kazot.
         be.PST.3FSG   DAT.1SG   car(F) such
      b. ?Haya   li   mexonit kazot.
         be.PST.3MSG   DAT.1SG   car(F) such
         'I had such a car.'

(43) a. ?Hayta   lanu   et   ha- mexonit hazot od
         be.PST.3FSG   DAT.1PL   ACC the- car(F) this still

         kše   garnu   be tel aviv.
         when   live.PST.1PL in Tel Aviv
      b. Haya   lanu   et   ha- mexonit hazot od
         be.PST.3MSG   DAT.1PL   ACC the- car(F) this still

         kše   garnu   be tel aviv.
         when   live.PST.1PL in Tel Aviv
         'We had this car when we were living in Tel Aviv.'

If we idealize the judgments[19] and read the question marks as asterisks, the result again clearly correlates agreement with the absence of Case.[20]

This seems to be a common pattern in languages with dependent-marking and a limited one-argument head-marking. We therefore consider Case marking to be the central construction, and hypothesize that agreement with a single argument is often triggered by Caselessness, rather than PIV status.[21]

The Case-marking facts themselves are more complex than the conventional view would have it, since the conventional view does not take into account such

---

19 There are two possible explanations for the uncertainty of the judgments reported by Ziv. One, Ziv's explanation, is that we are observing syntactic change in progress, and the fuzziness is a result of the transitional stage the language is in now. An alternative explanation might be the influence of prescriptive norms, which are very strong in Hebrew. Both explanations seem to me to be plausible, and in either case I think that idealizing the judgments is legitimate.
20 This is not the conclusion that Ziv reaches. For more discussion, see Falk (1996).
21 There are various ways this could be expressed formally. One would be to accept the idea that Case (K) is a functional category, and that Case-marked nominals are KP rather than NP or DP. Agreement could then be keyed to an absence of the K(P) category.

factors as differential marking of arguments based on such criteria as animacy and definiteness; nevertheless, it is correct in the sense that there is a clear tendency for PIVs to be unmarked for Case. Given the status of PIV as the distinguished element in the clause, often with a unique structural position, the lack of explicit dependent marking on PIV is unsurprising. Morphological identification is less important for the PIV than for other elements of the clause. A more complete approach to Case marking of core elements of the clause would include the following three (informal) constraints:

(44)   a. PIV is unmarked.
        b. ĜF is unmarked if it is higher than position x on the animacy/definiteness hierarchy.
        c. OBJ is unmarked if it is lower than position y on the animacy/definiteness hierarchy.

(For more on the animacy and definiteness hierarchies, see Comrie 1989, Dixon 1994, and references cited there.) Constraints (44b,c) are responsible for morphologically ergative languages,[22] split ergative Case marking, the absence of accusative Case on inanimate and/or indefinite objects in many nominative-accusative languages, and other Case-marking oddities related to ĜF and OBJ marking. Given the richness of typological and theoretical literature on these issues, and the peripherality of these issues to our interests in the present study, there is no point in rehashing the evidence here. In different languages, the constraints are ranked differently in terms of importance. This suggests an Optimality Theoretic approach; the constraints in (44b,c) have been partially formalized in OT by Aissen (1999, 2003). For our purposes, the important point is the frequent non-marking of the PIV, a consequence of the fact that it can often be identified by other means, and the concomitant triggering of agreement in single-agreement languages.

The agreement facts in exclusively head-marking languages are also interesting. Head-marking languages typically register all core arguments on the verb, so there is not one element triggering agreement. Nevertheless, there often is an agreement affix that is triggered by the PIV. This is true, for example, in the mixed-subject (syntactically ergative) Mayan languages. Consider the following data from Quiché (Larsen 1987):

(45)   a.   X-   at-   b'iin- ik.
            PERF- 2SG.ABS- walk- SUFF
            'You walked.'

---

22 For more on morphologically ergative languages, see section 6.3.3.4.

b. X-   oj-   b'iin- ik.
   PERF-   1PL.ABS-   walk- SUFF
   'We walked'
c. X-   at-   qa-   ch'ay- o.
   PERF-   2SG.ABS-   1plERG-   hit-   SUFF
   'We hit you.'
d. X-   oj-   a-   ch'ay- o.
   PERF-   1PL.ABS-   2SG.ERG-   hit-   SUFF
   'You hit us.'

It is clear from these examples that Quiché has agreement markers (glossed ABS) such as -*at*- for second person singular and -*oj*- for first person plural, which agree with the PIV regardless of whether it is G̃F or OBJ, while agreement with non-PIV G̃F is expressed with different morphemes (-*a*- and -*qa*-).

The conclusion is that inflectional morphology often does treat PIVs differently from other elements. As observed above, this is not surprising in light of the PIV's status as the designated element of the clause. However, such morphological effects are secondary to the syntactic properties of pivots.

3.6   Forthcoming attractions

In the last two chapters, we have factored the traditional grammatical function subject into two distinct, and intrinsically unrelated, grammatical functions: G̃F and PIV. We have shown that the properties of subjects, including the split in properties that one finds in split-subject languages, follow from this analysis: properties relating to argument hierarchies are G̃F properties, and properties relating to elements shared between clauses are PIV properties.

In the coming two chapters, we will further flesh out this picture by focusing on the analyses of extraction and control constructions, two central types of constructions. We will show how the notions of PIV and G̃F provide the basis for an explanation of the observed patterns.

4 Long-distance dependencies

4.1 About long-distance dependencies

In this chapter, we will discuss the nature of long-distance dependency constructions[1] (also known as unbounded dependencies, extraction, *wh*-movement, and Ā dependencies) and their interaction with subjecthood. We will see that the theory of pivots proposed in the previous chapter, combined with certain formal aspects of LFG, explains the special status of subjects in long-distance dependencies. In doing so, we will need to delve a little deeper into technical aspects of the LFG formalism.

Despite the image long-distance dependency constructions have as the epitome of the structure-dependent construction, it has long been known that subjecthood is relevant to long-distance dependency constructions. The fact that extraction of subjects is different from other types of extraction can be shown in many ways. For example, in many languages, only subjects (PIVs) can extract (Keenan and Comrie 1977) and subjects are often resistant to being resumptive pronouns (Keenan 1976). Subjects and non-subjects behave differently in across-the-board extraction. In English, matrix subject questions do not require *do* support. Subject extraction has been shown experimentally to involve a lower processing load than non-subject extraction (see references in Hawkins 1999). Paradoxically, subjects also sometimes appear to be harder to extract, as in the case of the infamous *that*-trace effect. The formal analysis of long-distance dependency constructions should allow for an elegant account of facts of this kind. In this section, we will examine the LFG analysis of long-distance dependencies and its interaction with the theory of subjecthood

---

[1] A better, though unwieldy, name for the construction would be "potentially long-distance dependency", since a construction of this type can involve a very local domain. We will retain the conventional name here.

being developed here. We will see that the higher ease of extracting subjects than non-subjects follows automatically. In subsequent sections we will examine other issues, such as across-the-board extractions and the *that*-trace effect.

4.1.1   Functional uncertainty

It is often supposed in the transformational literature that the essence of long-distance dependency constructions is displacement: an element appears in one part of the sentence even though it is semantically interpreted in a different part of the sentence. It has even been alleged that theoretical frameworks which claim to be non-transformational have what amounts to a notational variant of displacement. Thus, Chomsky and Lasnik (1993: 525) talk about "a relation between a 'displaced element' and the position in which such an element is standardly interpreted . . . Such displacement relations are a fundamental feature of human language, which must be captured somehow. Apparent differences among alternative formulations often dissolve, on inquiry, to notational questions about how this property is expressed . . ." In a similar vein, Chomsky (2000: 119–20) states about displacement constructions that "[s]uch phenomena are pervasive. They have to be accommodated by some device in any adequate theory of language, whether it is called 'transformational' or something else." However, this is not entirely accurate. Displacement is not an empirical observation, but rather a theoretical description based on an empirical observation.[2]

What lies at the heart of long-distance dependency constructions is the existence of a single element which bears two distinct functions, often in different clauses. For example, the italicized element in (1a) bears the two functions in (1b).

(1) a. [clause1 *Who* does Jerry think [clause2 that Elaine said [clause3 that Kramer claimed [clause4 saw Newman]]]]?
     b. FOCUS of clause1 and SUBJ ($\widehat{\text{GF}}$ + PIV) of clause4

Using the same curved-line notation that we have already used to show that a single element bears two grammatical functions, this can be represented with the following f-structure.

---

2 Despite this, we will continue to use the term "extraction" because of its intuitive appeal. This use is current in the constraint-based literature. The reader should mentally place scare quotes around the term wherever it appears.

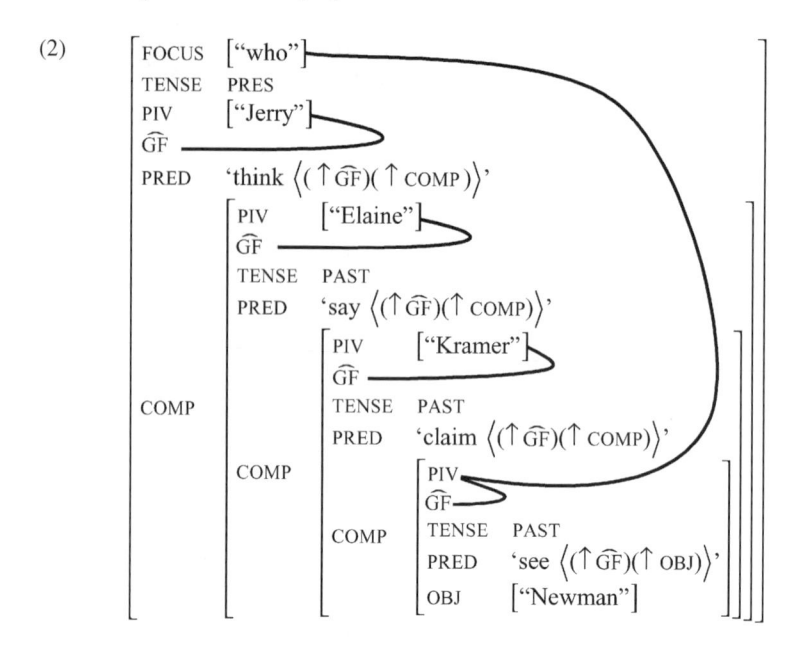

(2)
$$\begin{bmatrix} \text{FOCUS} & [\text{"who"}] \\ \text{TENSE} & \text{PRES} \\ \text{PIV} & [\text{"Jerry"}] \\ \widehat{\text{GF}} & \\ \text{PRED} & \text{'think} \langle (\uparrow \widehat{\text{GF}})(\uparrow \text{COMP}) \rangle \text{'} \\ \text{COMP} & \begin{bmatrix} \text{PIV} & [\text{"Elaine"}] \\ \widehat{\text{GF}} & \\ \text{TENSE} & \text{PAST} \\ \text{PRED} & \text{'say} \langle (\uparrow \widehat{\text{GF}})(\uparrow \text{COMP}) \rangle \text{'} \\ \text{COMP} & \begin{bmatrix} \text{PIV} & [\text{"Kramer"}] \\ \widehat{\text{GF}} & \\ \text{TENSE} & \text{PAST} \\ \text{PRED} & \text{'claim} \langle (\uparrow \widehat{\text{GF}})(\uparrow \text{COMP}) \rangle \text{'} \\ \text{COMP} & \begin{bmatrix} \text{PIV} & \\ \widehat{\text{GF}} & \\ \text{TENSE} & \text{PAST} \\ \text{PRED} & \text{'see} \langle (\uparrow \widehat{\text{GF}})(\uparrow \text{OBJ}) \rangle \text{'} \\ \text{OBJ} & [\text{"Newman"}] \end{bmatrix} \end{bmatrix} \end{bmatrix} \end{bmatrix}$$

This multifunctionality is, we believe, the observational core of long-distance dependency constructions – something every theory has to express somehow. Such a construction becomes a displacement only under two additional (and conceptually unnecessary) assumptions: first, that grammatical functions are invariably associated with specific constituent structure positions and, second, that only argument and adjunct functions (or positions) are relevant for "interpretation." Such assumptions lie at the heart of transformational grammar in its various incarnations, but are not part of the theoretical framework here. Without these additional assumptions, there is no reason to assume a movement (displacement) analysis.

From the perspective of the LFG formalism, a single element can have more than one function if there is a constraint (in the form of a functional equation) stating that the values of the two attributes (grammatical functions) are identical. Such constraints have already appeared in this study in our discussions in Chapter 3 about the assignment of the PIV function and the chaining construction. In the case of the present example, the following constraint, associated with the main clause, will license *who*, having both the upstairs FOCUS function and the downstairs PIV function, without any displacement.

(3) $(\uparrow \text{FOCUS}) = (\uparrow \text{COMP COMP COMP PIV})$

More generally, as first observed by Kaplan and Zaenen (1989), the relation between the two functions in a long-distance dependency can be expressed as follows (where DF means grammaticized discourse function):

(4)   (↑DF) = (↑ COMP* GF)

The use of the Kleene star is a formal expression of the unbounded nature of extraction: there is no principled limitation on the distance between the two functions of the extracted element. Such expressions are referred to as functional uncertainty, as there are potentially infinite f-structures that will satisfy them (because of the Kleene star).

An analysis of this kind has several advantages over a displacement analysis of long-distance dependencies. Conceptually, it is simpler, as it expresses the multifunctionality directly, without the need to refer to structural positions and movement. Empirically, as noted by Kaplan and Zaenen, one important advantage is the characterization of the path between the two functions in terms of grammatical functions. Cross-linguistic study reveals that the nature of this path varies from language to language; furthermore, grammatical functions are superior to constituent structure configurations as the description of this path. Here, we will (for the most part) abstract away from language-specific differences in the nature of the path, and simply represent the functional uncertainty equation as follows.

(5)   (↑ DF) = (↑ PathGF* GF)

The exact set of grammatical functions that make up PathGF will vary from language to language, resulting in different "island constraints" for different languages. Empirical evidence shows that island constraints are a matter of cross-linguistic variation; for example, while English prohibits extraction from PIV ("subject"), Tagalog requires extraction to be from PIV (Kroeger 1993). An LFG account also has no problem with multiple extractions in the same domain: some languages allow multiple focuses and topics in a single clause (modeled formally by allowing the functions FOCUS and TOPIC to take sets of f-structure elements as their values). One example of such a language is Russian, which has been discussed from an LFG perspective by King (1995).

To complete this picture, we need to consider the status of the functional uncertainty constraint (5). As we have seen, constraints in LFG are associated with nodes in the c-structure, either lexically (as parts of lexical entries) or constructionally (part of the phrase structure rules). Kaplan and Zaenen propose that the constraint is associated constructionally with the node occupied by the filler – [SPEC, CP] in the case of *wh* elements. However, this cannot be correct, since long-distance dependencies with no overt filler are possible. One clear example of this is the non-*wh* relative clause in English.

(6)   a. [The baby [that I think saw me]] is cute.
       b.

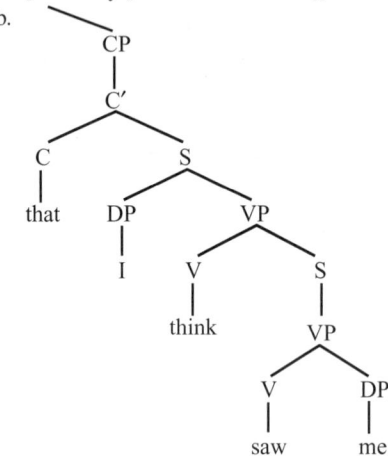

```
              CP
              |
              C'
             / \
            C   S
            |  / \
          that DP  VP
               |  / \
               I V   S
                 |   |
               think VP
                    / \
                   V   DP
                   |   |
                  saw  me
```

There is no [SPEC, CP] node here with which to associate the constraint. We propose that, for English at least, the constraint is associated lexically with the verb that heads the clause. Since this is redundantly a property of every clausal head (verb), it is a clausal property.

4.1.2   Pivots and non-pivots

Under Kaplan and Zaenen's formulation, the functional uncertainty expression in (5) is what licenses all long-distance dependencies. Extractions of different grammatical functions over various distances are all covered, without any need for displacement, null constituent structure, or any of the other machinery required in some other theoretical frameworks.

However, viewed from the perspective of the theory of subjecthood developed here, an additional consideration must be introduced. Recall that in Chapter 3 we formalized the nature of the PIV function by stating the Pivot Condition, which we repeat here.

(7)   *The Pivot Condition*
    Informal statement
    A path inward through f-structure into another predicate-argument domain or sideways into a coordinate f-structure must terminate in the function PIV.

Formal statement
In a functional designation of the form (↑ ... α ... β γ) where
α   or (φ(<∗ ... β γ)) or (φ(∗> ... β γ)), if β is a
(→ PRED ARGI)'
grammatical function and either γ=∅ or γ is a feature, β = PIV.

The functional uncertainty expression in (5) is a path inward through the f-structure. As such, it is subject to the Pivot Condition, and must terminate in the function PIV. Contrary to Kaplan and Zaenen's view, this mode of licensing long-distance dependencies should therefore only be able to license extraction of PIV.

As first noted by Keenan and Comrie (1977), PIVs are the most easily extractable function cross-linguistically. There are languages which conform to what appears to be the prediction made by the Pivot Condition, and only allow PIV to extract.[3]

(8)   **Tagalog** (Philippine-type, Schachter 1976)
   a.   Matalino   ang   lalaki- ng   bumasa   ng   diyaryo.
        intelligent NOM man-   LNK   PERF.ACT.read ACC   newspaper
        'The man who read a newspaper is intelligent.'

   b.   Interesante ang   diyaryo- ng   binasa   ng   lalaki.
        Interesting NOM   newspaper- LNK PERF.DO.read ERG   man
        'The newspaper that the man read is interesting.'

   c.   *Interesante ang   diyaryo- ng   bumasa   ang   lalaki.
        interesting NOM   newspaper- LNK PERF.ACT.read NOM   man
        'The newspaper that the man read is interesting.'

   d.   *Matalino ang   lalaki- ng   binasa   ang   diyaryo.
        intelligent NOM man-   LNK   PERF.DO.read NOM   newspaper
        'The man who read a newspaper is intelligent.'

(9)   **West Greenlandic Inuit** (syntactically ergative, Manning 1996)
   a.   nanuq   [Piita- P   tuqu- ta-   a]
        polar.bear Peter- ERG   kill- TR.PART-   3SG
        'a polar bear that Peter killed'

   b.   miiraq   [kamat- tu-   q]
        child.ABS angry-   REL.INTR- SG
        'the child who is angry'

   c.   *angut   [aallaat   tigu- sima-   sa-   a]
        man.ABS   gun.ABS   take- PERF-   REL.TR- 3SG
        'the man who took the gun'

---

3 In fact, as noted by Kroeger (1993) and mentioned above, in Tagalog the path has to consist only of the PIV function. The functional uncertainty equation for Tagalog reads:

(i)   (↑ DF) = (↑ PIV*)

(10) **Mam (Mayan)** (syntactically ergative, Manning 1996)
    a. Alkyee x- hi b'eet?
       who REC- 3Pl.ABS walk
       'Who walked?'

    b. Alkyee- qa x- hi tzaj t- tzyu- 7n Cheep?
       who- PL REC- 3PL.ABS DIR 3SG.ERG- grab- DIRS José
       'Who did José grab?'

    c. *Alkyee saj t- tzyu 7n kab' xiinaq?
       who REC.3SG.ABS.DIR 3SG.ERG- grab- DIRS two man
       'Who grabbed the men?'

    d. Alkyee saj tzyuu- n ky- e
       who REC.3SG.ABS.DIR grab- APASS 3PL- OBL
       kab' xiinaq?
       two man
       'Who grabbed the men?'

(11) **Chukchee** (syntactically ergative, Comrie 1979)
    a. E- tip?eyŋe kə- 1?- in ŋewəčqet
       NEG- sing- NEG- PART- ABS.SG woman.ABS.SG
       ragtə g?ə.
       go.home- 3SG
       'The woman who waw not singing went home'

    b. Igər a- yo?- kə- 1?- etə enm- etə mən- əlqən- mək.
       now NEG- reach- NEG- PART- to hill- to 1PL- go- 1PL
       'Now let us go to the hill which (someone) didn't reach.'

    c. En- agtat- kə- 1?- a qaa- k
       APASS- chase- NEG- PART- ERG reindeer- LOC
       ?aaček- a winret- ərkən- inet ŋewəčqet- ti.
       youth- ERG help- PRES-3SG.ERG.3PL.ABS woman- ABS.PL
       'The youth who does not chase the reindeer is helping the women.'

However, most languages do allow extraction of non-PIV elements as well.

To account for languages which allow non-PIVs to extract, we turn to another, independently motivated, formal tool in LFG. Since LFG functional equations are static constraints, there is no reason to limit paths through the f-structure to the inward (outside-in) ones we have seen up to this point. In principle, it should also be possible to specify paths that start on the inside and go outwards through the f-structure: inside-out paths.[4] An inside-out path is expressed formally by

---

[4] In more familiar tree-based terminology, outside-in corresponds to top-down, while inside-out corresponds to bottom-up. The difference in terminology comes from the difference in orientation between constituent structures and functional structures, and is a useful reminder that the

placing the "↑" specifying the starting position at the end of the expression. In the following examples, the starting point of the path is marked in the schematic f-structure as "↑", and the ending point of the path as f.

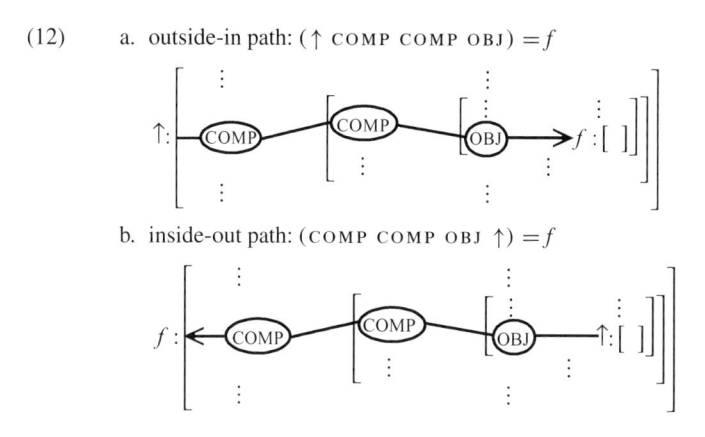

(12) a. outside-in path: (↑ COMP COMP OBJ) = f

$$\uparrow : \begin{bmatrix} \vdots \\ \text{COMP} \begin{bmatrix} \vdots \\ \text{COMP} \begin{bmatrix} \vdots \\ \text{OBJ} \rightarrow f : [\ ] \\ \vdots \end{bmatrix} \\ \vdots \end{bmatrix} \\ \vdots \end{bmatrix}$$

b. inside-out path: (COMP COMP OBJ ↑) = f

$$f : \begin{bmatrix} \vdots \\ \text{COMP} \begin{bmatrix} \vdots \\ \text{COMP} \begin{bmatrix} \vdots \\ \text{OBJ} \quad \uparrow : [\ ] \\ \vdots \end{bmatrix} \\ \vdots \end{bmatrix} \\ \vdots \end{bmatrix}$$

Inside-out paths are a formal device needed in LFG for reasons independent of our concerns here. They have been used primarily to model anaphoric properties (Dalrymple 1993) and to formalize certain properties of bound morphemes, such as Case (Nordlinger 1998). However, they can also be used, as in Bresnan (2001) and Falk (2001), to license long-distance dependencies. To be used for licensing long-distance dependencies, an inside-out expression needs to be combined with an outside-in expression designating the discourse function. Suppose that in (12b) the f-structure designated f contains a FOCUS. This FOCUS can be designated straightforwardly as (13a). If we wish to express this in terms of the f-structure designated ↑, we merely substitute for f the inside-out expression from (12b), as in (13b).

(13) a. (f FOCUS)
      b. ((COMP COMP OBJ ↑) FOCUS)

The formal difference between outside-in and inside-out expressions is important because long-distance dependencies licensed by inside-out functional designation are not subject to the Pivot Condition. In outside-in (top-down) licensing of long-distance dependencies, the licensing constraint is associated with the outer (upper) clause, the clause in which the extracted item has a discourse function. Since the constraint specifies an element of an inner (lower) clause,

relationships involved are not defined on constituent structure. Since the tree-based terminology is more familiar, we will usually include it in parentheses.

the clause where the extracted item has a locally licensed function, the Pivot Condition restricts the lower element to PIV. However, with inside-out (bottom-up) licensing, the constraint is associated with the clause of the inner (locally licensed) function, so the lower grammatical function is local to the constraint. Nothing rules out the specification by such a constraint of any local grammatical function. In other words, the Pivot Condition rules out the constraint in (14), but is irrelevant to the constraint in (15). These constraints license the same f-structure, one in which the FOCUS and the OBJ share a value.

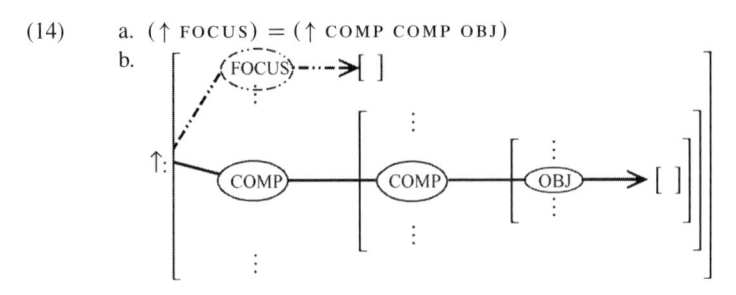

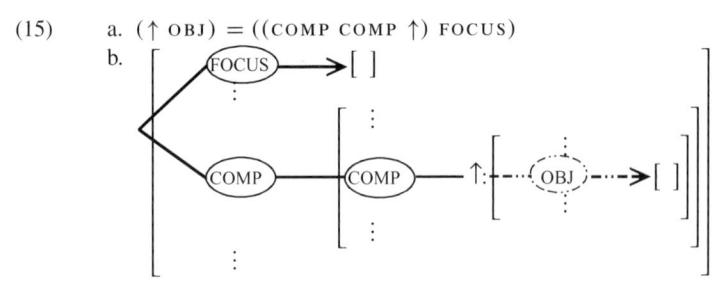

(14) a. (↑ FOCUS) = (↑ COMP COMP OBJ)
b. [diagram]

(15) a. (↑ OBJ) = ((COMP COMP ↑) FOCUS)
b. [diagram]

This is because the Pivot Condition does not directly limit structures, only the constraints that license them. The independently motivated availability of inside-out functional paths thus provides a loophole to the Pivot Condition, and allows the extraction of non-PIVs.

We will need a sister condition, one which disallows the use of inside-out licensing to license PIV extraction.[5]

(16) *Inside-Out LDD Condition*
A long-distance dependency in which the PIV function is involved may not be licensed by an inside-out constraint.

---

5 We will not state this condition formally because of the open question, to be discussed shortly, of the technicalities of inside-out licensing; specifically, whether or not it involves a trace. The inside-out constraint looks slightly different under the two approaches mentioned below.

While this condition does not derive directly from the function of the PIV, it has the effect of more sharply distinguishing PIV extraction from non-PIV extraction. It is thus functional, in that it provides more distance between related but different constructions.

The availability of two systems for licensing long-distance dependencies needs additional comment. In the terminology of Chapter 3, long-distance dependency (or, multifunctionality involving a discourse function) is a notional construction, and the two directions of licensing are two distinct formal constructions. Crucially, the distinction between outside-in licensing and inside-out licensing should not be taken to be a trick of the formal notation; the claim is that language makes use of the two directions of licensing for long-distance dependency constructions, and the formalism simply provides a way to express this. Most languages make use of both formal constructions. We consider the outside-in (top-down) construction to be unmarked relative to the inside-out (bottom-up) construction. While we know of no place in the LFG literature in which this has been stated explicitly, it seems to be implicit in much of the literature. It is computationally plausible, in that inside-out designation means a later specification of information. This may also account for the higher computational load that has been found for non-subject (non-PIV) extraction.

More important to the present study is the typological consequence of the lower markedness of the outside-in licensing construction. If we take the two licensing directions to be two distinct formal constructions, then a particular language might have both, or it might have only one of them. The markedness difference suggests that languages with only one of the two formal constructions will normally have only the unmarked construction. The typological consequence is that PIV-only extraction should be a more prevalent situation than no-PIV extraction. This, of course, correlates with the findings of Keenan and Comrie (1977) and others, as already discussed. On the other hand, given the vagaries of markedness, the approach taken here leaves open the possibility that there may be languages that only make use of the more marked inside-out licensing. Such a language would disallow PIV extraction, and is predicted to be impossible under a strict reading of Keenan and Comrie. One such language is the uniform-subject language Imbabura Quechua (Cole 1982). In subordinate clauses[6] in Imbabura Quechua, any element other than the subject may be extracted; the subject may not.[7]

---

6 Matrix clauses are different. We will return to this point shortly.
7 This constraint can be circumvented by pied-piping the entire subordinate clause. This is possible as an alternative for questioning non-subjects as well.

116 *Subjects and their properties*

(17) a. Juan wagra- ta randi- shka- ta ya- ni.
    Juan cow- ACC buy- NMNL- ACC think- 1
    'I think Juan bought a cow.'

   b. *Pi- taj ya- ngui wagra- ta randi- shka- ta ?
    who- Q think- 2 cow- ACC buy- NMNL- ACC
    'Who do you think bought a cow?'

   c. Ima- ta- taj ya- ngui Juan randi- shka- ta ?
    what- ACC- Q think- 2 Juan buy- NMNL- ACC
    'What do you think Juan bought?'

We propose that this is due to the availability of inside-out licensing and the (marked) unavailability of outside-in licensing. The existence of such a language confirms the treatment of outside-in licensing and inside-out licensing as two distinct formal constructions.

We need to discuss, albeit tangentially, the relation between inside-out designation and null constituent structure elements (empty categories or traces). To date, LFG implementations of inside-out licensing have had the inside-out constraint associated with an empty category in the constituent structure. The position of the empty category is taken to be responsible for the identification of the lower grammatical function, and its existence to be responsible for the constraint. To make this concrete, in a sentence like (18a) with the f-structure (18b), the lowest clause would have the c-structure (18c). The empty category in the c-structure, under such an analysis, is associated with the constraint (18d).

(18) a. Who does Jerry think that Elaine said that Kramer claimed that Newman saw?

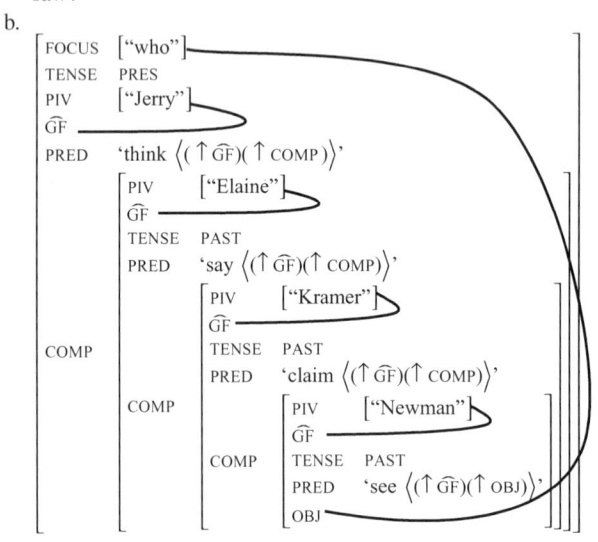

   b.
$$\begin{bmatrix}
\text{FOCUS} & [\text{``who''}] \\
\text{TENSE} & \text{PRES} \\
\text{PIV} & [\text{``Jerry''}] \\
\widehat{\text{GF}} & \\
\text{PRED} & \text{`think} \langle (\uparrow \widehat{\text{GF}})(\uparrow \text{COMP}) \rangle \text{'} \\
\text{COMP} & \begin{bmatrix}
\text{PIV} & [\text{``Elaine''}] \\
\widehat{\text{GF}} & \\
\text{TENSE} & \text{PAST} \\
\text{PRED} & \text{`say} \langle (\uparrow \widehat{\text{GF}})(\uparrow \text{COMP}) \rangle \text{'} \\
\text{COMP} & \begin{bmatrix}
\text{PIV} & [\text{``Kramer''}] \\
\widehat{\text{GF}} & \\
\text{TENSE} & \text{PAST} \\
\text{PRED} & \text{`claim} \langle (\uparrow \widehat{\text{GF}})(\uparrow \text{COMP}) \rangle \text{'} \\
\text{COMP} & \begin{bmatrix}
\text{PIV} & [\text{``Newman''}] \\
\widehat{\text{GF}} & \\
\text{COMP} & \begin{bmatrix}
\text{TENSE} & \text{PAST} \\
\text{PRED} & \text{`see} \langle (\uparrow \widehat{\text{GF}})(\uparrow \text{OBJ}) \rangle \text{'} \\
\text{OBJ} &
\end{bmatrix}
\end{bmatrix}
\end{bmatrix}
\end{bmatrix}
\end{bmatrix}$$

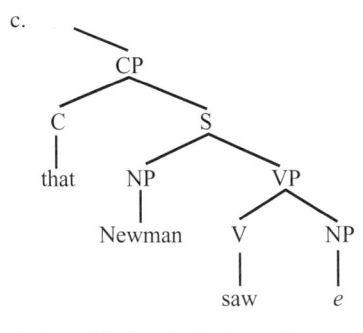

c.

```
         CP
        /  \
       C    S
       |   / \
     that NP  VP
          |   / \
       Newman V  NP
              |   |
             saw  e
```

d. ↑ = ((Path_GF* GF ↑) DF)

Such an analysis contrasts with one involving only outside-in licensing, in which there is no trace. While the evidence for the existence of the two different constructions is clear, and a theory which only recognizes outside-in licensing is therefore inferior, the question of the necessity of positing traces cannot be ignored. An analysis with trace has been motivated by Bresnan (1995) and Falk (2001), and argued against (within LFG) by Dalrymple *et al.* (2001). However, on closer inspection it transpires that the issue of traces is partially distinct from the question of inside-out licensing of long-distance dependencies, so the viability of the inside-out licensing analysis should not be judged on the basis of the trace question.

The fact of the matter is that inside-out licensing does not force us to use traces. An alternative method of licensing long-distance dependencies inside-out would be, as has been done in HPSG (e.g., Ginzburg Sag 2000), to hypothesize the c-structure in (19a) and for the verb (*saw* in [8]) to carry the optional lexical specification (19b).

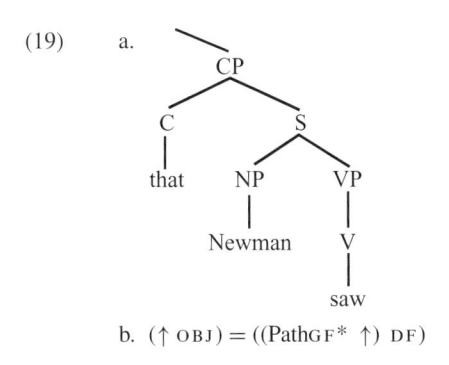

(19) a.

```
         CP
        /  \
       C    S
       |   / \
     that NP  VP
          |    |
       Newman  V
                |
               saw
```

b. (↑ OBJ) = ((Path_GF* ↑) DF)

This would achieve the same effect, and do it without the trace. Such an account would also need to allow for the extraction of adjuncts, which in turn would require reference to adjuncts in the lexical entry of the verb, along the lines proposed in the HPSG study of Bouma *et al.* (2001). An account of this kind is not unproblematic, however, as it is functionally inappropriate to specify adjuncts lexically. However these issues are to be resolved, the claim that non-PIV extraction is licensed inside-out is neutral on the question of traces.

To our mind, the most important consideration in the trace debate is that the trace analysis and the lexical analysis differ in their typological implications. The trace analysis predicts that, subject to island constraints (i.e., constraints on PathGF), a language which allows inside-out licensing of long-distance dependencies should allow extraction of any function. This is because, if one allows phrasal positions to remain empty, the phrasal positions in question should not be constrained by grammatical function. On the other hand, the lexical analysis predicts that gaps, like null pronouns (discussed in Chapter 2), should be subject to the relational hierarchy. If it is the lexical head that determines gap status for its arguments, the relational hierarchy, in addition to island constraints, will determine the distribution of gaps. Although it has been claimed (e.g., by Keenan and Comrie 1977) that the distribution of gaps is constrained by the relational hierarchy, the evidence for this is much less convincing than the evidence for the special status of pivots.[8] An examination of the typology of extractability is beyond the scope of the present study. Ultimately, though, such typological considerations will have to join with issues like *wanna* contraction (an argument for traces which has been largely debunked; Pullum 1997) and

---

8 Here is an example of the pitfalls of typological work done on this question. The oblique functions (in LFG, the OBL_θ family of grammatical functions) are ranked lower than the object function(s). The prediction is thus that there should be languages in which objects can extract but obliques cannot. Keenan and Comrie claim that this is the case; one of the languages they cite in this context is Hebrew. But the situation in Hebrew is more complex, and does not appear to support Keenan and Comrie's claim. In Hebrew, as in English, oblique arguments are realized structurally as PPs, with an embedded NP as the object of the preposition. Presumably, the entire PP is the oblique argument; the embedded NP is, depending on one's analysis, either the object of the head preposition or a co-head with the preposition. The problem is that what Keenan and Comrie mean when they say that obliques do not extract is the NP. That is to say, Hebrew disallows preposition stranding. The entire oblique PP, on the other hand, extracts as easily as an object. In fact, the same observation can be made concerning objects themselves. If they have the accusative preposition-like particle *et*, the *et* must front with the rest of the object. These facts are obscured somewhat by Keenan and Comrie's focus on relative clauses, as opposed to other long-distance dependency constructions. Since the element extracted in a relative clause is almost always an NP, the extractability of PPs did not come up in their study. However, the object/oblique distinction appears to be the crux of the claim that extraction is governed by the relational hierarchy. Until the true status of oblique extraction is clarified, we will not know whether the relational hierarchy is or is not relevant.

weak crossover effects (the core of Bresnan's argument) in determining whether traces exist or not.

In any case, the question of traces in long-distance dependency constructions remains an open question, but one which is tangential to our concerns. In the remainder of this study, we will assume an implementation with empty c-structure nodes, partially for the sake of concreteness and partially because this expresses our current analytic inclination. However, readers who find empty c-structure nodes objectionable should feel free to mentally replace the analysis invoking them with a lexical account of inside-out licensing.

To conclude, PIV extraction and non-PIV extraction are licensed by different formal devices. PIV extraction is licensed by the unmarked outside-in functional uncertainty; the Inside-Out LDD Condition blocks inside-out licensing. Non-PIV extraction is licensed by the more marked inside-out functional uncertainty, with the Pivot Condition blocking outside-in licensing. Thus, as in early constraint-based theories (Gazdar 1981, Falk 1983) we draw a sharp distinction between "subject" and non-"subject" extraction, with traces only (possibly) relevant for the latter.

4.1.3   Matrix subjects

One final point we need to address is the status of matrix subjects in extraction constructions: do matrix "extracted" subjects occupy the normal extracted position ([SPEC, CP] for *wh* elements) or are they in the normal subject position? The issue comes up clearly in English questions. In a subject question with an auxiliary, either c-structural analysis is plausible.

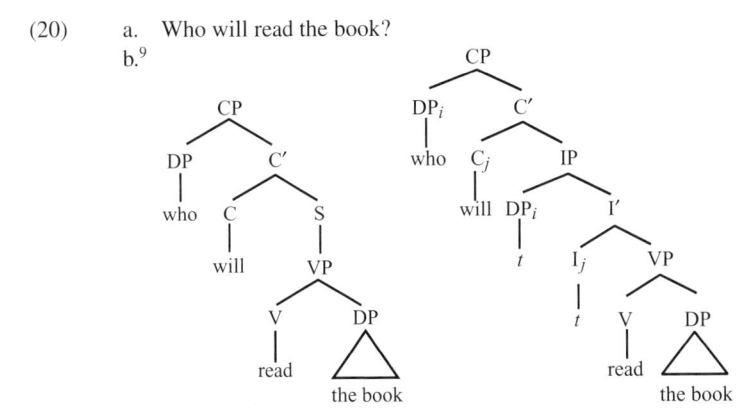

(20) a.   Who will read the book?
      b.[9]

[Tree 1: CP → DP (who), C' → C (will), S → VP → V (read), DP (the book)]

[Tree 2: CP → DP_i (who), C' → C_j (will), IP → DP_i (t), I' → I_j (t), VP → V (read), DP (the book)]

---

[9] For those readers who are more conversant with the constituent structures of transformational theory, I have included the transformational version of this structure (with traces of the movement of *who* and *will*) in addition to the structure assigned by the framework which underlies this study.

c.
```
        IP
       /  \
      DP   I'
      |   /  \
     who I    VP
         |   /  \
       will V    DP
            |    △
          read  the book
```

Either way, *who* will have to have a discourse function in addition to ĜF and PIV.

(21)
$$\begin{bmatrix} \text{FOCUS} & [\text{"who"}] \\ \text{PIV} \\ \widehat{\text{GF}} \\ \text{TENSE} & \text{FUT} \\ \text{PRED} & \text{'read} \langle (\uparrow \widehat{\text{GF}})(\uparrow \text{OBJ}) \rangle \text{'} \\ \text{OBJ} & [\text{"the book"}] \end{bmatrix}$$

The crucial evidence comes from subject questions with no auxiliary. If the *wh* element is in [SPEC, CP], we would expect obligatory *Do* Support and Subject-Aux Inversion, placing *do* in the head C position. If the *wh* element is in subject position, on the other hand, supportive *do* should be possible only if the sentence is emphatic, as in ordinary declarative clauses. Since the behavior of these sentences is the same as declaratives, it suggests a non-[SPEC, CP] analysis for matrix subject extraction.

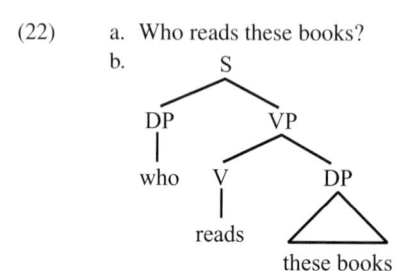

(22) a. Who reads these books?
b.
```
         S
        / \
       DP  VP
       |   / \
      who V   DP
          |   △
        reads these books
```

We hypothesize that, since PIV is an overlay function, it has an affinity for other overlay functions, and can be assigned one locally.

Other languages may or may not license matrix PIV "extraction" in similar fashion. For example, we have seen (see [17] above and the accompanying discussion) that Imbabura Quechua disallows the extraction of an embedded

PIV, and have conjectured that it lacks the normal outside-in licensing. However, matrix subjects can be involved in a dependency with a discourse function in the same clause (Cole 1982).[10]

(23) a. Ñuka wawki- ka   ñuka mama- man ali   wagra- ta
       my   brother- TOP my   mother- to good cow-   ACC
       kara- rka.
       give- PST.3
       'My brother gave my mother a good cow.'
    b. Pi- taj kan- paj mama- man ali   wagra- ta kara- rka ?
       who- Q you- POSS mother- to   good cow-   ACC give- PST.3
       'Who gave your mother a good cow?'

This would follow if matrix *wh* PIVs can receive a discourse function in situ; the (marked) lack of outside-in licensing in Imbabura Quechua would then be irrelevant. On the other hand, Clements *et al.* (1983) present evidence that matrix PIVs do extract in Icelandic, so Icelandic apparently lacks this option for matrix PIVs. This is apparently a parameter of cross-linguistic variation.

There are thus three different ways in English for a discourse function to be identified with a clause-internal function, or, alternatively, three different formal constructions corresponding to the notional construction of extraction/long-distance dependency.

(24) a. Lexically encoded property of verbs:[11]
       $(\uparrow DF) (\uparrow PIV) \Rightarrow (\uparrow DF) = (\uparrow PathGF^+ PIV)$
    b. Constraint associated with null c-structure nodes:
       $\uparrow = ((PathGF^* GF \uparrow) DF)$
    c. IP/S →   NP   I'/VP
                ($\uparrow$PIV) = ↓ $\uparrow$=↓
                (($\uparrow$DF) =↓)

Variants on these are evident in other languages, but the basic patterns are the same.

Each of these has its own formal nature, and therefore its own unique properties. There is no single set of properties for long-distance dependencies.

---

10 Cole's sentence includes two adjuncts, which have been omitted here.
11 Two technical notes about the formulation here. First, the condition has been added to prevent a subject/discourse function element from also being assigned to a lower PIV. Second, since local DF/PIV identification is specified in situ, the path in this case has to have length of at least one; the Kleene star has been replaced by a Kleene plus.

The outside-in (top-down) construction is unbounded and restricted to PIV, the inside-out (bottom-up) construction is unbounded and limited to non-PIVs, and the matrix-subject construction is local and restricted to PIV. Languages may use one, two, or all three of these constructions.

4.2 Across-the-board extraction

One place where subject/non-subject asymmetries have been observed is in across-the-board extractions in coordinate structures. In English, across-the-board extraction can involve subjects at the top level of the coordination in all clauses, or other elements in all clauses (non-subjects and embedded subjects), but not a combination of top-level subjects and other elements.[12]

(25) a. Who did you claim [[visited our house] and [saw the baby]]?
      b. What do you think [[I brought back] and [everyone thinks will entertain the baby]]?
      c. *Who do you think [[the baby likes] and [was smiled at]]?

In order to understand how this works, and how it interacts with the theory of pivots, we need a brief overview of the analysis of coordination in LFG.

Coordination in LFG is analyzed as involving a set of f-structures (Kaplan and Maxwell 1995), licensed by the following phrase structure schema:

(26)   XP → XP*   CONJ   XP
                ↓∈↑   ↓∈↑

It has been shown by Dalrymple and Kaplan (2000) and Dalrymple (2001) that coordinate structures have a hybrid character, being both f-structure entities in their own right and sets of f-structure entities. Conceptually, this means that, unlike sets of adjuncts, the whole coordinate structure is a functional unit just as much as the individual conjuncts. Features of coordinate structures are either distributive or non-distributive: non-distributive features are features of the coordination as a whole, while distributive features are features of the conjuncts. Grammatical functions are distributive; as we saw in Chapter 3, a

---

12 An anonymous reader suggests that the following is not as bad as one might expect:

(i)   Who do you think the elderly will vote for and {so/as a result} will win the election.

I agree that the imposition of an expression like *so* or *as a result* makes the sentence much better. While I do not fully understand why this would improve the sentence, it seems likely to me that the anaphoric nature of these expressions may be involved.

grammatical function which is present once in the c-structure, above the level of the coordination, becomes part of each conjunct functionally.

Across-the-board extraction of top-level subjects follows automatically. The outside-in constraint licensing PIV extraction will terminate at the coordinated complement. Essentially, the result is an f-structure like the following:

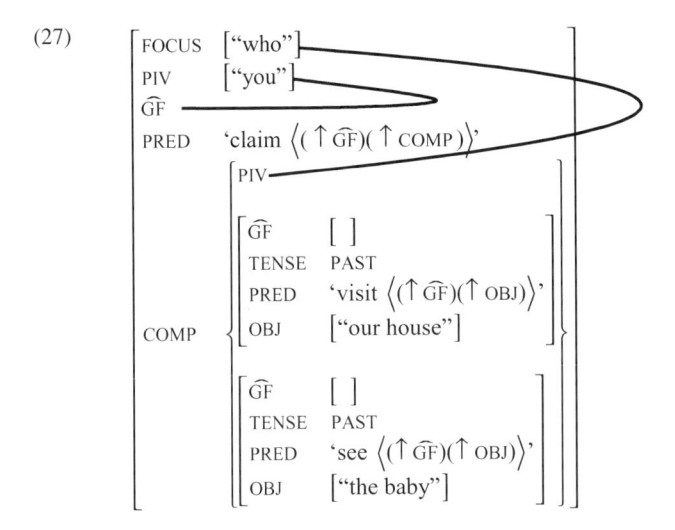

(27)
$$\begin{bmatrix} \text{FOCUS} & [\text{``who''}] \\ \text{PIV} & [\text{``you''}] \\ \widehat{\text{GF}} & \text{\textemdash} \\ \text{PRED} & \text{`claim} \langle (\uparrow \widehat{\text{GF}})(\uparrow \text{COMP}) \rangle\text{'} \\ \text{COMP} & \left\{ \begin{bmatrix} \text{PIV} & \\ \widehat{\text{GF}} & [\ ] \\ \text{TENSE} & \text{PAST} \\ \text{PRED} & \text{`visit} \langle (\uparrow \widehat{\text{GF}})(\uparrow \text{OBJ}) \rangle\text{'} \\ \text{OBJ} & [\text{``our house''}] \end{bmatrix} , \begin{bmatrix} \widehat{\text{GF}} & [\ ] \\ \text{TENSE} & \text{PAST} \\ \text{PRED} & \text{`see} \langle (\uparrow \widehat{\text{GF}})(\uparrow \text{OBJ}) \rangle\text{'} \\ \text{OBJ} & [\text{``the baby''}] \end{bmatrix} \right\} \end{bmatrix}$$

However, since PIV is a distributive attribute, this is equivalent to:

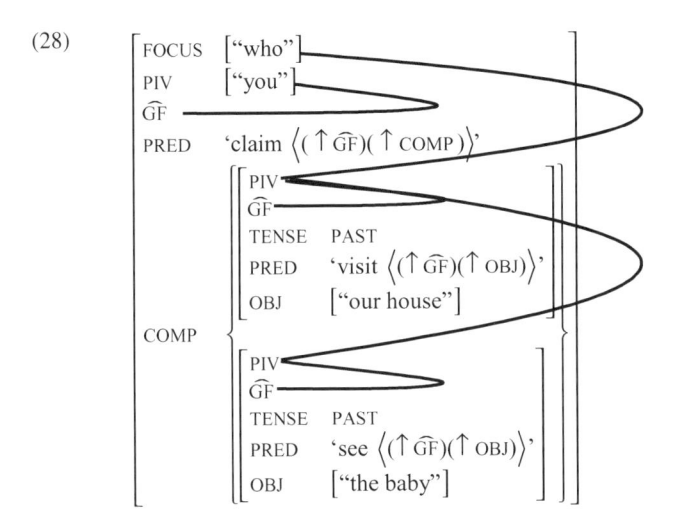

(28)
$$\begin{bmatrix} \text{FOCUS} & [\text{``who''}] \\ \text{PIV} & [\text{``you''}] \\ \widehat{\text{GF}} & \text{\textemdash} \\ \text{PRED} & \text{`claim} \langle (\uparrow \widehat{\text{GF}})(\uparrow \text{COMP}) \rangle\text{'} \\ \text{COMP} & \left\{ \begin{bmatrix} \text{PIV} & \\ \widehat{\text{GF}} & \\ \text{TENSE} & \text{PAST} \\ \text{PRED} & \text{`visit} \langle (\uparrow \widehat{\text{GF}})(\uparrow \text{OBJ}) \rangle\text{'} \\ \text{OBJ} & [\text{``our house''}] \end{bmatrix} , \begin{bmatrix} \text{PIV} & \\ \widehat{\text{GF}} & \\ \text{TENSE} & \text{PAST} \\ \text{PRED} & \text{`see} \langle (\uparrow \widehat{\text{GF}})(\uparrow \text{OBJ}) \rangle\text{'} \\ \text{OBJ} & [\text{``the baby''}] \end{bmatrix} \right\} \end{bmatrix}$$

Across-the-board extraction of PIVs as in (25a) is thus straightforward.

Things get more complicated with non-PIVs. As we have seen, non-PIV extraction is licensed from the lower end of the dependency by inside-out designation. In the case of coordination, this means that the path must cross from the f-structure element representing the conjunct to the f-structure element corresponding to the coordinate structure. However, since there is no grammatical function on the path between these, no specification of Path$_{GF}$ will license "escaping" the conjoined structure. In the following, there is no way to specify a path from the f-structure element labeled f (the first conjunct) to the one labeled g (the whole coordinate structure). "↑" marks the starting point of the inside-out designination.

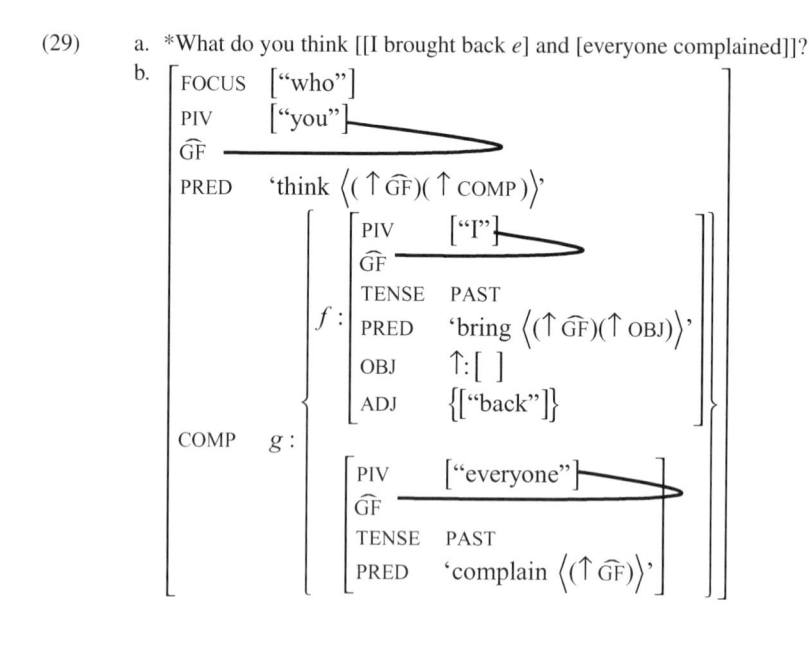

(29)   a.   *What do you think [[I brought back e] and [everyone complained]]?

b.
$$\begin{bmatrix} \text{FOCUS} & [\text{"who"}] \\ \text{PIV} & [\text{"you"}] \\ \widehat{\text{GF}} & \text{———} \\ \text{PRED} & \text{'think} \langle (\uparrow \widehat{\text{GF}})(\uparrow \text{COMP}) \rangle' \\ \text{COMP} & g: \left\{ f: \begin{bmatrix} \text{PIV} & [\text{"I"}] \\ \widehat{\text{GF}} & \text{———} \\ \text{TENSE} & \text{PAST} \\ \text{PRED} & \text{'bring} \langle (\uparrow \widehat{\text{GF}})(\uparrow \text{OBJ}) \rangle' \\ \text{OBJ} & \uparrow:[\ ] \\ \text{ADJ} & \{[\text{"back"}]\} \end{bmatrix}, \begin{bmatrix} \text{PIV} & [\text{"everyone"}] \\ \widehat{\text{GF}} & \text{———} \\ \text{TENSE} & \text{PAST} \\ \text{PRED} & \text{'complain} \langle (\uparrow \widehat{\text{GF}}) \rangle' \end{bmatrix} \right\} \end{bmatrix}$$

The Coordinate Structure Constraint thus follows from the LFG theory of coordination.

Now suppose that the following constraint is associated with the conjunction of the coordinate structure.

(30) $(\uparrow \text{DF}) = ((\text{Path}_{GF}* \uparrow) \text{DF})$

This licenses a discourse function in the coordinate structure which has the same value as a discourse function higher (or farther out) in the structure, a "cloned" discourse function.

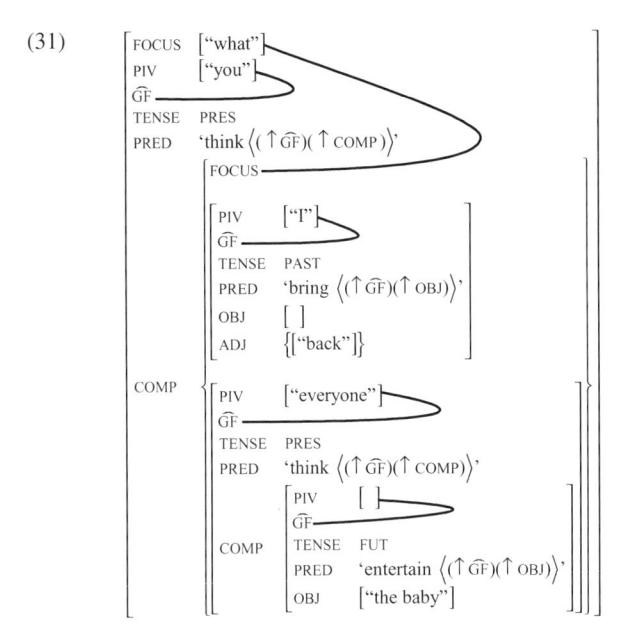

(31)
$$\begin{bmatrix} \text{FOCUS} & [\text{"what"}] \\ \text{PIV} & [\text{"you"}] \\ \widehat{\text{GF}} \\ \text{TENSE} & \text{PRES} \\ \text{PRED} & \text{'think} \langle (\uparrow \widehat{\text{GF}})(\uparrow \text{COMP}) \rangle \text{'} \\ \text{COMP} & \begin{Bmatrix} \begin{bmatrix} \text{FOCUS} \\ \text{PIV} & [\text{"I"}] \\ \widehat{\text{GF}} \\ \text{TENSE} & \text{PAST} \\ \text{PRED} & \text{'bring} \langle (\uparrow \widehat{\text{GF}})(\uparrow \text{OBJ}) \rangle \text{'} \\ \text{OBJ} & [\ ] \\ \text{ADJ} & \{[\text{"back"}]\} \end{bmatrix} \\ \begin{bmatrix} \text{PIV} & [\text{"everyone"}] \\ \widehat{\text{GF}} \\ \text{TENSE} & \text{PRES} \\ \text{PRED} & \text{'think} \langle (\uparrow \widehat{\text{GF}})(\uparrow \text{COMP}) \rangle \text{'} \\ \text{COMP} & \begin{bmatrix} \text{PIV} & [\ ] \\ \widehat{\text{GF}} \\ \text{TENSE} & \text{FUT} \\ \text{PRED} & \text{'entertain} \langle (\uparrow \widehat{\text{GF}})(\uparrow \text{OBJ}) \rangle \text{'} \\ \text{OBJ} & [\text{"the baby"}] \end{bmatrix} \end{bmatrix} \end{Bmatrix} \end{bmatrix}$$

This "cloned" DF will be distributed between the conjuncts.

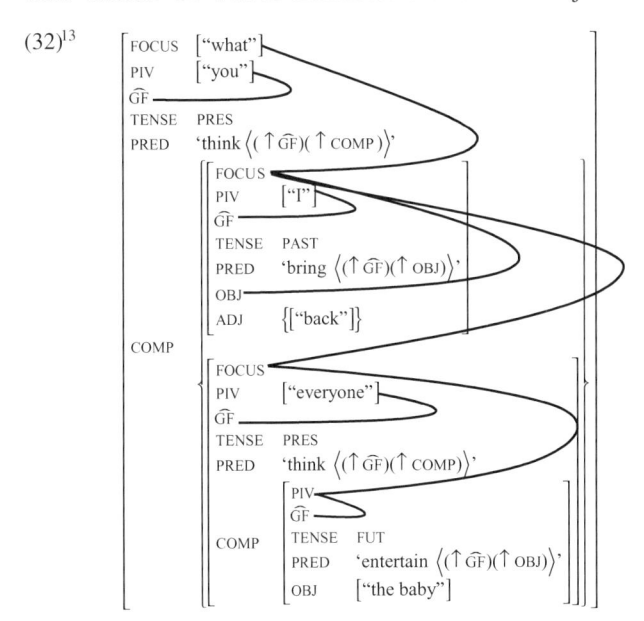

(32)[13]
$$\begin{bmatrix} \text{FOCUS} & [\text{"what"}] \\ \text{PIV} & [\text{"you"}] \\ \widehat{\text{GF}} \\ \text{TENSE} & \text{PRES} \\ \text{PRED} & \text{'think} \langle (\uparrow \widehat{\text{GF}})(\uparrow \text{COMP}) \rangle \text{'} \\ \text{COMP} & \begin{Bmatrix} \begin{bmatrix} \text{FOCUS} \\ \text{PIV} & [\text{"I"}] \\ \widehat{\text{GF}} \\ \text{TENSE} & \text{PAST} \\ \text{PRED} & \text{'bring} \langle (\uparrow \widehat{\text{GF}})(\uparrow \text{OBJ}) \rangle \text{'} \\ \text{OBJ} \\ \text{ADJ} & \{[\text{"back"}]\} \end{bmatrix} \\ \begin{bmatrix} \text{FOCUS} \\ \text{PIV} & [\text{"everyone"}] \\ \widehat{\text{GF}} \\ \text{TENSE} & \text{PRES} \\ \text{PRED} & \text{'think} \langle (\uparrow \widehat{\text{GF}})(\uparrow \text{COMP}) \rangle \text{'} \\ \text{COMP} & \begin{bmatrix} \text{PIV} \\ \widehat{\text{GF}} \\ \text{TENSE} & \text{FUT} \\ \text{PRED} & \text{'entertain} \langle (\uparrow \widehat{\text{GF}})(\uparrow \text{OBJ}) \rangle \text{'} \\ \text{OBJ} & [\text{"the baby"}] \end{bmatrix} \end{bmatrix} \end{Bmatrix} \end{bmatrix}$$

[13] This f-structure is rather busy. *What* here has six grammatical functions: FOCUS of the main clause, FOCUS and OBJ of the *bring* clause, FOCUS of the *think* clause, and PIV and $\widehat{\text{GF}}$ of the *entertain* clause.

This distribution of the cloned discourse function results in the across-the-board effect: each conjunct has its own internal long-distance dependency. There is nothing to block the gap from being a non-PIV or an embedded PIV. Thus, a sentence like (25b) is licensed.

However, the cloned discourse function cannot be the PIV of the same clausal level in which it is located. The outside-in functional uncertainty constraint that licenses PIV extraction requires a path of at least one member, since matrix PIVs are assigned a discourse function in situ. There is no way to license a sentence like (25c).

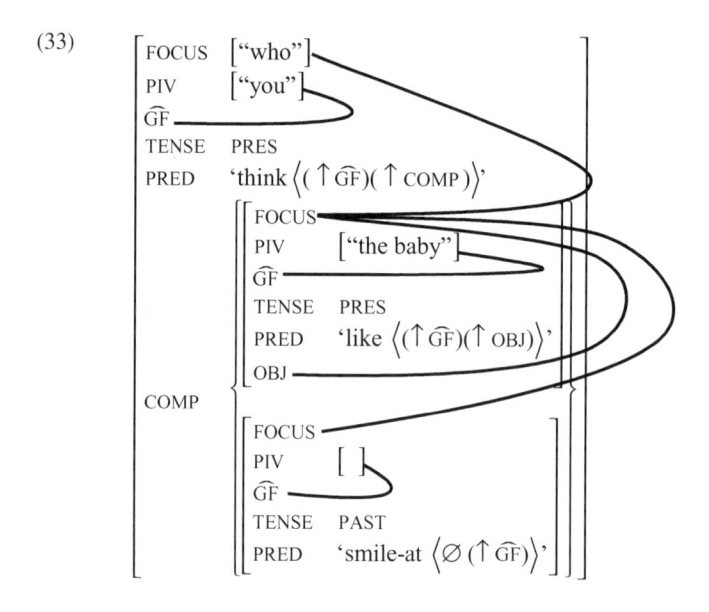

(33) $\begin{bmatrix} \text{FOCUS} & [\text{"who"}] \\ \text{PIV} & [\text{"you"}] \\ \widehat{\text{GF}} \\ \text{TENSE} & \text{PRES} \\ \text{PRED} & \text{'think}\langle(\uparrow\widehat{\text{GF}})(\uparrow\text{COMP})\rangle\text{'} \\ \text{COMP} \left\{\begin{bmatrix} \text{FOCUS} \\ \text{PIV} & [\text{"the baby"}] \\ \widehat{\text{GF}} \\ \text{TENSE} & \text{PRES} \\ \text{PRED} & \text{'like}\langle(\uparrow\widehat{\text{GF}})(\uparrow\text{OBJ})\rangle\text{'} \\ \text{OBJ} \end{bmatrix} \begin{bmatrix} \text{FOCUS} \\ \text{PIV} & [\ ] \\ \widehat{\text{GF}} \\ \text{TENSE} & \text{PAST} \\ \text{PRED} & \text{'smile-at}\langle\varnothing(\uparrow\widehat{\text{GF}})\rangle\text{'} \end{bmatrix}\right\} \end{bmatrix}$

Since the FOCUS and the PIV in the second conjunct cannot be identified with each other, the second conjunct is ill-formed: the FOCUS is not properly integrated into the clause (technically, a violation of the Extended Coherence Condition) and the ĜF argument of the predicate is missing (a violation of the Completeness Condition).

Other languages have slightly different patterns. For example, according to Saiki (1985), in Japanese no subject–non-subject combination is permitted in across-the-board extraction, regardless of degree of embedding.

(34) a. [Takashi o   nagutte] [[[Satoru o   ketobashita] to
         Takashi ACC hit   Satoru ACC kicked   COMP

         Reiko ga   omotteiru] to   Sachiko ga   shinjiteiru] otoko
         Reiko NOM think   COMP Sachiko NOM believe   man
         'the man who hit Takashi and Sachiko believes Reiko thinks kicked
         Satoru'

      b. [Takashi ga   nagutte] [Reiko ga   [Satoru ga
         Takashi NOM hit   Reiko NOM   Satoru NOM

         ketobashita] to   utagatteiru] otoko
         kicked   COMP doubt   man
         'the man who Takashi hit and Reiko doubts that Satoru kicked'

      c. *[Takashi ga   nagutte] [[[Satoru o   ketobashita] to
          Takashi NOM hit   Satoru ACC kicked   COMP

         Reiko ga   omotteiru] to   Sachiko ga   shinjiteiru] otoko
         Reiko NOM think   COMP Sachiko NOM believe   man
         'the man who Takashi hit and Sachiko believes Reiko thinks kicked
         Satoru'

      d. *[Takashi o   nagutte] [Reiko ga   [Satoru ga
          Takashi ACC hit   Reiko NOM   Satoru NOM

         ketobashita] to   utagatteiru] otoko
         kicked   COMP doubt   man
         'the man who hit Takashi and Reiko doubts that Satoru kicked'

Saiki proposes that the outside-in constraint (under our analysis, the one which licenses PIV extraction) is associated with the root of the relative clause.

(35)   NP →   S   NP
                   ↓ ∈ (↑ ADJ)   ↑ = ↓
                (↓ DF PRED) = 'PRO'
                ((↓ DF) = (↓ GF* PIV))

This analysis of Japanese differs from our analysis of English in that the licensing constraint for PIV extraction is associated with the root of the clause, not with the verb. Put slightly differently, Saiki's analysis treats the licensing of PIV extraction as a constructional property of relative clauses, while our analysis of English treats it as a more general clausal property. This difference is plausible, since English deploys long-distance dependencies more generally than Japanese; Japanese leaves *wh* elements in situ, for example. We also assume, following Falk (1983), that it is possible to associate certain constraints with the conjuncts of a coordinate structure *as long as it is annotated to all of them*. We hypothesize that the PIV extraction constraint is one of these.

128 *Subjects and their properties*

(36)
S →   S   CONJ   S
          ↓ ∈ ↑   ((↑ DF)=((PathGF* ↑) DF))   ↓ ∈ ↑
    ((↑ DF)=(↑ PathGF* PIV))   ((↑ DF)=(↑ PathGF* PIV))

This difference results in the different judgments in English and Japanese. In Japanese, PIV extraction has to be across the board.

4.3 The *that*-trace effect

One of the best known, and least understood, constraints on extraction is the "*that*-trace effect." The theory of pivots proposed here provides a new approach,[14] one which is more principled and less arbitrary than other analyses that have been proposed. The facts are well known:

(37)   a. I think Gabi hugged Pnina.
        b. I think that Gabi hugged Pnina.

(38)   a. Who do you think Gabi hugged ____?
        b. Who do you think that Gabi hugged ____?

(39)   a. Who do you think ____ hugged Pnina??
        b. *Who do you think that ____ hugged Pnina??

In the Government/Binding framework, this has been generally seen as a consequence of a locality condition on traces: the Empty Category Principle (ECP), which requires a trace to be "properly governed."

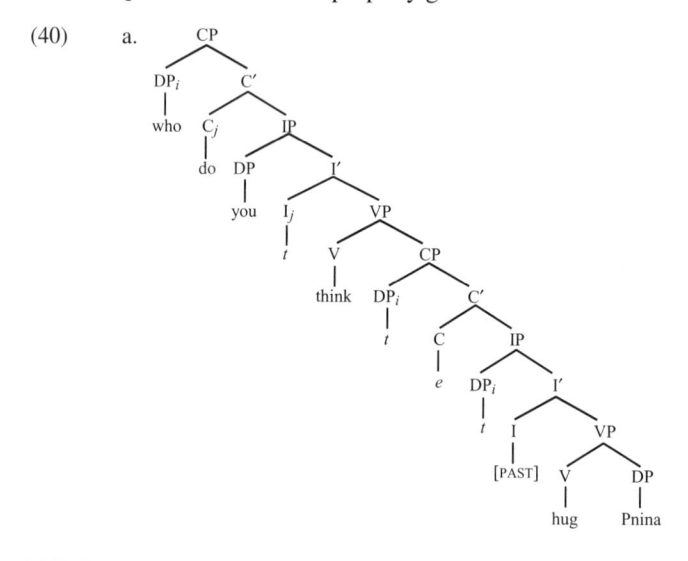

(40) a.

```
        CP
       /  \
     DPᵢ   C'
      |   /  \
    who  Cⱼ   IP
         |
         do  DP  I'
             |  /  \
            you Iⱼ  VP
                |   / \
                t  V   CP
                   |   / \
                 think DPᵢ C'
                       |  / \
                       t C   IP
                         |
                         e  DPᵢ  I'
                             |   / \
                             t  I   VP
                                |   / \
                             [PAST] V  DP
                                    |   |
                                   hug Pnina
```

---

14 Earlier versions of this analysis have been outlined in Falk (2000, 2001).

b.

```
        CP
       /  \
     DPᵢ   C'
      |   / \
     who Cⱼ  IP
         |  / \
         do DP  I'
            |  / \
           you Iⱼ  VP
               |  / \
               t  V   CP
                  |  / \
                 think DPᵢ  C'
                       |   / \
                       t  C   IP
                          |  / \
                         that DPᵢ  I'
                              |   / \
                              t  I    VP
                                 |   / \
                              [PAST] V  DP
                                     |   |
                                    hug Pnina
```

In (40a), the subject trace is hypothesized to be properly governed, while in (40b) it is not. How to achieve this result formally has turned out to be something of a puzzle, since, under GB assumptions, there is no difference in structure between the sentence with the complementizer and the one without. Several versions of this have been proposed, such as Chomsky's (1986) minimality-based approach to government, and Rizzi's (1990) conjunctive statement of the ECP (antecedent government *and* head government) combined with relativized minimality. The essential problem with approaches of this kind is that the *that*-trace effect is not really a locality effect; the *wh* element is no more local in the absence of an overt complementizer than in its presence. The attempts to redefine locality to account for the *that*-trace effect are artificial.

There have been other approaches as well. For example, Ginzburg and Sag (2000) propose an analysis in HPSG, under which an extracted subject is present in the feature structure of the verb: the value of the SUBJ attribute is a *gap-synsem* object. (The Argument Realization Principle, which subtracts SLASH elements from the COMPS list, does not affect the SUBJ list.) The SUBJ list is passed to the VP and S which the verb heads. Unlike ordinary Ss, which have an empty SUBJ list, the S from which the subject has been extracted has this *gap-synsem* object in the value of its SUBJ attribute. So the subordinate S in (39) would have the following structure:

(41)

$$\begin{bmatrix} \text{SUBJ} & \langle \boxed{1} \rangle \\ \text{COMPS} & \langle \rangle \\ \text{SLASH} & \{\boxed{2}\} \end{bmatrix}$$

S

|
VP
$$\begin{bmatrix} \text{SUBJ} & \langle \boxed{1} \rangle \\ \text{COMPS} & \langle \rangle \\ \text{SLASH} & \{\boxed{2}\} \end{bmatrix}$$

V
$$\begin{bmatrix} \text{SUBJ} & \langle \boxed{1} \begin{bmatrix} \textit{gap-ss} \\ \text{LOC} & \boxed{2} \\ \text{SLASH} & \{\boxed{2}\} \end{bmatrix} \rangle \\ \text{COMPS} & \langle \boxed{3} \rangle \end{bmatrix}$$
|
hugged

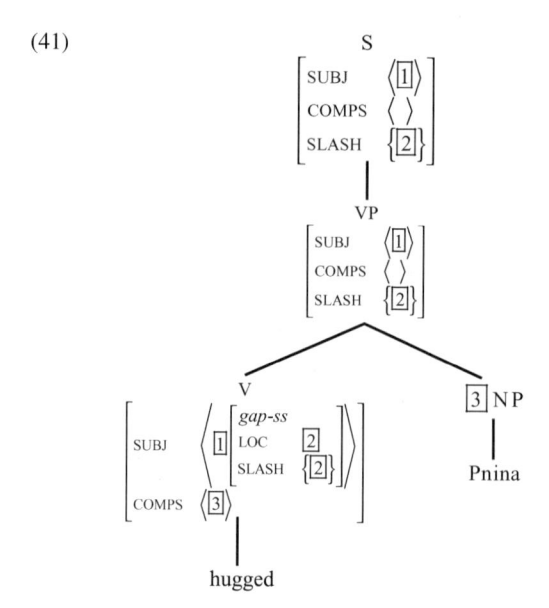

$\boxed{3}$ NP
|
Pnina

Such an S cannot be complement to the complementizer *that*, which selects a finite S with an empty SUBJ list:

(42)
$$\begin{bmatrix} \text{PHON} & \langle \text{that} \rangle \\ \text{ARG-ST} & \langle \begin{bmatrix} \text{S} \\ \text{INV} & - \\ \text{VFORM} & \textit{fin} \\ \text{SUBJ} & \langle \rangle \end{bmatrix} \rangle \end{bmatrix}$$

Like the analysis we will propose, this is a lexical analysis, not a structural one. However, it is arbitrary: it does not explain why SUBJs should be different, or why the complementizer *that* should be subcategorized for an S with an empty SUBJ list rather than just an S. Therefore, like the ECP analysis, it is inadequate.

We begin by observing that, contrary to what is generally supposed, the *that*-trace effect is a lexical property of the head complementizer. For example, as observed by Shlonsky (1988), in Hebrew the complementizer *še* 'that' does not induce the *that*-trace effect, while *im* 'if' does.[15]

---

15 Shlonsky attributes this to *še* cliticizing to the element to its right. He claims that *še* is a "phonetic clitic" on the grounds that it is not related to another word (the way English *that* is), it cannot be contrastively stressed, and cannot occur in isolation. He then argues for the possibility of syntactic cliticization on the basis of a problematic (by his own admission) analysis of multiple *wh* constructions and on the basis of a particular analysis of free relatives in Hebrew. The argument for *še* even being a phonetic clitic is weak, as *that* is also resistant to contrastive stress and cannot occur (as a complementizer) in isolation.

(43) a. Mi   ata xošev   še   xibek   et   Pnina ?
         who you think.PRES that hug.PST ACC Pnina
         'Who do you think hugged Pnina??'
      b. *Mi šaalta   im xibek   et   Pnina ?
         who ask.PST.2MSG.SUBJ if   hug.PST ACC Pnina
         'Who did you ask if hugged Pnina?'

A similar pattern has been claimed for some speakers of English by Sobin (1987), for whom the effect obtains with *if* but not with *that*. The existence of differences between complementizers in some languages indicates that the *that*-trace effect cannot be the result of some general structural principle involving complementizers, but must be an individual lexical property of specific complementizers. So the *that*-trace effect must be due to some marking in the complementizer's lexical entry. This contrasts sharply with the attempt in transformational theory to make the *that*-trace effect be a result of structural constraints.

The second observation about the *that*-trace phenomenon comes from the functionalist literature: different types of complement clauses are more or less closely bound to the main clause. For example, Givón (1990: 517) divides complement-taking verbs into three classes:

(44)   a. Modality verbs ('want,' 'begin,' 'finish,' 'try,' etc.)
       b. Manipulative verbs ('make,' 'tell,' 'order,' 'ask,' etc.)
       c. Cognition-utterance verbs ('know,' 'think,' 'say,' etc.)

Givón observes that the cognition-utterance verbs involve a weaker bond between the main clause and subordinate clause than the other two types. He also discusses different types of complements, and observes that finite complements involve a weaker bond than non-finite. These two observations are related to each other, since verbs of cognition and utterance are more likely to take finite complements. Givón also presents a scale of syntactic complement types, from strongest bond to weakest bond:

(45)   predicate-raised (e.g., *let go*) > bare infinitive > *to* infinitive > *for-to* infinitive > subjunctive > "indirect quote" (i.e., *that*) > direct quote

Our hypothesis is that the *that*-trace effect is a grammaticalization of these differences in clausal bond. The concept of grammaticalization is familiar from the functionalist literature: functionally motivated distinctions become fossilized in the grammar of the language. When this happens, they often lose their original functional motivation and become mere formal constraints.

From our mixed functional–formal perspective, we need to ask how Givón's observation might be expressed formally in the grammars of languages, and thus become grammaticalized. It seems to us that there are two primary ingredients to such a grammaticalization of this functional notion of bond. The first ingredient is the concept of different types of clauses. Since the type of clause is lexicalized in the complementizer, it is plausible that properties which are a consequence of the type of clause will be encoded as lexical properties of the complementizer. Note that this means that, since (as noted above) grammaticalization tends to lose the original functional conditioning, omitting the complementizer provides a loophole to escape the properties in question. In the context of the *that*-trace effect, if the effect is a consequence of the higher independence of finite clauses, omitting the complementizer *that* should cancel the effect. It does.

The second ingredient is the concept of the bond between main and subordinate clause. We have already identified the PIV as the element that links a subordinate clause to the clause in which it is embedded. It stands to reason, then, that the relative independence of certain types of clauses should be expressed as a limitation on the PIV; some constraint that requires the clause to have "its own" PIV, rather than a PIV which is also part of a higher clause.

We propose that the lexical entry of *that* includes a constraint which we can express informally as:

(46)   The clause has its own PIV.

This is exactly the right thing to say about the *that*-trace effect: it is a property of the complementizer, and it affects the PIV. We formalize this in terms of the c-structure–f-structure mapping.[16]

(47)   If the PIV is overtly represented in the c-structure, it must be represented in the c-structure of *that*'s clause.

The f-structure–c-structure mapping relation is called ϕ^{-1} in the LFG literature. We can thus restate the constraint in the lexical entry of *that* as:

(48)   If $\phi^{-1}(\uparrow \text{PIV})$ exists, one of the nodes in $\phi^{-1}(\uparrow)$ must immediately dominate one of the nodes in $\phi^{-1}(\uparrow \text{PIV})$.

---

[16] This differs from the formulation in Falk (2000). There, the formulation was purely in terms of f-structure properties, disallowing the PIV from being identical to an element in any higher clause. The reformulation here follows Falk (2002), and takes into account the common use of resumptive pronouns as a way of circumventing *that*-trace effects (Sells 1984).

Long-distance dependencies 133

More formally, we can define an f-structure-aware notion of immediate dominance, similar to such concepts as f-precedence. We will call this the f–ID relation.

(49)   For any f-structures f_1 and f_2, f_1 f–IDs f_2 ($f_1 \rightarrow_f f_2$) iff there exists a node n_1 in $\phi^{-1}(f_1)$ and a node n_2 in $\phi^{-1}(f_2)$ such that n_1 immediately dominates n_2.

We can now state the lexical constraint on *that*-trace complementizers formally:

(50) $\phi^{-1}(\uparrow \text{PIV}) \Rightarrow \uparrow \rightarrow_f (\uparrow \text{PIV})$

The lexical constraint (50) will be associated with different complementizers in different languages, although always taken from the bottom of Givón's scale. Languages will differ in the extent to which the independence of subordinate clauses is grammaticalized. In standard English, *that*, *if*, and *whether* will all be marked with (50); in the dialects described by Sobin (1987), only *if* and *whether*. Similarly, in Hebrew *im* 'if' will have (50) in its lexical entry, but *še* will not.

The c-structure and f-structure of the ungrammatical (39b) are:

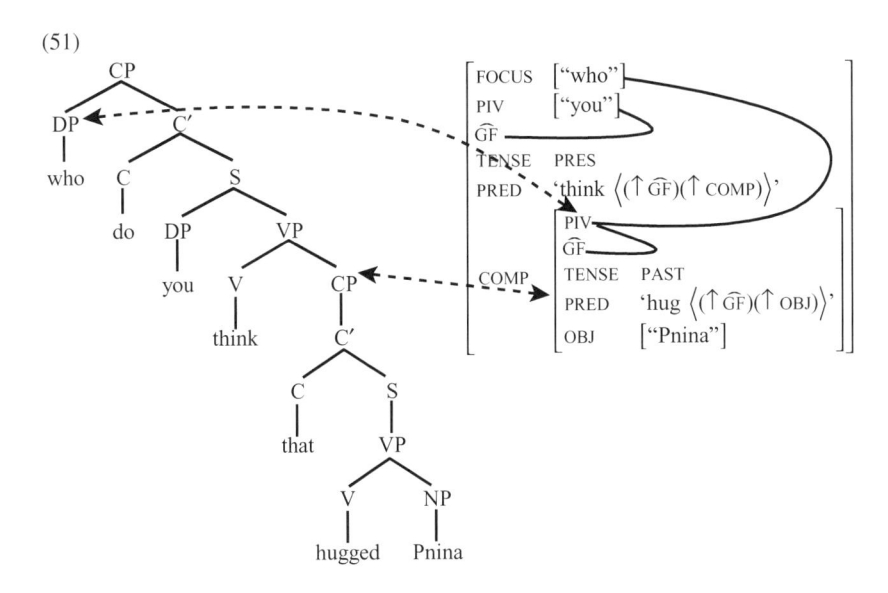

(51)

The highest c-structure node corresponding to *that*'s f-structure is indicated here, as is the c-structure node corresponding to the PIV of *that*'s f-structure.

Contrary to the requirements of the lexical constraint on *that*, the latter is not contained in the former.[17]

We also note that this analysis is consistent with what is often a problem for analyses of the *that*-trace effect: the *that* relative.

(52)   the book [that interests me]

In such a relative clause, the relative pronoun is not overtly expressed in the c-structure. If the relative pronoun is the PIV, as it is here, the premise of the conditional in (50) is not met. We therefore do not need any special exemptions for relative clauses in this analysis.

Most importantly, this analysis of the *that*-trace effect is explanatory. It combines the functionally based observation of Givón's with the formal/functional theory of pivothood developed here, to provide an account which does not just stipulate the effect.[18]

4.4   Summary

In this chapter, we have seen that the special status of subjects in long-distance dependency constructions follows from the theory of pivothood. The PIV is the only subordinate element that can be directly referred to by the unmarked outside-in functional uncertainty constraint licensing long-distance dependencies. Other elements can only be licensed as extractees through the more marked inside-out constraint. Asymmetries in across-the-board extraction follow from this distinction. Finally, the theory of pivothood provides the basis for an explanatory account of the *that*-trace effect.

17 It should be noted that this only works if there is no empty element (trace) in the lower CP corresponding to the PIV. This follows from our analysis, as PIV extraction is always licensed by an outside-in constraint; outside-in constraints do not involve traces under anybody's conception.
18 As has been pointed out to me by Edit Doron (personal communication), data from mixed-subject languages would help argue that it is PIV that is relevant for the *that*-trace effect. Unfortunately, a search of the literature and query on the LINGUIST List (issue 13.2132, August 20, 2002) have not turned up any mixed-subject languages that have the effect.

5 *Control constructions*

5.1 Overview of the issues

One of the most interesting constructions to be explained in a discussion of subject properties is the class of constructions that can be grouped under the rubric "control." Under the most inclusive definition, control constructions are all those in which an argument of a subordinate clause is not expressed overtly, but understood either as identical with some other element (usually an element in the immediately superordinate clause) or as generic/arbitrary. The unexpressed element is the controllee, and the understood reference is the controller. Control in this sense encompasses cases where the controller is a thematic argument in its own clause (equi, or control in the narrower sense) and cases where the controller is not a thematic argument in its own clause (raising).

We take the core control constructions to be what can be referred to as complement equi, constructions in which there is a subordinate clause (generally non-finite in languages that have a finite/non-finite distinction) which is a complement to a verb, with one of the arguments of the subordinate clause unexpressed and understood as being coreferential with one of the arguments of the main verb. English examples include sentences such as the following:

(1) a. The student tried [to understand the material]. (understood subject of *understand* is *the student*)
     b. The landlord agreed [to decrease the rent]. (understood subject of *decrease* is *the landlord*)
     c. The child persuaded her father [to read another story]. (understood subject of *read* is *her father*)

When we use the term "control" in this chapter with no modification, we refer to constructions of this kind. Less central constructions include non-complement equi (where the subordinate clause is not a complement of the main clause) and

Raising.[1] We will have less to say about these other constructions, especially non-complement equi.

Control, as understood here, crucially excludes constructions in which the subordinate clause has explicit marking that indicates that its subject is coreferential and/or non-coreferential with the subject of the higher clause. These constructions, usually called switch-reference, were discussed in Chapter 2 in the context of anaphoric constructions. The distinction between control and switch-reference was motivated there.

The conventional wisdom is that the controllee in all control constructions must be a "subject." In transformational theory, various explanations have been proposed for this, as consequences of the special structural position which subjects occupy combined with stipulated properties of the position and of the empty subjects. For example, the limitation of equi-type controllees to subject is attributed by Chomsky (1981) to the lack of government of the subject position, combined with the otherwise unmotivated stipulation that the empty subject PRO is a pronoun-reflexive hybrid (pronominal "anaphor") and thus must be ungoverned in order to escape the conflicting demands made by Binding Theory on pronouns and reflexives. On the other hand, Chomsky and Lasnik (1993) claim that PRO carries a special abstract Case feature (called null Case) which only Equi *to*[2] is capable of assigning. While theoretical proposals such as these may provide an analysis within the context of particular theoretical assumptions, they cannot be described as explanatory.

The interesting question in the context of the present study is whether being a controllee is a property of the ĜF or a property of the PIV. Such a question cannot, of course, be answered with reference to uniform-subject languages, since it is impossible to distinguish between ĜF and PIV. Examination of mixed-subject languages reveals a puzzling situation: in some the controllee in a (core) control construction is the ĜF (e.g. Inuit, which we showed in Chapter 1 is a syntactically ergative language [Manning 1996] [2]), while in others it is the PIV (e.g. Balinese, which we showed in Chapter 1 is a Philippine-type language [Arka 1998] [3]).

---

1 We consider sentences like the following to be examples of the Raising construction, and not "Exceptional Case Marking":

   (i)   Babies believe dirt [to be edible].

2 But crucially not the superficially identical *to* which heads Raising clauses, as discussed briefly in Chapter 1.

(2) a. Miiqqat [qiti- ssa- llu- tik] niriusui- pp- u- t.
 children dance- FUT- INF- REFL.PL] promise- IND- INTR- 3PL
 'The children promised to dance.'

 b. Miiqqat [Juuna ikiu- ssa- llu- gu] niriusui- pp- u- t.
 children Juuna help- FUT- INF- 3SG promise- IND- INTR- 3PL
 'The children promised to help Juuna.'

(3) a. Ia edot [meriksa dokter].
 3 want ACT.examine doctor
 'He wants to examine a doctor.'

 b. Ia edot [periksa dokter].
 3 want DO.examine doctor
 'He wants a doctor to examine [him].' / 'He wants to be examined by a doctor.'

 c. *Tiang edot [dokter periksa].
 1 want doctor DO.examine
 'I want to examine a doctor.'

This difference is all the more surprising since it is the only subject property which appears not to be consistent cross-linguistically. All other properties are consistently typical of $\widehat{GF}$ or consistently typical of PIV.

In this chapter, we will show that a proper understanding of the control construction, combined with the theory developed in this study, provides an explanation for the properties of control constructions, including the apparently contradictory behavior of mixed-subject languages. The required ingredients are an interaction between semantics and syntax, and the LFG distinction between anaphoric control and functional control.

5.2 The semantic basis of control

We begin by considering the semantic basis of the control construction. Although generative linguistics has a long tradition of treating control as a purely syntactic phenomenon, it is clear that semantics plays a role (as originally noted by Jackendoff 1972). The question of the semantic basis of control has been thoroughly examined by Sag and Pollard (1991).

Sag and Pollard observe that if control were purely a lexically governed syntactic property, one would expect to find a fair degree of idiosyncrasy. Instead, we find a predictable system of control verbs. Sag and Pollard classify these verbs as follows in English:

(4) a. *Influence verbs: the order/permit class (object controller)*[3] order, persuade, bid, charge, command, direct, enjoin, instruct, advise, authorize, mandate, convince, impel, induce, influence, inspire, motivate, move, pressure, prompt, sway, stir, talk (into), compel, press, propel, push, spur, encourage, exhort, goad, incite, prod, urge, bring, lead, signal, ask, empower, appeal (to), dare, defy, beg, prevent (from), forbid, allow, permit, enable, cause, force

b. *Commitment verbs: the promise class (subject controller)* promise, swear, agree, contract, pledge, vow, try, intend, refuse, choose, decline, decide, demand, endeavor, attempt, threaten, undertake, propose, offer, aim

c. *Orientation verbs: the want/expect class (subject control)* want, desire, fancy, wish, ache, hanker, itch, long, need, hope, thirst, yearn, hate, aspire, expect

They note that the following generalization holds:[4]

(5) Given a non-finite VP or predicate complement C, whose semantic content C' is the soa-arg of a soa s whose relation is R, the unexpressed subject of C is linked to:
A. the influenced participant of s, if R is of influence type,
B. the committor participant of s, if R is of commitment type,
C. the experiencer participant of s, if R is of orientation type.

That is to say, the choice of controller is based on the semantics of the control verb.

Sag and Pollard are less committal about the choice of controllee, which is the focus of our interests here. They note that there must be a syntactic component to the choice of controllee, as evidenced by sentences such as the following.

(6) a. Lee persuaded Tracy to examine Kim.
b. Lee persuaded Tracy to be examined by Kim.

The fact that the controllee is the subject both in the active and the passive makes it clear that the only possible generalization is that the controllee is the subject of the subordinate clause. However, having said this, they proceed to observe that there are semantic constraints on the controllee, at least for some verbs. Specifically, in the case of influence (*order/permit*) verbs and commitment (*promise*) verbs, the complement must have an intentional Agent, and it is this intentional Agent which is the controllee. Where this does not happen, as in (6b), the reading undergoes causative coercion, as imperatives do when the $\widehat{GF}$

---

[3] Some of these (*allow, permit, cause, force*) are ambiguous; they also have a meaning where the influenced entity is not present, generally a raising verb.
[4] As is standard in the HPSG literature, *soa* here is an abbreviation for "state of affairs."

addressee is not an intentional Agent; (6b) means something like 'Lee persuaded Tracy to cause herself to be examined by Kim.'[5] Languages that do not allow causative coercion do not accept sentences like (6b), as discussed by Kroeger (1993), so the choice of controllee is determined by both syntactic and semantic factors. The situation is very similar to the addressee of imperatives, discussed in Chapter 2.

We can approach this from a slightly different perspective. Consider the lexical-conceptual representation proposed for the verb *try* by Jackendoff (1990):

(7)
$$\left[\begin{array}{l} \text{AFF}_{+\text{vol}} \; ([\;\;]^{\alpha}, \;) \\ \text{CS}^{u} \; ([\alpha], \; [_{\text{Event}} \; \text{AFF} \; ([\alpha], \;)]) \end{array} \right]_{\text{Event}}$$

The top line of this representation expresses the existence of a volitional Actor: specifically, it states that there is situation of volitional affecting ($\text{AFF}_{+\text{vol}}$), in which the affecting entity (Actor) is an argument (designated α). The bottom line says that this α instigates (or causes: CS) a further (embedded) event, with uncertain success (the u superscript on CS). In this embedded event the same argument α is the Actor. To paraphrase, this representation says that 'a volitional actor does something, and exerts an effort towards the goal of self doing something.' The important part of this is the embedded event (i.e. the "self doing something" part, or $[_{\text{Event}} \; \text{AFF} \; ([\alpha],)]$ in Jackendoff's formal notation). This embedded event is not expressed in *try*'s clause; rather, it is expressed by the complement clause. The lexical conceptual representation specifies semantic identity between the Actor/Agent of *try* and the Actor of the subordinate clause. This relation, the semantic side of control, is inherent in the meaning of the verb *try*. As a result of its meaning, the verb *try* must appear in a syntactic context which allows semantic identity between these two elements.

Despite the differences in approach between Sag and Pollard and Jackendoff, the conclusion is the same. Control is, at its source, a consequence of the semantics of control verbs, not just a syntactic construction. By virtue of its meaning, such a verb must appear in a syntactic structure which allows coreference between the appropriate argument of the control verb and an intentional Agent in the subordinate clause.

---

5 Sag and Pollard deny that this semantic restriction holds for orientation verbs, and they demonstrate the lack of causative coercion with such verbs. On the other hand, Dixon (1994) includes verbs like 'want' and 'hope' among those verbs which have a semantically based same-subject constraint universally, so he apparently considers orientation verbs to be the same as the other classes.

5.3 Syntactic types of control

While control is based in semantics, it must be executed in the syntax. For this reason, control has both a semantic/conceptual aspect, which we discussed in the previous section, and a formal syntactic aspect. This corresponds to the distinction we made in Chapter 3 between notional constructions and formal constructions. The semantic side constitutes a notional construction, but what interests us is the nature of the formal construction(s). It is the imperfect match between notional constructions and formal constructions that results in the apparent typological complexity of the control construction.

In fact, the formal tools available for expressing the identity of argument between main verb and subordinate verb are two of the three tools available for argument sharing across coordination discussed in Chapter 3. To review, we saw that if one wants to express a shared argument of coordinate clauses only once, there are three ways to achieve this syntactically: coordination of a subclausal constituent, such as VP, with the concomitant distribution of any higher clausal element; the use of a null (or incorporated) pronoun; or multifunctionality involving multiple clauses. In control, subclausal coordination is not available, since it is a subordination construction and therefore does not involve coordination. However, null anaphora and multifunctionality are both possible.

The use of null anaphora is illustrated by (8): the element in the subordinate clause is an unexpressed pronoun which is coindexed with the element of the main clause. This is analogous to the standard transformational analysis of control in terms of the null pronominal element PRO.[6] Like any null pronoun, an unexpressed pronoun with control properties is licensed lexically by the verb of which it is an argument.

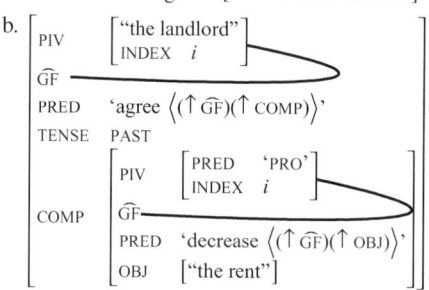

(8)   a. The landlord agreed [to decrease the rent].

b.
$$\begin{bmatrix} \text{PIV} & \begin{bmatrix} \text{``the landlord''} \\ \text{INDEX} \quad i \end{bmatrix} \\ \widehat{\text{GF}} & \\ \text{PRED} & \text{`agree} \langle (\uparrow \widehat{\text{GF}})(\uparrow \text{COMP}) \rangle \text{'} \\ \text{TENSE} & \text{PAST} \\ \text{COMP} & \begin{bmatrix} \text{PIV} & \begin{bmatrix} \text{PRED} & \text{`PRO'} \\ \text{INDEX} & i \end{bmatrix} \\ \widehat{\text{GF}} & \\ \text{PRED} & \text{`decrease} \langle (\uparrow \widehat{\text{GF}})(\uparrow \text{OBJ}) \rangle \text{'} \\ \text{OBJ} & [\text{``the rent''}] \end{bmatrix} \end{bmatrix}$$

---

[6] As already noted, we reject the idea that PRO is also a kind of reflexive anaphor. As discussed in Chapter 2, it is simply an unexpressed pronoun; there is no formal distinction between PRO and *pro*.

The other possibility is cross-clausal multifunctionality. In such a case, the complement can be thought of as a kind of predicate which is predicated of the relevant element of the main clause, rather than a true propositional complement. This predicative (or open) complement has a grammatical function which is called XCOMP in the LFG literature, and the governing verb (*try* in this case) specifies that one of its arguments (the ĜF here) has an additional function in the XCOMP.

(9) a. The landlord tried to increase the rent.
b. $\begin{bmatrix} \text{PIV} & [\text{``the landlord''}] \\ \widehat{\text{GF}} & \\ \text{PRED} & \text{`try} \langle (\uparrow \widehat{\text{GF}})(\uparrow \text{XCOMP}) \rangle \text{'} \\ \text{TENSE} & \text{PAST} \\ \text{XCOMP} & \begin{bmatrix} \text{PIV} \\ \widehat{\text{GF}} \\ \text{PRED} & \text{`increase} \langle (\uparrow \widehat{\text{GF}})(\uparrow \text{OBJ}) \rangle \text{'} \\ \text{OBJ} & [\text{``the rent''}] \end{bmatrix} \end{bmatrix}$

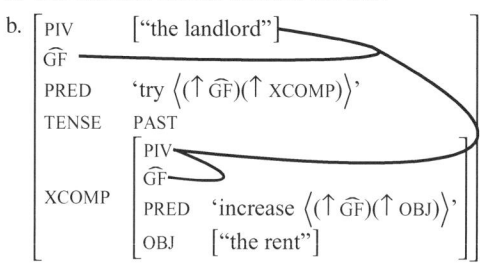

It should be noted that the availability of both of these options for control constructions is a consequence of the general LFG theory of syntax. Excluding one of them would require additional machinery in the theory. Thus, the use that we will be making of the existence of the two constructions is additional confirmation of an existing theory, not an ad hoc extension that we have made.

Work on control in LFG has recognized the existence of both of these options since the seminal study of Bresnan (1982). The anaphoric construction (8) is usually called **anaphoric control**, and the one involving multifunctionality (9) is called **functional control**. In a parallel-architecture theory, it is to be expected, as we have already noted, that a single notional construction type may correspond to more than one formal construction. Such a theory receives independent confirmation if it turns out that the availability of more than one formal construction results in an explanation of differing patterns of properties. We have already seen this with coordination chaining (Chapter 3) and long-distance dependencies (Chapter 4). In the case of control, too, the existence of more than one formal construction receives empirical support. We will see in the next section how it accounts for the initially puzzling behavior of control constructions in mixed-subject languages. For now, we note, following Falk (2001), that the effects are present even in English. Under the semantic analysis of Sag and Pollard (1991), as noted above, *agree* and *try* both belong to the class of commitment verbs. As a result, both require control by the committor argument; the subject of the active forms of these verbs. The semantics predicts that these verbs will have the same control properties. However, it turns out that they have different properties at the level of syntax. For example, if we passivize the verbs, the committor argument (the controller) is no longer expressed as an argument: it is either omitted or expressed as a *by*-phrase adjunct. In anaphoric control, this should not matter: the antecedent of a pronominal element need not be linguistically present and, if it is linguistically present, the grammatical function it bears is irrelevant. However, in functional control the controllee is identified with a linguistically expressed controller whose properties the governing verb can specify (i.e. a core argument function); if the controller is not present syntactically, the construction should be ungrammatical.[7] The verbs *agree* and *try* differ in exactly this way. (Bresnan 1982 refers to the inability of a passive agent to be a functional controller as Visser's Generalization.)

(10) a. It was agreed (by the landlord) to decrease the rent.
      b. *It was tried (by the landlord) to increase the rent.

As we noted in Chapter 3, null anaphora constructions can be expected to allow greater flexibility in the identity of the antecedent: anaphoric control in English allows split controllers, while functional control, naturally, does not.

(11) a. Yoni said that Michal agreed to go to the movies together.
         (subject of *go* is Yoni+Michal)
      b. *Yoni said that Michal tried to go to the movies together.

Such facts confirm the existence of both anaphoric and functional control in a single language, independently of issues of subjecthood.

5.4 Subjecthood and control

5.4.1 General

We turn now to the question of subjecthood in control constructions. It is conventionally believed that the controllee must be a subject, but in the context of the theory proposed here the question is whether it is the $\widehat{\text{GF}}$ or the PIV. As we have seen, the evidence from mixed-subject languages on this is ambiguous. We will argue here that the controllee in anaphoric control constructions is $\widehat{\text{GF}}$, but it is PIV in functional control constructions.

---

7 In the passive, the committor argument can be expressed as a *by* phrase, which we take to be an adjunct, but has also been analyzed as an oblique argument. Due to the nature of the licensing of functional control, neither an adjunct nor an oblique can be a controller; only core functions can (Bresnan 1982). As a result, the control facts are the same with or without a *by* phrase.

In (2) and (3) above we have seen examples of control in two mixed-subject languages: Inuit and Balinese. Closer inspection shows that these two languages have different control constructions. It is observed by Manning (1996: 124 fn. 41) that control in Inuit need not involve strict identity between controller and controllee, but instead can involve overlapping reference. As we have discussed, departures from strict identity are the hallmarks of anaphoric constructions, and impossible in multifunctionality constructions. In addition, it appears that passive agents (even when unexpressed) can control. While Manning's example involves an adjunct, his surrounding discussion suggests that this is true for all cases of control.

(12) Uumasuq [pikin-   naviir-   lu-   gu] qilirsur- niqar-
      animal   kick.about- prevent- INF- 3SG tie.up-   PASS-
      p-   u-   q.
      IND- INTR- 3SG
      'The animal$_j$ was tied up (by somebody$_i$) (PRO$_i$) preventing (it$_j$) from kicking about.'

Functional control by an unexpressed element is impossible. Control in Inuit must therefore be anaphoric control, the formal construction in which the controllee is an unexpressed anaphoric element which is coreferential with the controller. In Balinese, on the other hand, in accordance with Visser's Generalization, passive agents cannot be controllers (Arka & Simpson 1998, Arka personal communication).

(13) a. Ci nyanjiang   ia [meli   montor].
         you ACT.promise he ACT.buy   motor.bike
         'You promised him to buy a motor bike.'
      b. Ia janjiang   ci   [meli   montor]
         he DO.promise you ACT.buy   motor.bike
         'You promised him to buy a motor bike.'
      c. *Ia janjiang- a   teken ci   [meli   montor].
          he promise-   PASS   by   you ACT.buy   motor.bike
         'He was promised by you to buy a motor bike.'

In addition, any unexpressed subject must be identical with an element in the governing clause (Arka 1998). Balinese control thus has the properties of the multifunctionality construction – functional control.[8] Despite superficial

---

8 Our analysis differs from that of Arka (1998). He claims that Balinese has both functional and anaphoric control, the difference being marked (in part) by the conjunction/complementizer

appearances, then, Inuit control and Balinese control are distinct formal constructions: anaphoric control in the case of Inuit, and functional control in the case of Balinese.

We have already discussed the essentials of anaphoric control, the control construction used in Inuit, in Chapter 2. Anaphoric control involves a null pronoun, just like pro-drop. As we saw in Chapter 2, a null pronoun is licensed by the verb of which it is an argument, with a lexical specification of the following type:

(14)   ($\uparrow$ GF) = "pronominal properties," where GF is chosen from a language-specific set Γ of argument functions.

One set of "pronominal properties" that can be specified in such a constraint is whatever properties characterize the pronominal controllee (such as capacity for arbitrary reference and dispreference for discourse antecedence). The choice of grammatical functions that can be members of the set Γ is governed by the relational hierarchy. As a consequence, the most likely anaphoric controllee will be $\widehat{\text{GF}}$. With control, unlike ordinary pro-drop, there is little possibility that a language will allow Γ to go any farther down the relational hierarchy. This is because of the semantic constraints on control. As we have seen, at least two of Sag and Pollard's three classes of control verbs require the controllee to be an intentional Agent. Since the normal mapping of Agent is to $\widehat{\text{GF}}$, it makes functional sense for languages to stop at $\widehat{\text{GF}}$ in specifying anaphoric controllees. In this sense, anaphoric control is similar to the imperative construction, where similar considerations apply with respect to the addressee. We thus predict that anaphoric controllees are most likely to be limited to $\widehat{\text{GF}}$, and in any case will include $\widehat{\text{GF}}$. As we have seen, the Inuit controllee conforms to this prediction: it must be $\widehat{\text{GF}}$. To account for the Inuit example (2b) above, repeated below as (15a), the grammar of Inuit will include the lexical entry (15b); the f-structure of the sentence is (15c).

> *apang*. However, the evidence he brings does not support this analysis. The basic difference between clauses with *apang* and clauses without is semantic: non-*apang* clauses involve a greater degree of control over the subordinate clause. In a sentence like 'He wants to be rich,' where there is a lesser degree of control, *apang* can appear in the subordinate clause, while in a sentence like 'He wants to eat a mango,' where there is a greater degree of control, it cannot. However, the facts of control are the same in all cases: the unexpressed element is obligatorily controlled. In sentences with an overt subject, *apang* is optional in both kinds of clauses. While these overt-subject sentences display differences in the anaphoric possibilities depending on the presence of *apang* and the semantic nature of the control over the event, non-control sentences do not bear on the nature of control.

(15) a. Miiqqat [Juuna ikiu- ssa- llu- gu] niriusui- pp- u- t.
children Juuna help- FUT- INF- 3SG promise- IND- INTR- 3PL
'The children promised to help Juuna.'

b. *ikiussallugu* ($\uparrow$ PRED) = 'help $\langle(\uparrow \widehat{GF})(\uparrow OBJ)\rangle$'
   ($\uparrow \widehat{GF}$) = "control pronominal properties"
   ($\uparrow$ PIV) = ($\uparrow$ OBJ)
   . . .

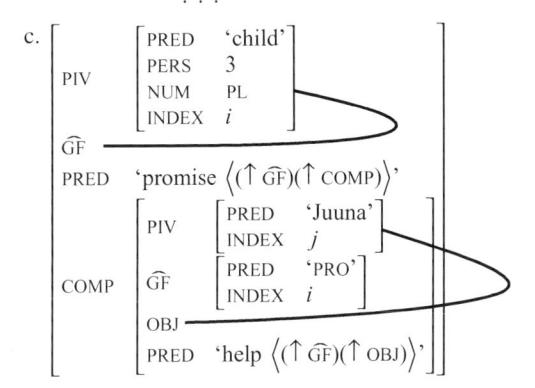

c. $\begin{bmatrix} \text{PIV} & \begin{bmatrix} \text{PRED} & \text{'child'} \\ \text{PERS} & 3 \\ \text{NUM} & \text{PL} \\ \text{INDEX} & i \end{bmatrix} \\ \widehat{\text{GF}} & \\ \text{PRED} & \text{'promise} \langle(\uparrow \widehat{GF})(\uparrow \text{COMP})\rangle\text{'} \\ \text{COMP} & \begin{bmatrix} \text{PIV} & \begin{bmatrix} \text{PRED} & \text{'Juuna'} \\ \text{INDEX} & j \end{bmatrix} \\ \widehat{\text{GF}} & \begin{bmatrix} \text{PRED} & \text{'PRO'} \\ \text{INDEX} & i \end{bmatrix} \\ \text{OBJ} & \\ \text{PRED} & \text{'help} \langle(\uparrow \widehat{GF})(\uparrow OBJ)\rangle\text{'} \end{bmatrix} \end{bmatrix}$

The prediction of our theory, that anaphoric control involves a $\widehat{GF}$ controllee, is thus confirmed by Inuit: the control is anaphoric control, and the controllee is $\widehat{GF}$.

On the other hand, functional control, the control construction used in Balinese, is a lexical property of the governing verb, which specifies that one of its arguments bears an additional function as an element in the XCOMP (Bresnan 1982). Schematically:

(16)   ($\uparrow$ Controller) = ($\uparrow$ XCOMP Controllee)

The specification of the controllee here differs from anaphoric control. It is specified by the higher verb, and thus involves reference to an element of a lower clause. By the Pivot Condition, such specification can only target the PIV. The controllee in functional control must therefore be the PIV of its clause.

(17)   ($\uparrow$ Controller) = ($\uparrow$ XCOMP PIV)

This prediction is confirmed by Balinese, as we have seen with the example (3b), repeated here as (18a). The Balinese lexicon will include the entry in (18b), and the f-structure of the sentence is (18c).

(18) a. Ia edot [periksa dokter].
3 want DO.examine doctor
'He wants a doctor to examine [him].'/ 'He wants to be examined by a doctor.'

b. *edot* (↑ PRED) = 'want ⟨(↑ ĜF) (↑ XCOMP)⟩'
(↑ PIV) = (↑ ĜF)
(↑OBJ) = (↑ XCOMP PIV)

c.
$$\begin{bmatrix} \text{PIV} & [\text{``mother''}] \\ \text{ĜF} & [\text{``father''}] \\ \text{OBJ} & \\ \text{PRED} & \text{`tell } \langle(\uparrow \text{ĜF})(\uparrow \text{OBJ})(\uparrow \text{XCOMP})\rangle\text{'} \\ \text{TENSE} & \text{NONFUT} \\ \text{XCOMP} & \begin{bmatrix} \text{PIV} \\ \text{ĜF} & [\text{``doctor''}] \\ \text{OBJ} \\ \text{PRED} & \text{`examine } \langle(\uparrow \text{ĜF})(\uparrow \text{OBJ})\rangle\text{'} \end{bmatrix} \end{bmatrix}$$

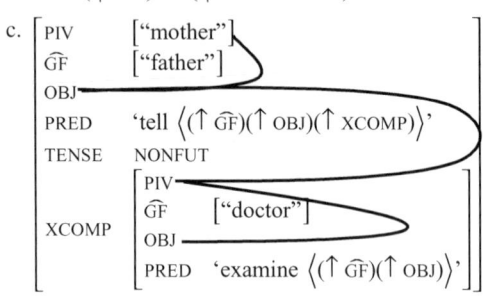

In uniform-subject languages, anaphoric and functional control cannot be distinguished by the identity of the controllee: since the same element functions as both ĜF and PIV, the controllee is the A argument in either case. However, in mixed-subject languages, the difference is clear.

In syntactically ergative languages that do not allow causative coercion, the use of functional control poses a potential problem. In intransitive clauses control will work as expected, at least those intransitives with agentive ĜFs. With a transitive clause, however, it will be impossible to create a control construction in which both syntactic and semantic constraints can be met. The syntax will designate the PIV (OBJ) as the controllee, but since the OBJ is not agentive it is not semantically compatible with the status of controllee. This can be overcome in a language which allows causative coercion, but a language that does not allow it will have no way to produce a grammatical control construction with a transitive subordinate clause. As a result, one might expect such languages to allow control into intransitive clauses only. As we saw in Chapter 3, this is what Van Valin and LaPolla (1997) claim is the pattern in the Mayan language Jakaltek. This apparently bizarre restriction of control to intransitive clauses is less bizarre under the current theory: it is simply a consequence of an irresolvable clash between the semantic and syntactic requirements in transitive complements.

The LFG distinction between anaphoric and functional control thus allows us to explain the apparent breakdown in the otherwise predictable division of labor between ĜF and PIV in mixed-subject languages. It turns out that the distinction between two types of control, rather than being an embarrassment for the theory, receives confirmation from these languages, which were not considered when the theory was initially designed.

5.4.2 Case study: Tagalog

One interesting mixed-subject language whose control constructions have been discussed in the literature is Tagalog. Tagalog is a Philippine-type language, in which the choice of PIV is marked morphologically on the verb. Although Schachter's (1976) original description stated that the ĜF is always the controllee, subsequent work has made it clear that control of both ĜF and PIV exist in the language. The discussion here is based heavily on the very insightful analysis of various aspects of Tagalog syntax by Kroeger (1993). Kroeger's analysis is far-reaching and covers some of the same questions we are addressing. It is expressed within the same formal framework as the present study (LFG), making comparisons easier. While we will disagree with some of Kroeger's conclusions (Kroeger assumes a version of the inverse-mapping approach), we are heavily indebted to Kroeger. To increase readability of the Tagalog examples, subordinate clauses are bracketed; the main clause PIV is in **boldface**; the subordinate clause PIV is in *italics*; and the subordinate clause ĜF is underlined. If any of these items is unexpressed, it is represented as "∅."

In the usual control construction, the one described by Schachter, the controllee is the ĜF regardless of whether it is also the PIV. PIV-hood also has nothing to do with determining the controller.

(19) (from Kroeger [2.35])
  a. Um-   iwas **ako**   [-ng   tumingin   kay   Lorna <u>∅</u>].
     PERF.ACT- avoid me.NOM COMP ACT.look.at DAT Lorna

  b. Um-   iwas **ako**   [-ng   tingn-   an   *∅*   *si*   *<u>Lorna</u>*].
     PERF.ACT- avoid me.NOM COMP look.at- IO   NOM Lorna

  c. In-   iwas- an ko   [**-ng   tumingin   kay   Lorna** <u>∅</u>].
     PERF- avoid- IO me.ERG COMP ACT.look.at DAT Lorna

  d. In-   iwas- an ko   [**-ng   tingn-   an** *∅* *si*   *<u>Lorna</u>*].
     PERF- avoid- IO me.ERG COMP look.at- IO   NOM Lorna
     'I avoided looking at Lorna.'

Kroeger identifies this construction as anaphoric control. This is in accord with the theory of control proposed here, under which we expect the controllee in an anaphoric control construction to be ĜF, regardless of PIV choice. Taking (19b) as an example, the verb in the subordinate clause has the lexical entry (20a) and the full f-structure is (20b).

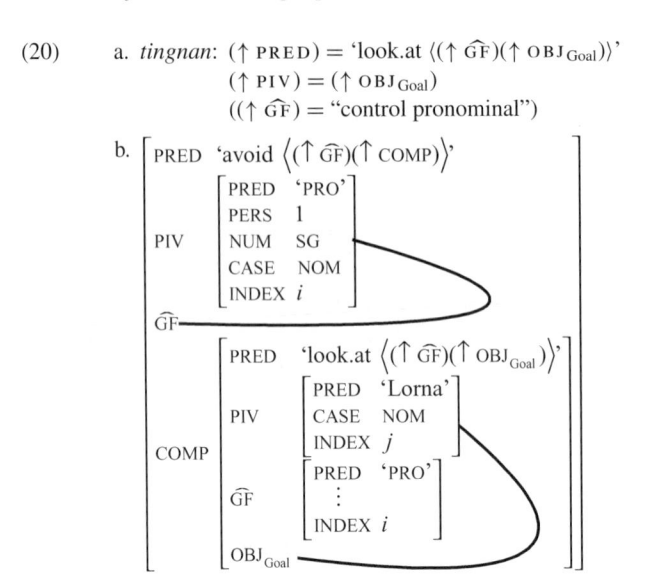

(20) a. *tingnan*: $(\uparrow \text{PRED}) = \text{'look.at} \langle (\uparrow \widehat{\text{GF}})(\uparrow \text{OBJ}_{\text{Goal}}) \rangle\text{'}$
$(\uparrow \text{PIV}) = (\uparrow \text{OBJ}_{\text{Goal}})$
$((\uparrow \widehat{\text{GF}}) = \text{"control pronominal"})$

b.
$$\begin{bmatrix} \text{PRED} & \text{'avoid} \langle (\uparrow \widehat{\text{GF}})(\uparrow \text{COMP}) \rangle\text{'} \\ \text{PIV} & \begin{bmatrix} \text{PRED} & \text{'PRO'} \\ \text{PERS} & 1 \\ \text{NUM} & \text{SG} \\ \text{CASE} & \text{NOM} \\ \text{INDEX} & i \end{bmatrix} \\ \widehat{\text{GF}} & \\ \text{COMP} & \begin{bmatrix} \text{PRED} & \text{'look.at} \langle (\uparrow \widehat{\text{GF}})(\uparrow \text{OBJ}_{\text{Goal}}) \rangle\text{'} \\ \text{PIV} & \begin{bmatrix} \text{PRED} & \text{'Lorna'} \\ \text{CASE} & \text{NOM} \\ \text{INDEX} & j \end{bmatrix} \\ \widehat{\text{GF}} & \begin{bmatrix} \text{PRED} & \text{'PRO'} \\ \vdots \\ \text{INDEX} & i \end{bmatrix} \\ \text{OBJ}_{\text{Goal}} & \end{bmatrix} \end{bmatrix}$$

However, Kroeger denies that the controllee is selected syntactically. He claims "that the identity of the controller is determined by the lexical semantics of the matrix verb (following Sag and Pollard, 1991), and that the identity of the controllee is primarily determined by universal semantic constraints on this class of Equi constructions" (1993: 39). Specifically, he argues that the controllee must be a volitional Agent expressed as a core argument. Since Agent always[9] maps to $\widehat{\text{GF}}$ there is no need for a syntactic constraint that requires the controllee to be $\widehat{\text{GF}}$. This differs from our analysis, which claims that there are both semantic and syntactic constraints on the controllee. One possible piece of evidence in favor of a mixed syntactic-semantic approach is that the restriction to $\widehat{\text{GF}}$ holds for Sag and Pollard's class of orientation verbs as well, verbs which they claim do not impose a semantic restriction on the controllee.

Better evidence against Kroeger's position comes from the behavior of verbs in non-volitive mood. Ordinary ("volitive") mood involves intentional action; non-volitive mood is unspecified for intentionality. Involuntary actions must be expressed with the non-volitive mood. This is illustrated in the following examples from Kroeger, in which the accidental reading of the non-volitive mood is a pragmatic inference which is unavailable for the volitive mood sentence.

---

9 Tagalog does not have a passive construction.

(21) a. Naka- inum siya ng lasun.
ACT.NONVOL.PERF- drink 3SG.NOM ACC poison
'He [accidentally] drank poison.'

b. Um- inum siya ng lasun.
ACT.PERF- drink 3SG.NOM ACC poison
'He {intentionally drank/tried to drink} poison.'

The non-volitive mood entails that the event actually took place. Notions like trying can only be expressed with the volitive mood. Crucially, control complements, since they involve intention, are normally expressed with volitive mood. However, if the governing verb does not require control, it is possible to have a non-volitive complement: the $\widehat{GF}$ is then null, and receives arbitrary interpretation.

(22) a. Nag- atubili **si Maria**[-ng ma- bigy- an
PERF.ACT- hesitate NOM Maria COMP NONVOL- give- IO
∅ ng pera si Ben].
ACC money NOM Ben
'Maria hesitated for (someone) to give the money to Ben.'

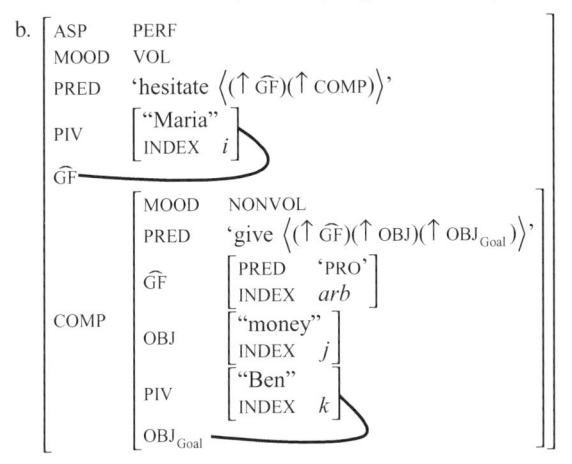

b. $\begin{bmatrix} \text{ASP} & \text{PERF} \\ \text{MOOD} & \text{VOL} \\ \text{PRED} & \text{'hesitate} \langle (\uparrow \widehat{GF})(\uparrow \text{COMP}) \rangle \text{'} \\ \text{PIV} & \begin{bmatrix} \text{"Maria"} \\ \text{INDEX} \quad i \end{bmatrix} \\ \widehat{GF} & \\ \text{COMP} & \begin{bmatrix} \text{MOOD} & \text{NONVOL} \\ \text{PRED} & \text{'give} \langle (\uparrow \widehat{GF})(\uparrow \text{OBJ})(\uparrow \text{OBJ}_{\text{Goal}}) \rangle \text{'} \\ \widehat{GF} & \begin{bmatrix} \text{PRED} & \text{'PRO'} \\ \text{INDEX} & arb \end{bmatrix} \\ \text{OBJ} & \begin{bmatrix} \text{"money"} \\ \text{INDEX} \quad j \end{bmatrix} \\ \text{PIV} & \begin{bmatrix} \text{"Ben"} \\ \text{INDEX} \quad k \end{bmatrix} \\ \text{OBJ}_{\text{Goal}} & \end{bmatrix} \end{bmatrix}$

The question is how this sentence is licensed. According to Kroeger, arbitrary interpretation (represented here as the feature [INDEX *arb*]) is a property of anaphoric control; pro-drop in Tagalog does not allow it.[10] This unexpressed $\widehat{GF}$ must therefore be licensed by the same mechanism that licenses anaphoric

---

10 See the discussion of null pronominals in Tagalog in Chapter 2 .

control, not the constraint that licenses pro-drop. In this case, it cannot be the semantics of the control construction, because those semantics rule out control with a non-volitive complement. It must be a syntactic specification allowing an unexpressed pronoun with control properties as $\widehat{\text{GF}}$. We hypothesize that Tagalog verbs have both of the following optional specifications:

(23)   a. (↑ GF) = "referential pronoun properties" where GF ∈ $\{\widehat{\text{GF}}, \text{OBJ}, \text{OBJ}_\theta\}$ in decreasing order of naturalness
         b. (↑ GF′) = "control pronoun properties" where GF′ ∈ $\{\widehat{\text{GF}}\}$

This analysis is only possible if anaphoric control constructions are licensed syntactically (as well as semantically).

Tagalog also has a second type of control. As Kroeger (1993: 71) puts it,

> certain Equi predicates allow the controllee to be either the Actor [= $\widehat{\text{GF}}$] or the subject [= PIV] of the complement clause. But we shall see that the syntactic constraints vary depending on which of these two options is selected. Tagalog thus provides evidence for two different kinds of control relations, one involving a semantic identification of controller with controllee, the other involving a syntactic unification. This contrast is quite parallel to the distinction drawn by Bresnan (1982) between anaphoric and functional control.

In this construction, controller and controllee are both PIV. The following examples show the same verb used in both constructions.

(24)   a. Nagpilit   si   Maria[-ng   bigy- an ng   pera
           PERF.ACT.insist.on NOM Maria COMP give- IO ACC money
           <u>ni   Ben ∅</u>].
           ERG Ben
           'Maria insisted on being given the money by Ben.'
         b. Nagpilit   si   Maria[-ng   bigy- an <u>∅</u>
           PERF.ACT.insist.on NOM Maria COMP give- IO
           ng   pera   si   **Ben**].
           ACC money NOM Ben
           'Maria insisted on giving money to Ben.'

In the above quotation, Kroeger identifies the normal control construction with the $\widehat{\text{GF}}$ controllee as anaphoric control, and the lexically governed one with PIV controller and controllee as functional control. This is in accordance with our predictions. In anaphoric control, the controllee is based (at least on the syntactic side) on the relational hierarchy. In functional control (which is a lexical property of the governing predicate) the controllee must be PIV. The f-structures of the sentences in (24) are:

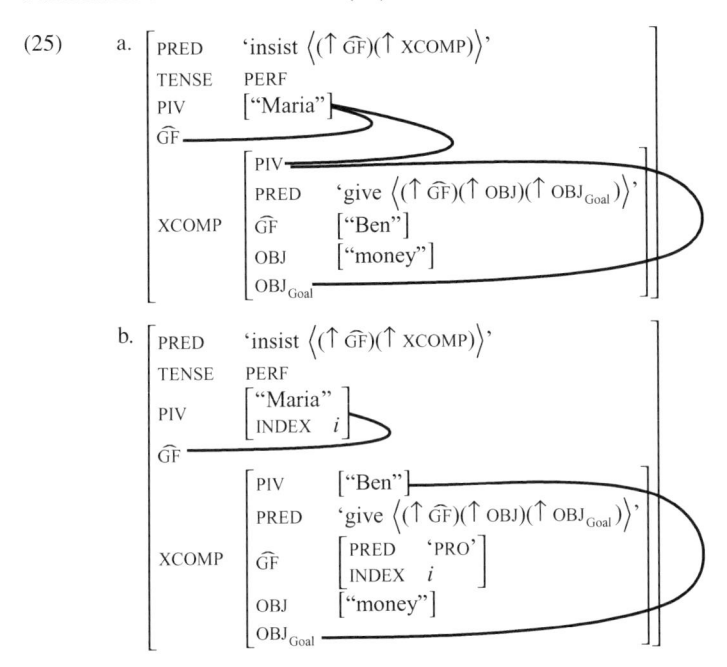

(25) a.
$$\begin{bmatrix} \text{PRED} & \text{'insist} \langle (\uparrow \widehat{\text{GF}})(\uparrow \text{XCOMP}) \rangle \text{'} \\ \text{TENSE} & \text{PERF} \\ \text{PIV} & [\text{"Maria"}] \\ \widehat{\text{GF}} & \\ \text{XCOMP} & \begin{bmatrix} \text{PIV} \\ \text{PRED} & \text{'give} \langle (\uparrow \widehat{\text{GF}})(\uparrow \text{OBJ})(\uparrow \text{OBJ}_{\text{Goal}}) \rangle \text{'} \\ \widehat{\text{GF}} & [\text{"Ben"}] \\ \text{OBJ} & [\text{"money"}] \\ \text{OBJ}_{\text{Goal}} & \end{bmatrix} \end{bmatrix}$$

b.
$$\begin{bmatrix} \text{PRED} & \text{'insist} \langle (\uparrow \widehat{\text{GF}})(\uparrow \text{XCOMP}) \rangle \text{'} \\ \text{TENSE} & \text{PERF} \\ \text{PIV} & \begin{bmatrix} \text{"Maria"} \\ \text{INDEX} & i \end{bmatrix} \\ \widehat{\text{GF}} & \\ \text{XCOMP} & \begin{bmatrix} \text{PIV} & [\text{"Ben"}] \\ \text{PRED} & \text{'give} \langle (\uparrow \widehat{\text{GF}})(\uparrow \text{OBJ})(\uparrow \text{OBJ}_{\text{Goal}}) \rangle \text{'} \\ \widehat{\text{GF}} & \begin{bmatrix} \text{PRED} & \text{'PRO'} \\ \text{INDEX} & i \end{bmatrix} \\ \text{OBJ} & [\text{"money"}] \\ \text{OBJ}_{\text{Goal}} & \end{bmatrix} \end{bmatrix}$$

We tentatively suggest that there is another case of functional control in Tagalog. Recall that anaphoric control complements must be in the volitive mood, since the intentionality of the Agent is required by the semantics of the governing verb. We saw that verbs that do not require control can also take non-volitive complements. Interestingly, non-volitive complements are also possible for verbs whose semantics require control. Due to the non-volitive mood, the $\widehat{\text{GF}}$ of the subordinate clause cannot be the controllee. In fact, there must be an overt $\widehat{\text{GF}}$. But some argument other than the $\widehat{\text{GF}}$ will be controlled (with a coerced intentional-agent reading). The anaphoric control of a non-$\widehat{\text{GF}}$ argument is not licensed by the syntax of Tagalog. This suggests that the formal construction involved in these cases is functional control: a non-$\widehat{\text{GF}}$ can be functionally controlled, though, as long as it is also the PIV. As the examples below (from Kroeger) show, the controlled non-$\widehat{\text{GF}}$ argument has to also function as the PIV.[11]

[11] This is also possible, optionally, for verbs that do not require control.

(26) a. *In-   utus- an ko   si   Maria[-ng
        PERF- order- IO me.ERG NOM Maria   COMP
        ma-   halik- an ∅ si   Pedro].
        NONVOL- kiss- IO   NOM Pedro
        'I ordered Maria to kiss Pedro.'

    b. In-   utus- an ko   si   Maria [-ng
       PERF- order- IO me.ERG NOM Maria   COMP
       ma-   halik- an ni   Pedro ∅].
       NONVOL- kiss- IO ERG Pedro
       'I ordered Maria (to allow herself) to be kissed by Pedro.'

Kroeger does not have an explanation of the restriction of the controllee to PIV in this construction, which he seems to consider to be anaphoric control. If it is functional control, the restriction to PIV is automatically accounted for. We propose the following f-structure.

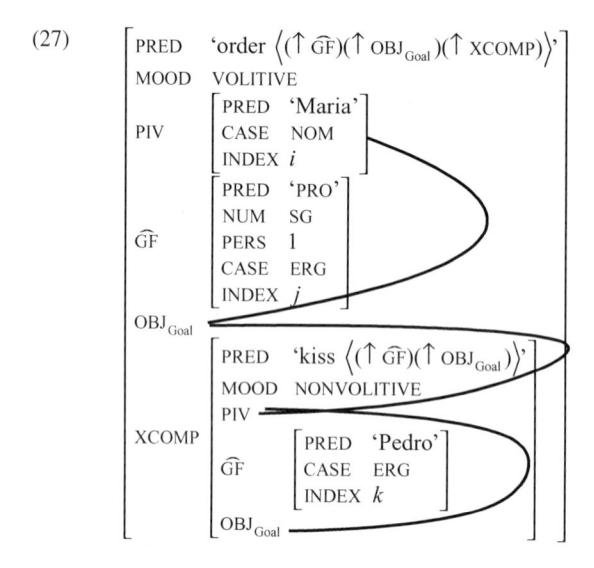

(27)
$$\begin{bmatrix} \text{PRED} & \text{'order} \langle (\uparrow \widehat{\text{GF}})(\uparrow \text{OBJ}_{\text{Goal}})(\uparrow \text{XCOMP}) \rangle \text{'} \\ \text{MOOD} & \text{VOLITIVE} \\ \text{PIV} & \begin{bmatrix} \text{PRED} & \text{'Maria'} \\ \text{CASE} & \text{NOM} \\ \text{INDEX} & i \end{bmatrix} \\ \widehat{\text{GF}} & \begin{bmatrix} \text{PRED} & \text{'PRO'} \\ \text{NUM} & \text{SG} \\ \text{PERS} & 1 \\ \text{CASE} & \text{ERG} \\ \text{INDEX} & j \end{bmatrix} \\ \text{OBJ}_{\text{Goal}} & \\ \text{XCOMP} & \begin{bmatrix} \text{PRED} & \text{'kiss} \langle (\uparrow \widehat{\text{GF}})(\uparrow \text{OBJ}_{\text{Goal}}) \rangle \text{'} \\ \text{MOOD} & \text{NONVOLITIVE} \\ \text{PIV} & \\ \widehat{\text{GF}} & \begin{bmatrix} \text{PRED} & \text{'Pedro'} \\ \text{CASE} & \text{ERG} \\ \text{INDEX} & k \end{bmatrix} \\ \text{OBJ}_{\text{Goal}} & \end{bmatrix} \end{bmatrix}$$

This differs from the previous case of functional control in that the controller here need not be the PIV, but nothing in our theory requires this.

5.4.3 A non-problem in Balinese

In this section, we will discuss a potential problem for theories of control that has been raised on the basis of facts from Balinese, and show that the theory proposed here can account for these facts without any change. The material in this section is based on Arka and Simpson (1998).

Balinese, which we discussed briefly above, is a mixed-subject language of the Philippine type; that is to say, it has morphological marking on the verb overtly indicating which argument is the PIV. Unlike Tagalog, the "voice" system consists of only two forms: agentive and objective. Agentive voice, as in Tagalog, assigns the PIV function to the $\widehat{\text{GF}}$; objective voice assigns it to (at least) the OBJ or OBJ$_\theta$ (secondary object). Thus, in an applicative verb, the objective form of the verb allows either object to be the PIV. (In Balinese sentences, the PIV precedes the verb.)

(28) a. Ia nanem- in teban- ne kasela-kutuh.
3 ACT.plant- APPL backyard- 3POSS cassava
'(S)he planted cassava in his/her backyard.'

b. Kasela-kutuh tanem- in=a teban- ne.
cassava DO.plant- APPL backyard- 3POSS
'(S)he planted cassava [i.e. nothing else] in his/her backyard.'

c. Teban- ne tanem- in=a kasela-kutuh.
backyard- 3POSS DO.plant- APPL cassava
'In his/her backyard, (s)he planted cassava.'

As we have seen, Balinese uses the functional control construction, and the controllee is the PIV of its clause. Here is a further example:

(29) a. Tiang tawang= a [ng- alih Luh Sari].
me DO.know= 3 ACT- look.for Luh Sari
'Of me she knew I was looking for Luh Sari.'

b. *Tiang tawanga= a [Luh Sari alih].
me DO.know= 3 Luh Sari DO.look.for
'Of me (s)he knew that Luh Sari was being looked for by me.'

The problem Arka and Simpson raise has to do with the controlled clause itself. Theories of control identify the controlled clause as a complement; in LFG, specifically an XCOMP. Arka and Simpson claim that sentences such as (30b) are problematic for any such theory of control.

(30) a. Tiang negarang [naar ubad ento].
me ACT.try ACT.eat medicine that

b. [Naar ubad ento] tegarang tiang.
ACT.eat medicine that DO.try me
'I tried to take the medicine.'

In (30a), the controlled clause is some sort of complement. The alleged problem is (30b). Under Arka and Simpson's analysis, the clause bears the SUBJ function. Theories of control do not recognize subject as a grammatical function for a core control clause; control of subject clauses is always optional control, often involving an arbitrary reading. Under the analysis proposed here, this problem does not exist. The controlled clause is the PIV of the main clause, but this has no bearing on controllability. The controlled clause can still be analyzed as an XCOMP; in fact, it could not bear the argument function $\widehat{\text{GF}}$, since the voice marking on the verb 'try' is objective. All we need to say is that Balinese has the (apparently unusual) property of allowing XCOMPs to be PIVs,[12] a functional assignment associated with objective voice. Unlike the analysis assumed by Arka and Simpson, being PIV does not exclude the possibility of bearing the XCOMP function. The f-structure of (30b) is the following; note that the controlled clause bears the XCOMP function.

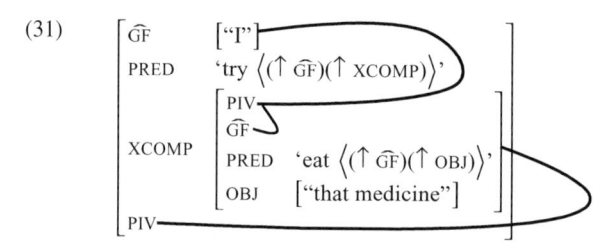

(31) $\begin{bmatrix} \widehat{\text{GF}} & [\text{"I"}] \\ \text{PRED} & \text{'try} \langle (\uparrow \widehat{\text{GF}})(\uparrow \text{XCOMP}) \rangle \text{'} \\ \text{XCOMP} & \begin{bmatrix} \text{PIV} \\ \widehat{\text{GF}} \\ \text{PRED} & \text{'eat} \langle (\uparrow \widehat{\text{GF}})(\uparrow \text{OBJ}) \rangle \text{'} \\ \text{OBJ} & [\text{"that medicine"}] \end{bmatrix} \\ \text{PIV} \end{bmatrix}$

Under the approach to control and to pivothood taken here, Balinese does not pose a theoretical challenge. This is specifically a consequence of taking pivothood to be independent of argument mapping. We take such results to be confirmation of the correctness of our view of pivothood, as well as the analysis of functional control.

5.5 Other control constructions

5.5.1 Non-complement equi

We do not have much to say about non-complement control constructions. These come in two varieties: non-(X)COMP arguments (usually subjects) and adjuncts. The former should be restricted to anaphoric control, since it involves a closed-function argument. It should therefore be limited to $\widehat{\text{GF}}$ controllees. For

---

12 There is a complication which is not relevant for the issues here, but does suggest a need to enrich the LFG theory of open functions. According to Arka (1998), not all controlled clauses can be PIV. He distinguishes between term (core) complements and non-term (non-core) complements, with only the former having the ability to be PIV. This may mean that there is more than one open complement function, perhaps a core XOBJ and a non-core XCOMP; see Falk (2005). This does not materially change the point being made here, however.

example, the following Tagalog construction, with arbitrary control, appears to be of this kind:

(32) a. Magastos [i- bili Ø ng bigas sa groseri ang pamilya].
 expensive BEN- buy   ACC rice DAT supermarket NOM family
 'It is expensive to buy rice for a family at a supermarket.'

b. $\begin{bmatrix} \text{PRED} & \text{'expensive} \langle (\uparrow \widehat{\text{GF}}) \rangle' \\ \widehat{\text{GF}} & \begin{bmatrix} \text{MOOD} & \text{VOL} \\ \text{PRED} & \text{'give} \langle (\uparrow \widehat{\text{GF}})(\uparrow \text{OBJ})(\uparrow \text{OBL}_{\text{Ben}}) \rangle' \\ \widehat{\text{GF}} & \begin{bmatrix} \text{PRED} & \text{'PRO'} \\ \text{INDEX} & arb \end{bmatrix} \\ \text{OBJ} & [\text{"rice"}] \\ \text{ADJ} & \{[\text{"at a supermarket"}]\} \\ \text{PIV} & [\text{"family"}] \\ \text{OBL}_{\text{Ben}} \end{bmatrix} \\ \text{PIV} \end{bmatrix}$

c. Mabuti- ng [bigyan Ø ng pera ang mga mahihirap].
 good- LNK give.IO ACC money NOM PL poor
 'It is good to give money to the poor.'

Functional control of non-(X)COMP arguments should be ungrammatical. We therefore predict that controllee choice in these constructions should never be pivot-dependent.

Adjuncts, on the other hand, can be either closed (ADJ) or open (XADJ) (Bresnan 1982). Closed adjuncts should have $\widehat{\text{GF}}$ controllees, while open adjuncts should have PIV controllees. We therefore make no prediction about adjuncts in general.

The main problem with coming to a typological conclusion about non-complement control phenomena is that much less has been said about them in the literature. Studies of non-complement control constructions in individual languages are needed to get a clearer picture of what the empirical facts are.

5.5.2 Raising

Raising is a control construction in which the controller is not a thematic argument of its verb. An anaphoric analysis is not possible, because that would leave the controller without a thematic role.[13] Under a functional control analysis, on the other hand, since the controller and controllee are the same entity, as

---

13 Technically, in LFG, a violation of the Coherence Condition.

long as the controllee gets a thematic role there is no meaningful element in the sentence which does not receive a thematic role. Raising must therefore be analyzed as a functional control construction (Bresnan 1982, Falk 2001). The raising verb lexically requires its non-thematic argument to be identical to the subordinate clause's PIV.

In terms of the present study, then, we would expect that the controllee in raising constructions must be PIV. So far as it can be tested (raising appears to be rare in mixed-subject languages), this is true outside of the Polynesian languages. Note the following Tagalog examples from Kroeger (1993). ([34c] is a non-Raising use of the same verb.)

(33)   a. Pinang- aakalaan **si**   **Fidel** [na   makakagawa
            IMPERF- think.IO NOM Fidel COMP ACT.NONVOL.FUT.do

            ng   mabute $\emptyset$].
            ACC good
            'Fidel is thought to be able to do something good.'

      b. Malapit   na   **si**   **Manuel** [na   hulihin   <u>ng</u>   <u>polis</u> $\emptyset$].
            STAT.close already NOM Manuel COMP catch.DO ERG police
            'Manuel is about to be arrested by the police.'

(34)   a. Inasah- an ko   **ang**   **pambansang awit** [na   awit- in
            expect- IO I.ERG NOM national anthem   COMP sing- DO

            <u>ni</u>   <u>Linda</u> $\emptyset$].
            ERG Linda
            'I expected the national anthem to be sung by Linda.'

      b. *Inasah- an ko   **si**   **Linda** [na   awit- in   <u>$\emptyset$</u>
            expect- IO I.ERG NOM Linda COMP sing- DO

            ang   *pambansang awit*].
            NOM national anthem
            'I expected Linda to sing the national anthem.'

      c. Inasah- an ko   **[na**   **awit- in**   <u>**ni**</u>   <u>**Linda**</u>
            expect- IO I.ERG COMP sing- DO ERG Linda

            ang   *pambansang awit*].
            NOM national anthem
            'I expected that Linda would sing the national anthem.'

The f-structures of (34a,b) are as follows:[14]

---

14 A couple of notes: one about analysis and one about notation. I am assuming, on the basis of the voice marking on the verb, that the controller is a secondary (indirect) object. As for notation, placing the function name outside of the angle brackets in the f-structure representation of argument structure indicates that it is a non-thematic argument.

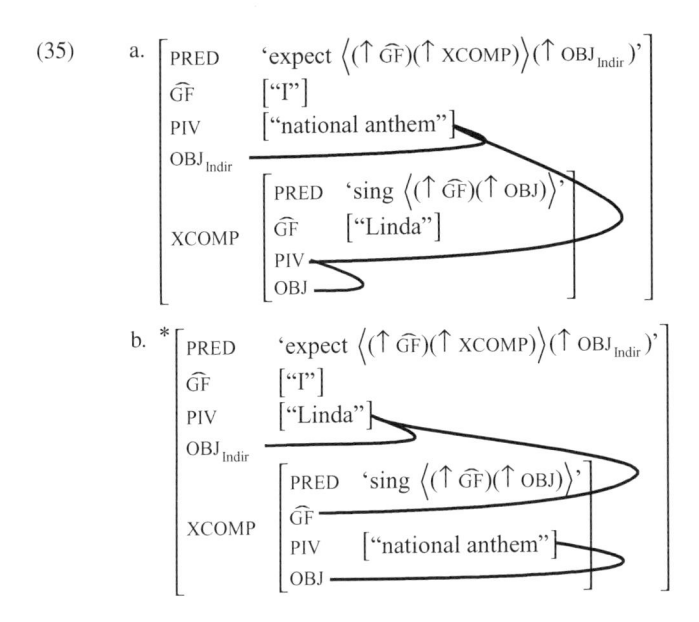

(35) a.
$$\begin{bmatrix} \text{PRED} & \text{'expect} \langle (\uparrow \widehat{\text{GF}})(\uparrow \text{XCOMP}) \rangle (\uparrow \text{OBJ}_{\text{Indir}})' \\ \widehat{\text{GF}} & [\text{``I''}] \\ \text{PIV} & [\text{``national anthem''}] \\ \text{OBJ}_{\text{Indir}} \\ \text{XCOMP} & \begin{bmatrix} \text{PRED} & \text{'sing} \langle (\uparrow \widehat{\text{GF}})(\uparrow \text{OBJ}) \rangle' \\ \widehat{\text{GF}} & [\text{``Linda''}] \\ \text{PIV} \\ \text{OBJ} \end{bmatrix} \end{bmatrix}$$

b. *
$$\begin{bmatrix} \text{PRED} & \text{'expect} \langle (\uparrow \widehat{\text{GF}})(\uparrow \text{XCOMP}) \rangle (\uparrow \text{OBJ}_{\text{Indir}})' \\ \widehat{\text{GF}} & [\text{``I''}] \\ \text{PIV} & [\text{``Linda''}] \\ \text{OBJ}_{\text{Indir}} \\ \text{XCOMP} & \begin{bmatrix} \text{PRED} & \text{'sing} \langle (\uparrow \widehat{\text{GF}})(\uparrow \text{OBJ}) \rangle' \\ \widehat{\text{GF}} \\ \text{PIV} & [\text{``national anthem''}] \\ \text{OBJ} \end{bmatrix} \end{bmatrix}$$

Note also that the controller in the raising construction in Tagalog also must have the function of PIV. It is thus exactly the same as Tagalog functional-control Equi.

However, consideration of the discussion in the previous chapter leads us to conclude that the situation may not be quite so simple. We saw there, in discussing long-distance dependency constructions, that LFG hypothesizes a loophole to the Pivot Condition, the source of our prediction that functional controllees will be PIVs. This loophole is inside-out (bottom-up) licensing of cross-clausal identity. Since in inside-out licensing the starting point is the controllee's clause, the Pivot Condition is inapplicable; a constraint associated with the same clause as the controllee could designate anything as a functional controllee. We suggested that such an option is marked, but available in principle. This leads us to expect that, while raising of PIV is the norm, there may be languages that allow raising of non-PIVs, a possibility that appears not to have been raised previously in the LFG literature. While this option appears to be relatively rare (much rarer than inside-out licensing of long-distance dependencies), inside-out functional control appears to exist in languages of the Austronesian family, primarily Polynesian languages.[15]

15 Some such analysis may also be appropriate for some of the cases of equi and raising in Daghestanian languages discussed by Kibrik (1987).

158 *Subjects and their properties*

In the Polynesian language Niuean (Seiter 1983, Chung and Seiter 1980), for example, G̑F and OBJ can both raise, although oblique arguments cannot.

(36) a. Kua   kamata [ke   hala he   tama tāne e   akau].
        PERF begin   SBJCT cut ERG child male ABS tree
        'The boy has begun to cut down the tree.' (Literally: 'It has begun that the boy cut down the tree.')

     b. Kua   kamata [e   tama tāne] [ke   hala e   akau].
        PERF begin   ABS child male   SBJCT cut ABS tree
        'The boy has begun to cut down the tree.'

     c. Kua   kamata [e   akau] [ke   hala he   tama tāne].
        PERF begin   ABS tree   SBJCT cut ERG child male
        'The tree has begun to be cut down by the boy.'

(37) a. To   kamata [ke   fakahū e   Pita e   tau tohi ki
        FUT begin   SBJCT send   ERG Peter ABS PL letter to
        a   Sione].
        PERS John
        'Peter's going to begin sending letters to John.' (Literally: 'It is going to begin that Peter sends letters to John.')

     b. *To   kamata [a   Sione] [ke   fakahū e   Pita
         FUT begin   ABS John   SBJCT send   ERG Peter
         e   tau tohi ki ai].
         ABS PL letter to PRON
         'John is going to begin being sent letters by Peter.'

While it is not clear from the literature what the PIV is in Niuean, it cannot be the case that it is simply indeterminate, and that G̑F and OBJ can both serve as PIV. Languages which allow both G̑F and OBJ to function as PIV are Philippine-type languages, and mark the identity of the PIV morphologically on the verb. We hypothesize that in Niuean the raising verb selects the open XCOMP function, but functional control is licensed by the subordinate verb, which carries the optional lexical specification:[16]

(38)   (↑GF) = ((XCOMP ↑) GF'), where GF ∈ {G̑F, OBJ}

---

16 Note that the options for controllee in Niuean are taken from the top of the relational hierarchy. This is what is expected under our analysis. Since the control equation is associated with the subordinate verb, which picks one of its arguments as controllee, the construction involves a verb specifying information about an argument – this should be subject to the relational hierarchy as discussed in Chapter 2.

Rotuman, related to the Polynesian languages but not itself Polynesian, allows raising of a wider variety of grammatical functions (Besnier 1988); the following examples show raising of G̃F, OBJ, and two cases of OBL$_{Goal}$.

(39) a. Dou pa?es [?e Jone] [lala?].
       me want OBJ Jone go
       'I want Jone to go.'

  b. Dou pa?es [?e Jone] [la   ?ɛe lakel].
       me want OBJ Jone COMP you see
       'I want Jone to be seen by you.'

  c. Dou pa?es [?e Jone] [la   ?ɛe lafɛeaŋ se].
       me want OBJ Jone COMP you speak to
       'I want Jone to be spoken to by you.'

  d. Dou pa?es [?e Jone] [la   ?ɛe lala? se].
       me want OBJ Jone COMP you go   to
       'I want Jone to go to you.'

Here again, we hypothesize that the argument sharing is licensed inside-out, and the constraint is thus associated with the clause containing the controllee.

The hypothesis that these cases of non-PIV raising involve inside-out licensing makes one expect this construction to be similar to long-distance dependency constructions, where inside-out licensing, though marked, is prevalent cross-linguistically. One interesting similarity with long-distance dependencies is the use of resumptive pronouns. For example, along with the ordinary Raising that we discussed earlier, Tagalog allows raising of a non-PIV G̃F if the controllee position has a resumptive pronoun. Kroeger (1993) calls this construction Copy-Raising.

(40) a. Gusto ko   **si** **Charlie** [na   lutu- in   niya/*∅
        want me.ERG NOM Charlie COMP cook- DO 3SG.ERG

       ang   suman].
       NOM rice.cake
       'I want Charlie to cook the suman.'

  b. Inasahan   ko   **si**   **Charlie** [na   bibigyan
       PERF.expect.IO me.ERG NOM Charlie COMP FUT.give.DO

       niya/*∅   ng   pera   *si*   *Linda*].
       3SG.ERG ACC money NOM Linda
       'I expected Charlie to give Linda some money.'

160 *Subjects and their properties*

The verbs involved here are clearly raising verbs, and their semantics shows this: the controller is not a thematic argument of its verb. (This is also true of the examples below.) These are not ordinary anaphoric constructions. The use of a resumptive pronoun in a raising construction makes sense if the construction is licensed from the controllee position. It thus provides evidence for the inside-out licensing analysis of non-PIV raising.

Another language in which resumptive pronouns are possible in raising is the Polynesian language Tuvaluan (Besnier 1988). The sentences below exemplify raising of ĜF, OBJ, OBL_Dir, and OBL_Ben, respectively:

(41) a. Koo   ttau [Niu] [o   ssala   (nee ia) tena manuia].
         INCH must Niu   COMP look.for ERG he his   luck
         'Niu must go and seek his fortune.'

      b. Koo   ttau [Niu] [o   polopolooki Nee   ana maatua (a   ia)].
         INCH must Niu   COMP scold   ERG his parents ABS he
         'Niu ought to be scolded by his parents.'

      c. Koo   ttau [iaa Niu] [o   faipati au ki ei].
         INCH must at Niu   COMP Speak me to PRON
         'I must have a word with Niu.' (Literally: 'Niu must [I speak to him].')

      d. Koo   Ttau [iaa Niu] [o   maua mai   se sulu   foou
         INCH must at Niu   COMP get   DEICT A loincloth new
         Moo ia].
         BEN he
         'Niu must be given a new loincloth.'

Resumptive pronouns are optional in Tuvaluan for the raising of ĜF and OBJ, and obligatory for OBL_Dir and OBL_Ben.

Similarly, in Samoan (a mixed-subject "syntactically ergative" language), modal verbs govern raising of the subordinate ĜF (not the PIV);[17] a resumptive pronoun is possible although dispreferred (Chung 1978). Other verbs that govern raising allow both ĜF and OBJ to be controllee (Chung 1978, Mosel and Hovdhaugen 1992). Nothing forces a language with inside-out licensing to allow resumptive pronouns, of course, just as not all languages with inside-out licensing of long-distance dependency constructions have resumptive pronouns. However, the fact that at least some of the languages with non-PIV raising allow resumptive pronouns is significant.

The possibility of inside-out licensing of functional control, inherent in the formalism of LFG, thus seems to be realized in some languages. Nevertheless,

---

17 In Tongan, the sole raising verb, *lava* 'be possible, be able, manage' is like this (Chung 1978), apparently without the resumptive pronoun option.

such languages appear to be relatively rare, much rarer than languages that use inside-out licensing for long-distance dependencies. The rareness of such languages may be due to the fact that functional control is fundamentally a lexical property of the governing verb, so there is stronger functional pressure for the governing verb to provide the licensing.

5.6 Conclusion

What we have seen in this chapter is that the properties of control constructions are the result of a complex interplay between semantics and syntax. The core instance of control, complement equi, is a construction which results from the semantics of the control verb but is licensed syntactically. The availability of two different syntactic constructions, anaphoric control and functional control, results in both the $\widehat{GF}$ and the PIV being potential controllees. (The possibility of inside-out licensing of functional control, which allows additional possibilities, seems to be taken primarily by Austronesian languages in raising constructions.) Some languages, like Tagalog, use both constructions, while others pick one: anaphoric control in the case of Inuit, functional control in the case of Balinese. For many languages that have been discussed in the literature, there is no independent evidence available for the identity of the control construction, but it is plausible to hypothesize at this stage that other languages in which the controllee is $\widehat{GF}$ – such as Chukchee (Comrie 1979) – are like Inuit in using anaphoric control exclusively, while languages in which the controllee is PIV – such as Toba Batak (Manning 1996), Indonesian (Arka & Manning 1998), Dyirbal (Dixon 1972, 1994), and Yidin^y (Dixon 1977) – are functional control languages. We are aware of no counterexamples, languages in which other evidence for the nature of the control construction clashes with our prediction as to the nature of the controller. Such languages would pose a serious challenge to the theory proposed here, but if, as seems to be the case, languages of that kind do not exist, our theory provides an explanation for the cross-linguistic distribution of controllees.

Explaining the identity of the controllee cross-linguistically is a particularly difficult challenge for theories of syntax, especially in light of the superficially puzzling behavior of mixed-subject languages. Past attempts at explaining the strong affinity of control to subjects have foundered in one way or another. Accounts in the transformational tradition posit unwarranted constituent structure and arbitrary stipulated properties, and provide no way to explain the inconsistent behavior of mixed-subject languages. Functionalist and typological accounts have typically fallen back on stipulating different pivots for different constructions, and not explaining the existence of the options which exist. Many accounts, including previous LFG analyses, simply stipulate that the subject is the controllee. The theory of subjecthood proposed here, combined with the standard LFG theory of control, allows us to explain the cross-linguistic behavior of control constructions elegantly, and with no arbitrary stipulations.

6 Universality

6.1 Non-subject languages

The question has often been raised whether the concept of subject is relevant for the grammars of all languages. As noted in Chapter 1, such a claim has been made for a class of languages which we have referred to as non-subject languages. In this chapter, we will explore the question of the universality of the subjecthood functions.

In a sense, we have already answered the question about universality of the SUBJ function in the negative. In the theory proposed here, subject is not a universal grammatical function: it is merely the intersection of the grammatical functions $\widehat{\text{GF}}$ and PIV in those languages (the uniform-subject languages) in which they always coincide. In mixed-subject languages there is no equivalent to the notion subject. However, this just pushes the question back a step; the same question can be asked about the functions $\widehat{\text{GF}}$ and PIV. Are they a necessary part of the grammar of every language? In this chapter, we explore this question.

The question of the applicability of the theory we have developed here to non-subject languages has important implications for linguistic theory, and the concept of Universal Grammar. It is part of a broader question: the universality of grammatical functions in general. The conception of grammar that we have adopted here assigns grammatical functions an important role in determining the properties of syntactic constructions. If it were to turn out that there are languages in which grammatical functions can be argued not to exist, it would pose a major challenge for such a theory. An illuminating analog comes from constituent-structure-centric theories: if it can be argued (as it has been by many researchers in LFG; see Nordlinger 1998 for a recent survey) that not all languages have a constituent structure in which the subject asymmetrically c-commands the object, the potential universality of theories that require such a structural asymmetry to account for the differing properties of subjects and objects is seriously compromised. Similarly, if we argue that the properties of subjects are a result of the grammatical functions that they bear, the discovery of languages in which grammatical functions do not play a role is potentially very damaging.

On the other hand, we must be careful in evaluating claims that particular languages may lack grammatical functions (just as we must be careful in evaluating claims about lack of particular types of constituents in a particular language). Certainly, nothing in the theory presented here prevents semantic or pragmatic factors from entering into determining the properties of a particular construction; in fact, a parallel-architecture theory like LFG leads one to expect multiple dimensions of language to interact. We have already seen interactions of this kind in anaphoric binding (Chapter 2), the *that*-trace effect (Chapter 4), and control constructions (Chapter 5). The parallel-architecture approach to language, while clearly superior, makes the job of the typologist much more difficult.

We also must be careful not to draw conclusions which go beyond the evidence available. Consider two examples from phonological distinctive features. Not all features play a role in every language; for example, the feature [±distributed] (or whatever feature one's phonology uses to distinguish dentals from alveolars) is not necessary in describing the phonology of English, as there are no pairs of phonemes which are distinguished by this feature, so it does not define a natural class of English sounds. However, demonstrating that [±distributed] plays no role in the phonology of English does not result in any questioning of the role of distinctive features per se; it simply means that different languages deploy the features differently. The other example from phonology concerns a feature that may exist in a language but the class it defines happens not to play a direct role in the phonology of the language. Thus, if a language has labial phonemes it makes active use of the feature [labial] in defining its sounds, but there may be no phonological rule that refers to this feature. We are not then free to try to analyze the phonology of the language in such a way as to eliminate the feature [labial]. We must therefore be careful both to ensure that if we discover that a particular language lacks a particular grammatical function we do not conclude that the language has no grammatical functions, and to keep the purpose of the grammatical functions in mind, and not to conclude that if a particular class of rules does not refer to a particular grammatical function that the grammatical function does not exist. The view of Universal Grammar that we take here is what Jackendoff (2002) calls the "toolbox" view.

Returning to syntax, we can draw a parallel to the earlier observation of constituent structure. If we conclude, following the literature cited, that there exist languages in which subjects and objects exist but are not distinguished by occupying distinct positions in constituent structure, we are not automatically free to conclude that constituent structure has no role to play in the grammar of the language. In fact, research in LFG has (correctly, we believe) consistently assumed that constituent structure exists in all languages, and what differs is the nature of the mapping between constituent structure positions and grammatical functions.

Part of the problem with claims about the irrelevance of grammatical functions for a particular language is that they often derive from a prejudice against syntax. Consider Van Valin and LaPolla (1997), for example. Section 6.2.1 of their book is entitled "Do all languages have grammatical relations?" The first sentence of the section reads, "The question here is quite straightforward: is it the case that in every language, one or more grammatical relations can be identified which cannot be reduced to any other type of relation, in particular to semantic or pragmatic relations?" The clear implication is that if one can do without reference to syntax-internal relations, one should. This is no better than the opposite extreme of syntactic imperialism in which many formalist syntacticians indulge. Since, under our conception of grammar, the different dimensions of language are in relations of correspondence with each other, we can expect syntactic, semantic, and pragmatic relations roughly to coincide. Our guiding assumption here is that all of these aspects of language exist, and that none has primacy over another. The question is how to disentangle the roles of the various dimensions.

One final problem with most attempts to determine whether grammatical functions are universal is a faulty conception (or no conception) of the nature of grammatical functions. In Chapter 1, we outlined several approaches to the nature of notions like subjecthood, and argued for an approach that takes the function part of grammatical function seriously. We have subsequently specified the nature of the functionality of subjects, identifying and distinguishing the functions $\widehat{GF}$ and PIV, and shown how properties of various constructions follow from the nature of these types of functionality. Our exploration of the question of universality will be based on the understanding reached in earlier parts of this study of the nature of the grammatical functions $\widehat{GF}$ and PIV.

We will conclude in this chapter that the $\widehat{GF}$ function appears to be used in all languages, while there may be languages that do not make use of the PIV function. In the course of reaching these conclusions, we will also show that some languages which have been claimed to be pivotless do, in fact, have pivots. We will discuss the typological distinction between subject-oriented and topic-oriented languages, and its relationship to pivothood. We will also provide some conjectural comments on morphologically ergative languages.

166 *Subjects and their properties*

6.2 The realization of arguments

We begin with exploring the universality of the $\widehat{\text{GF}}$ function. What does it mean to ask if $\widehat{\text{GF}}$ is universal? $\widehat{\text{GF}}$ is an argument function: the grammatical expression of an argument – specifically, the most prominent argument. Taken literally, claiming that $\widehat{\text{GF}}$ is not universal would mean that there are languages that have no grammatical way of expressing the most prominent argument. Naturally, this is not what is meant.

Instead, the claim that has been made is that in certain languages arguments express thematic roles directly, with no need for an intermediate level of syntax (grammatical functions). These kinds of claims are made primarily for what are often called "active languages," where the expression of the sole argument of an intransitive verb is based on whether or not it is agentive. We presented examples of active languages in Chapter 1; we repeat them here.

(1) **Manipuri**
    a. əy-   nə   celli
       I-   ERG ran
       'I ran.'

    b. əy sawwi
       I   got.angry
       'I got angry.'

    c. Nuŋsit- nə   ce   cèlli.
       wind-   ERG paper carried
       'The wind carried away the paper.'

(2) **Lakhota**
    a. Wa-   i'.
       1SG.AGT- arrive
       'I arrived.'

    b. Ma-   si'ca.
       1SG.PAT- bad
       'I am bad.'

    c. Ma-   ya-   kte.
       1SG.PAT- 2SG.AGT- kill
       'You kill me.'

(3) **Acehnese**
    a. Gopnyan ka=   geu=   jak u= keude.
       he   already 3.AGT go to market
       'He went to market.'

    b. Gopnyan sakêt= geuh.
       he   sick   3.PAT
       'He is sick.'

c. Ji=   kap= keuh.
   3.AGT bite 2.PAT
   'It'll bite you.'

More fine-grained typological distinctions are sometimes made. For example, Dixon (1994) distinguishes between languages with semantically based marking, split-S languages, and fluid-S languages. These distinctions are largely based on Case marking/agreement. In semantically based marking, the Case marking on the nouns reflects their semantic properties in the particular event described, rather than being a grammaticalized property of the verb. In split-S languages, the arguments of transitive verbs are uniformly marked, but the marking of arguments of intransitive verbs depends on whether the verb prototypically takes agentive or non-agentive argument. In fluid-S languages the arguments of intransitive verbs are marked based on the particular event described, not grammaticalized by the verb. However, Dixon does not deny the relevance of the argument-expressing grammatical functions to the description of these languages; he merely claims that they are less important. This is an important distinction: nothing in our theory prevents morphological marking from mirroring thematic roles, informational status, or other non-syntactic properties. This does not render grammatical functions nonexistent; simply irrelevant (in those languages) for specifying the morphological markings under consideration. However, we believe that Dixon has overstated the case for the irrelevance of grammatical functions.

Consider pronominal clitics in Acehnese. We presented some data from Acehnese above; we give further examples here. These examples are taken from a discussion of these clitics in Van Valin and LaPolla (1997), based on Durie (1985). The basic observation is that some arguments are registered on the verb by proclitics and some by enclitics.

(4)   a. (Lôn) lôn=   mat   =geuh.
         1POL 1POL= hold   =3
         'I hold him/her.'

      b. Geu=   jak (gopnyan).
         3POL= go   3POL
         'S/he goes.'

      c. Lôn   rhët (=lôn).
         1POL fall   =1POL
         'I fall.'

      d. *Lôn   lôn=   rhët.
         1POL 1POL= fall
         'I fall.'

168 *Subjects and their properties*

The descriptive question is how to characterize which arguments trigger proclisis and which enclisis. The description preferred by Durie and by Van Valin and LaPolla is to say that the syntax makes direct reference to the thematic roles: proclitics are Agents and enclitics are Patients. Such a description allows one to avoid reference to grammatical functions. However, this is not the only possible way to describe the situation. Suppose, as we suggested in Chapter 2, that active languages differ from the more familiar variety in that, instead of mapping their arguments as in (5a), they map them as in (5b).[1]

(5)   a. The highest available argument maps to the highest available grammatical function, the next argument to the next grammatical function, and so on.
        b. The highest argument role maps to the highest grammatical function, the next argument to the next grammatical function, and so on. Grammatical functions whose corresponding argument role is missing are skipped.

Under this sort of active argument mapping, an Agent (as in non-active languages) is predictably $\widehat{\text{GF}}$, since Agent is the highest thematic role, but, unlike in non-active languages, a Patient (the second role on the thematic hierarchy) maps to the second grammatical function on the relational hierarchy: OBJ.[2] If this is the correct description of Acehnese, the lexical entries of the verbs will include the following arguments.

(6)   a. 'hold $\langle(\uparrow \widehat{\text{GF}})(\uparrow \text{OBJ})\rangle$'
        b. 'go $\langle(\uparrow \widehat{\text{GF}})\rangle$'
        c. 'fall $\langle(\uparrow \text{OBJ})\rangle$'

The agreement clitics can now be described in terms of grammatical functions: $\widehat{\text{GF}}$ triggers proclisis and OBJ triggers enclisis.

(7)   V' →   CL   V   CL
                    $(\uparrow \widehat{\text{GF}})=\downarrow$ $\uparrow=\downarrow$ $(\uparrow \text{OBJ})=\downarrow$

The difference between these two descriptions is primarily a theoretical question. And the center of the theoretical issue goes back to the question of what kind of entity "subject" is, an issue we addressed in Chapter 1.

In Chapter 1, we drew a distinction between the concepts of grammatical relation and grammatical function, and argued that the latter is preferable. It

---

[1] Again, as in Chapter 2, we are using an informal description of argument mapping. Within a framework like LFG's Lexical Mapping Theory, this could be formalized by requiring [−r] arguments to follow the default mapping to grammatical functions ([+o]) instead of allowing them to map to [−o] as an alternative.
[2] In multistratal theories like GB and RG, something like this is assumed for the initial mapping of arguments to the syntax even in languages like English, with a subsequent advancement or movement of the object to subject. This is what is often referred to as the Unaccusative Hypothesis, essentially the claim that underlyingly all languages are active.

is significant that the approaches that deny the need for notions like "subject" and "object" for languages like Acehnese are based on a notion of grammatical relations rather than grammatical functions. The question they ask is what kind of relations the agreement clitics mark, and the conclusion they come to is that they mark thematic relationships.

From our "grammatical functions" perspective, the question is different. We start by observing that there is some syntactic element which functions to express the Agent argument of a verb. There is also some syntactic element which functions to express the Patient argument of a verb. This differs from the situation in English, where the relation between thematic role and syntactic expression is less direct. The question, then, concerns the functional nature of these elements. They are either core functions or obliques. As we saw in Chapter 2, the core/non-core distinction expresses a difference in the syntactic nature of the expression of arguments. Obliques are little more than grammaticalizations of thematic roles;[3] we can thus come close to replicating the Durie – Van Valin-LaPolla answer by hypothesizing that in Acehnese, Agents and Patients, like other arguments, map to the syntax as obliques: OBL_{Agent} and $OBL_{Patient}$ in standard LFG terminology. Such analysis would retain the flavor of their conclusion, but without completely denying the existence of syntax-specific functions.

We are thus faced with two possible analyses of argument mapping in Acehnese: one in which Agents map to $\widehat{GF}$ and Patients to OBJ; and one in which both map to obliques. The distinction between these analyses is empirical: if Agents and Patients have special properties as core functions, the $\widehat{GF}/OBJ$ analysis is to be preferred, while if they do not the oblique analysis is preferable. Note that if Agents and Patients have core-function properties, one could choose to call these functions AGT and PAT, but as far as the syntax is concerned these are the same functions that we have been calling $\widehat{GF}$ and OBJ. They just map to the semantics differently. We prefer to retain the more consistent terminology for the grammatical functions in question.[4]

Durie (1985) refers to Agents and Patients (and some "Datives," which we assume are secondary objects, or OBJ_{Goal}) as core arguments. Core arguments in Acehnese are distinguished by certain syntactic characteristics. They need not be marked by a preposition, and they can occur in preverbal position. The

---

3 This is the intuition behind the idea in Jackendoff (2002) that f-structure should only include the core grammatical functions. On the other hand, we reject Jackendoff's actual proposal, since obliques *are* syntactically active at the functional level.

4 To put it slightly differently, if one chose to call these core grammatical functions AGT and PAT in Acehnese, one would have to do so for English as well, and say that the sole argument of an intransitive bears the grammatical function AGT regardless of its thematic role. The distinction between AGT/PAT and $\widehat{GF}/OBJ$ is purely notational.

unmarked core arguments (Agent and Patient) trigger agreement clitics on the verb, while other arguments (including core Datives) do not. The unmarked core arguments can incorporate into the verb, and they can also be null pronouns. The empirical evidence shows, then, that the syntax of Acehnese must distinguish between core argument functions and oblique argument functions.

We conclude, therefore, that Acehnese cannot be described as realizing thematic roles directly in the syntax. The syntactic distinction between core and non-core arguments is no less a part of the syntax of Acehnese than of other languages, and argument expression in Acehnese makes use of the grammatical functions $\widehat{\text{GF}}$, OBJ, and OBJ$_\theta$. We leave open the question of whether all non-subject languages are like Acehnese. There may be languages in which all arguments are mapped to the syntax as obliques, but we suspect that a closer look at other languages which have been claimed not to have subjects will reveal facts parallel to those in Acehnese. If this suspicion is correct, then all languages have the $\widehat{\text{GF}}$ function.

There is another sense in which subjects are sometimes thought to be universal. Most theories of syntax include a principle that requires every clause to have a subject, such as the Extended Projection Principle of transformational theory, the Final 1 Law of Relational Grammar, and the Subject Condition of LFG. At least in some formulations (including in LFG), this is specifically a requirement for subject as an argument, i.e., $\widehat{\text{GF}}$. Such a principle is appropriate for some languages, like English, but clearly not for others, like Acehnese. In this sense, $\widehat{\text{GF}}$-hood is not universal.

It is interesting that Van Valin and LaPolla assume that if there is a subject argument function, the sole argument of an intransitive must be subject. They consistently argue that a syntactic account of various phenomena would mean that Patient arguments of intransitives would have to pattern with Agents. That is to say, they assume, in our terms, that universality requires that every verb have a $\widehat{\text{GF}}$ argument. But there is no basis for such an assumption. Hypothesizing that a language has the $\widehat{\text{GF}}$ function does not entail that every verb has a $\widehat{\text{GF}}$ argument, any more than hypothesizing that a language has the OBJ function entails that every verb has an OBJ argument.

6.3 Universality of the Pivot Function

6.3.1 Case study: Acehnese

Universality of PIV is a more complicated question than universality of $\widehat{\text{GF}}$. Argument functions are necessary because every language needs a syntactic tool to express arguments. Unlike argument functions, however, there is no reason in principle that every language has to have a PIV. Conceptually, then, the possibility of pivotlessness is less problematic than ĜFlessness. However, as in the case of argument functions, a closer look is necessary to determine whether a particular language has a PIV or not.

We begin by taking another look at Acehnese, a language which has frequently been cited as not having a PIV (for example, by Dixon 1994 and Van Valin and LaPolla 1997). Durie (1987) puts it as follows.

> [I]t turns out that in Acehnese there is a dearth of evidence for what one might call a subject. The sense of subject I have in mind here is a syntactic relation which can be identified, from language-internal structures, as that borne by the single argument of an intransitive predicate, and by one of the two arguments of a transitive predicate, in short, a relation which is present in all or most clauses. . . . I will term a relation of this kind a SUBJECT.   (Durie 1987: 365)

> In a theory-driven formal analysis of the Acehnese facts, the conclusion developed here might seem untenable. It might turn out that for a theory which requires an analogue of the SUBJECT relation, as defined here, the properties of Core Status would have to be described by means of such a relation. However that, I suggest, would be a projection from the theory, not from the facts of Acehnese.   (Durie 1987: 396 fn. 24)

We disagree with the view expressed here by Durie, and suggest that what he refers to as Core Status can be shown to be intimately tied up with the PIV function on the basis of "the facts of Acehnese." However, as we will see, there is an interesting typological difference between pivothood in Acehnese (and probably in many other non-subject languages) and pivothood in uniform- and mixed-subject languages. It is lack of appreciation of this difference that has led some researchers, including Durie, to miss the evidence of pivots in Acehnese.

We begin with a consideration of word order in Acehnese. The language is essentially verb-initial, but optionally one argument of the verb can precede it. We mentioned this fact in passing in the previous section as one of the properties that distinguish core from non-core arguments in Acehnese: only core arguments (Durie's Agent, Patient, and Dative; our ĜF, OBJ, and OBJ Goal) can be initial (examples from Durie 1987, 1988).[5]

(8) a. Gopnyan ka   geu= côm lôn.
        3POL   INCH 3POL= kiss 1POL
        'She kissed me.'

---

5 If an "Agent" is postverbal, it is marked with the particle *lé*, which, following Durie (1988), is here glossed as ergative Case.

172 *Subjects and their properties*

    b. Lôn   ka   geu=   côm lé   gopnyan.
       1POL INCH 3POL= kiss ERG 3POL
       'She kissed me.'

    c. Ara nyan di=   pubeureusih.
       ara that 3FAM= tidy.up
       'They tidied up that *ara* tree.'

    d. Asèe nyan i=   kap =keuh.
       dog that 3FAM= bite =2POL
       'That dog will bite you.'

This preverbal element has some sort of discourse-level prominence, generally marking topic. Since it must be a core argument and is generally a topic, Durie calls it Core Topic. Our claim is that the Acehnese Core Topic is actually the PIV. We thus propose the following f-structures for (8a,b):

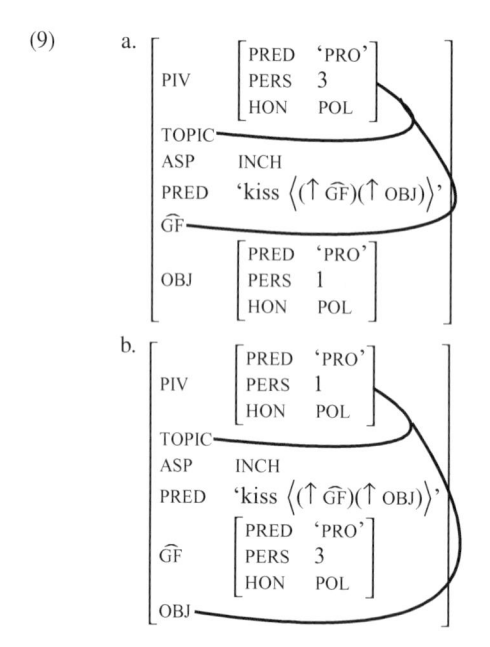

(9) a.
$$\begin{bmatrix} \text{PIV} & \begin{bmatrix} \text{PRED} & \text{'PRO'} \\ \text{PERS} & 3 \\ \text{HON} & \text{POL} \end{bmatrix} \\ \text{TOPIC} & \\ \text{ASP} & \text{INCH} \\ \text{PRED} & \text{'kiss} \langle (\uparrow \widehat{\text{GF}})(\uparrow \text{OBJ}) \rangle \text{'} \\ \widehat{\text{GF}} & \\ \text{OBJ} & \begin{bmatrix} \text{PRED} & \text{'PRO'} \\ \text{PERS} & 1 \\ \text{HON} & \text{POL} \end{bmatrix} \end{bmatrix}$$

b.
$$\begin{bmatrix} \text{PIV} & \begin{bmatrix} \text{PRED} & \text{'PRO'} \\ \text{PERS} & 1 \\ \text{HON} & \text{POL} \end{bmatrix} \\ \text{TOPIC} & \\ \text{ASP} & \text{INCH} \\ \text{PRED} & \text{'kiss} \langle (\uparrow \widehat{\text{GF}})(\uparrow \text{OBJ}) \rangle \text{'} \\ \widehat{\text{GF}} & \begin{bmatrix} \text{PRED} & \text{'PRO'} \\ \text{PERS} & 3 \\ \text{HON} & \text{POL} \end{bmatrix} \\ \text{OBJ} & \end{bmatrix}$$

Under this analysis, Acehnese bears some resemblance to the Philippine-type languages; different elements can bear the PIV function. Unlike the Philippine-type languages, however, the identity of the PIV is not morphologically encoded on the verb. We will discuss the nature of pivot choice in Acehnese in the following section.

Our analysis of Core Topic as PIV is supported by the properties of Core Topics, as described by Durie. Crucially, Core Topics display the same properties that PIVs have in other languages. Core Topichood does not matter for anaphora, which is subject to the thematic and relational hierarchies (which in Acehnese are the same) but for which PIVhood is irrelevant. It is also irrelevant for pro-drop, which is relatively free, and for equi controllee, which is limited to the Agent/ĜF argument, which, as we have seen, is one of the options made available by our theory. (By hypothesis, control in Acehnese is thus anaphoric control.)

However, Core Topichood is relevant for raising and extraction constructions. In Raising, the raised element is the "Core Topic" of the upstairs clause, and there is no (overt) "Core Topic" in the downstairs clause. This is exemplified in the following, from Durie (1987):

(10) a. Gopnyan teuntèe [geu=   woe].
        3POL   certain   3POL=   return
        '(S)he is certain to return'

   b. Gopnyan teuntèe [meungang =geuh].
        3POL   certain   win   =3POL
        '(S)he is certain to win.'

   c. Gopnyan teuntèe [geu=   beuet hikayat prang sabi].
        3POL   certain   3POL=   recite   epic   Prang Sabi
        'He/She is certain to recite the Prang Sabi epic.'

   d. Hikayat prang sabi teuntèe [geu=   beuet].
        epic   Prang Sabi certain   3POL=   recite
        'The epic Prang Sabi is certain to be recited (by him/her).'

The apparent obligatory lack of an overt Core Topic cannot be attributed to the agreement being an incorporated pronoun, since overt free subject pronouns are permitted as an option in Acehnese. It can be explained if we hypothesize that the Core Topic is the raising controllee. Under our theory, this would make it the PIV. As for the controller, while the theory does not require it to be PIV, we have seen that Tagalog has this property too. The lexical entry of 'certain' is (11a), and the f-structures of (10c,d) are (11b,c).

(11) a. *teuntèe*: (↑ PRED) = 'certain ⟨(↑ XCOMP)⟩ (↑ ĜF)'
              (↑ PIV) = (↑ CF)
              (↑ PIV) = (↑ XCOMP PIV)

b.
$$\begin{bmatrix} \text{PIV} & \begin{bmatrix} \text{PRED} & \text{'PRO'} \\ \text{PERS} & 3 \\ \text{HON} & \text{POL} \end{bmatrix} \\ \text{TOPIC} & \\ \text{PRED} & \text{'certain } \langle(\uparrow \text{XCOMP})\rangle(\uparrow \widehat{\text{GF}})\text{'} \\ \widehat{\text{GF}} & \\ \text{XCOMP} & \begin{bmatrix} \text{PIV} & \\ \text{TOPIC} & \\ \text{PRED} & \text{'recite } \langle(\uparrow \widehat{\text{GF}})(\uparrow \text{OBJ})\rangle\text{'} \\ \widehat{\text{GF}} & \\ \text{OBJ} & [\text{"epic Prang Sabi"}] \end{bmatrix} \end{bmatrix}$$

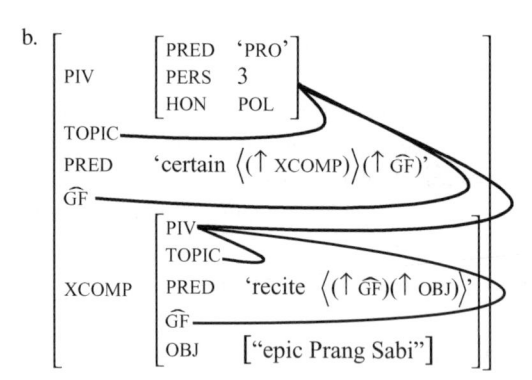

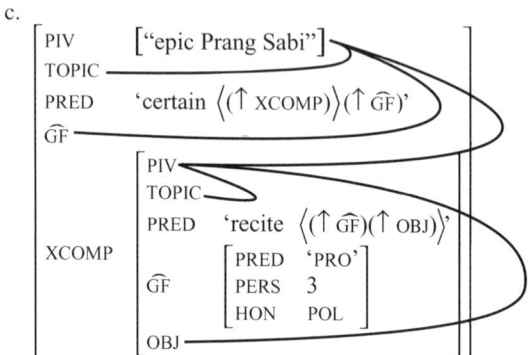

c.
$$\begin{bmatrix} \text{PIV} & [\text{"epic Prang Sabi"}] \\ \text{TOPIC} & \\ \text{PRED} & \text{'certain } \langle(\uparrow \text{XCOMP})\rangle(\uparrow \widehat{\text{GF}})\text{'} \\ \widehat{\text{GF}} & \\ \text{XCOMP} & \begin{bmatrix} \text{PIV} & \\ \text{TOPIC} & \\ \text{PRED} & \text{'recite } \langle(\uparrow \widehat{\text{GF}})(\uparrow \text{OBJ})\rangle\text{'} \\ \widehat{\text{GF}} & \begin{bmatrix} \text{PRED} & \text{'PRO'} \\ \text{PERS} & 3 \\ \text{HON} & \text{POL} \end{bmatrix} \\ \text{OBJ} & \end{bmatrix} \end{bmatrix}$$

Relative clauses display a similar pattern: no overt Core Topic.

(12) a. Gopnyan geu= bloe moto nyan.
       3POL   3POL= buy car that
       '(S)he bought that car.'

   b. Lôn= ngieng ureueng [nyang= bloe moto nyan].
      1POL= see   person REL=   buy car that
      'I saw the person who bought that car.'

   c. *Lôn= ngieng ureung [nyang= moto nyan (geu=) bloe].
      1POL= see   person REL=   car that 3POL= buy
      'I saw the person who bought that car.'

   d. Lôn= ngieng moto [nyang= geu=   bloe lé ureueng nyan].
      1POL= see   car REL=   3POL= buy ERG person that
      'I saw the car that was bought by that person.'

   e. *Lôn= ngieng moto [nyang= ureueng nyan geu= bloe].
      1POL= see   car REL=   person that 3POL= buy
      'I saw the car that was bought by that person.'

If we analyze the Core Topic as PIV, the lack of overt Core Topic is once again explained, and Acehnese turns out to be like other Austronesian languages in only allowing extraction of PIV.

The Acehnese Core Topic has other PIV-like properties. One is suggested by its linear position. Acehnese clauses are basically verb-initial, but the Core Topic precedes the verb. Plausibly, the basic verb-initial clause is a constituent, to which the Core Topic is a sister:

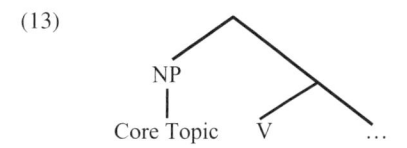

(13)

```
        /\
       /  \
      NP   /\
      |   /  \
 Core Topic V  ...
```

The Core Topic thus appears to have an external structural position, which we have seen is a property of PIV in many languages. In addition, it is not Case-marked (most striking with the ĜF, which is Case-marked *lé* if it is not the Core Topic), like PIVs in many languages. So, contrary to claims that have been made to the contrary, Acehnese turns out to have a PIV, but it can be any core argument, it is not obligatory, and it is also a discourse topic.

6.3.2 Topic prominence

While non-subject languages like Acehnese do seem to have pivots, there is a major difference between the nature of pivots in these languages and in more "conventional" languages, both uniform-subject and mixed-subject.

In uniform- and mixed-subject languages, PIV is identified with some argument function. It is the nature of this argument function that distinguishes these two types of languages. In Acehnese, as we have seen, this is not the case: Acehnese thus cannot be identified as either a uniform-subject language or a mixed-subject language. Instead, the PIV in Acehnese has two properties: it has one of the core argument functions, and it bears a discourse function, usually TOPIC. We will focus on the second of these here, and propose that the grammar of Acehnese specifies the following constraint as part of the lexical entry of every verb.

(14)   (↑ PIV) = (↑ DF)

We would like to suggest that this specification is part of the grammar of what Li and Thompson (1976) refer to as "topic-prominent" (as opposed to "subject-prominent") languages.

As described by Li and Thompson, languages can be organized on either a subject–predicate or topic–comment basis. Some of the differences that they identify between subjects and topics are the following:

(15) Topics must be definite, subjects need not be.
Topics need not be arguments, subjects must be.
Verb determines subject, not topic.
Topic has a consistent discourse role, subject doesn't.
Verb agrees with subject, not topic.
Topic always sentence-initial, subject not in all languages.
Subject plays a role in grammatical processes (reflexives, passive, equi, serial verbs, imperatives).

Topic-prominent languages, according to Li and Thompson, have consistent coding for topic, but not necessarily subject (Japanese and Korean have both: Japanese *wa* marks topics and *ga* marks subjects). They may have what appears to be a double subject construction, where both the topic and the subject are in specifier positions preceding the rest of the clause. Most interestingly, in topic-prominent languages, the topic need not be locally licensed (i.e., either an argument or an adjunct).

Our proposal is that Li and Thompson's topic prominence is a combination of two distinct properties. One of them is the possibility of a topic that is not locally licensed, as in the following examples from Li and Thompson.

(16) a. **Lahu**
[Hɛ chi tê pê?] ɔ̄ dà? jâ.
field this one CLASS rice very good
'This field, the rice is very good.'

b. **Mandarin**
[Nèi- chang huǒ] xìngkui xiāofang- duì laí de kwài.
that- CLASS fire fortunate fire- brigade come PART quick
'That fire, fortunately the fire brigade came quickly.'

c. **Korean**
[Siban- in] hakkjo- ga manso.
now- TOP school- NOM many
'The present time, there are many schools.'

d. **Japanese**
[Gakko- wa] buku- ga isogasi- kat- ta.
school- TOP I- NOM busy- PST
'School, I was busy.'

We propose that in topic-prominent languages in this sense discourse functions do not need to be identified with a locally licensed function; formally, the part of the Extended Coherence Condition that deals with discourse functions is inactive in these languages. Thus, for example, the Japanese sentence in (16d) has the following f-structure.

(17) $\begin{bmatrix} \text{TOPIC} & [\text{"school"}] \\ \text{PIV} & [\text{"I"}] \\ \widehat{\text{GF}} & \\ \text{PRED} & \text{'busy} \langle (\uparrow \widehat{\text{GF}}) \rangle \text{'} \\ \text{TENSE} & \text{PAST} \end{bmatrix}$

This f-structure would be ungrammatical in a non-topic-prominent language like English. In a topic-prominent language, it is possible for the TOPIC to be identified with an argument, but not necessary.[6]

There is a second aspect to Li and Thompson's topic prominence, which is the one which is relevant to our present concerns. This is the fact that, in many of these languages (roughly, the ones Li and Thompson identify as exclusively topic-prominent), the topic has properties that we have identified in this study as pivot properties. These two topic-prominent properties do not always coincide: in languages like Japanese the non–locally licensed topic does not have pivot properties, and in Acehnese the topic must be locally licensed. It is in this second sense that Acehnese is a topic-prominent language. (The restriction to core functions in Acehnese is either a second restriction on PIV, or an independent restriction on TOPIC.) A language which appears to be topic-prominent in both senses is Mandarin. Note the following examples of chaining in coordination in Mandarin.

(18) a. Nèike shù yèzi dà, suǒyi wǒ bu xǐhuān.
        that tree leaves big so I not like
        'That tree, the leaves are big so I don't like it/*them.'

    b. Nèi kuài tián dàozi zhǎngde hěn dà, suǒyi hěn zhíqián.
        that piece land rice grow very big so very valuable
        'That piece of land, rice grows very big so it [the land/*the rice] is very valuable.'

In general, an Acehnese-like analysis for Mandarin pivots looks very attractive. Due to the quirks of Mandarin word order (Li and Thompson 1981) the arguments are a little harder to make. In particular, both "topic" (PIV) and "agent" (ĜF) precede the verb, and other elements may also precede it optionally. This makes it harder to uniquely identify the Mandarin topic/PIV. However,

---

[6] Alternatively, topic-prominent languages have a non-overlay topic function (distinct from the overlay function TOPIC), which is not used in languages like English.

it appears that in long-distance dependency constructions and raising constructions the subordinate clause does not have an overt topic; if this is in fact the case, an analysis identifying the Mandarin topic with PIV is almost certainly correct.

Typologically, then, we can distinguish between two types of PIV choice: pivot choice on the basis of argument status (**argument-pivot languages**), and pivot choice on the basis of discourse status, particularly topichood (**topic-pivot languages**). Argument-pivot languages include both uniform-subject and mixed-subject languages; topic-pivot languages are those non-subject languages that have PIVs, are not part of the uniform-subject/mixed-subject distinction, and include many languages (such as Acehnese and Mandarin) that have been claimed in other studies to be pivotless.

Our approach differs fundamentally from that taken by studies like Van Valin and LaPolla (1997). In studies of that variety, the fact that pivot properties are not limited to a single argument of the verb is taken to be evidence that there is no pivot. Instead, the rules for constructions like relativization will refer to whatever relations at whatever level of structure are deemed appropriate. Under the approach we are taking, on the other hand, the function of cross-clausal continuity is PIV; any element that has this function is of necessity the PIV of its clause. The formal structure of syntax does not allow a language with no pivots to simply ignore the Pivot Condition: something with pivot properties must be a pivot. The prohibition against arguments from being referenced by superordinate predicates is an expression of the nature of their functionality as arguments; there is no reason to expect it to be suspended just because a language makes no use of the PIV function.

Nothing in our conception of pivothood rules out pivot choice on the basis of syntactically relevant discourse properties. Unlike Van Valin and LaPolla, we do not impose arbitrary a priori requirements that the PIV be uniquely identifiable in terms of predicate–argument relations. As a result, we have discovered that a class of languages chooses its pivots not on the basis of predicate–argument relations, but rather on the basis of grammaticized discourse relations. We believe that this is an important typological discovery; and it is one which is made possible by the framework within which we are working and the theory of pivothood which we have proposed here.

6.3.3 Pivotless languages
6.3.3.1 General considerations
We concluded in the previous section that a subset of languages which have been identified as pivotless do have pivots, but choose their pivots on the basis

of syntactically relevant topicality rather than argument structure. We consider this to be an important conclusion, but it still leaves open the question of whether pivotless languages exist. In this section, we will answer this question with a tentative "yes".

We need to begin by asking what a language with no PIV would look like. As we have seen, it is not a language in which the element with pivot properties is not uniquely determined by the argument structure; since in sentences of such languages there is an element with PIV properties, there must be a PIV which is chosen on some basis other than argument structure. We have argued that in such a language the PIV is chosen on the basis of syntacticized discourse functions. Instead, a truly pivotless language would be a language in which no element of any clause has pivot properties. For example, in a pivotless language there would be no reason to analyze one element of the clause as being singled out with special status, such as occupying a special position. Languages like Acehnese and (probably) Mandarin do have such an element, and therefore have a PIV. Furthermore, a pivotless language would tend to eschew pivot-sensitive constructions, such as long-distance dependencies or functional control constructions. Instead, it would generally achieve the requisite effects through other syntactic means. For example, instead of multifunctionality constructions (such as functional control and coordination chaining), it would use some variety of anaphoric construction: overt anaphoric element, null anaphoric element, or a switch-reference system; alternatively, instead of functional control it might use a complex predicate construction in which the higher and lower verbs merge functionally into a single argument-taking element. Instead of relative clauses of the familiar kind, it would have internally headed relative clauses or eschew relative constructions completely, using (anaphoric) control constructions instead of relative clauses. Instead of placing the *wh* element of a question in a special matrix position, it would keep it in its own clause, either in the appropriate place for its local function (often referred to as "in-situ" questions) or in a special position in its clause.

It is important to note, however, that, as always, there is no simple test. There could be a special position picked out for an element with discourse prominence, without it also being a PIV. A pivotless language could have long-distance dependency constructions, but license them inside-out (bottom-up); as we have seen, this is a frequently used loophole to the Pivot Condition in long-distance dependencies. This is marked, and generally does not exist in the absence of Pivot Condition–sensitive outside-in (top-down) licensing, but it is possible. We have even seen an example of a language that seems to have only inside-out licensing of long-distance dependency constructions,

180 *Subjects and their properties*

Imbabura Quechua. Inside-out licensing may also be possible for functional control, although it seems to be much more rarely used. Conversely, the use of some of the alternative non-pivot-dependent constructions does not automatically make a language pivotless. We take it, however, that when a language uses many of these and appears to be avoiding pivot-sensitive constructions it is plausible to hypothesize that it lacks a PIV completely.

There are two important points to make about these observations. In the first place, our theory of pivothood gives us a clear picture of what a pivotless language would look like. This is the advantage of an articulated theory such as we have proposed here. Secondly, there is nothing impossible in principle about a pivotless language. It would appear exotic in its grammatical structure, but it would have a full array of construction types. Since there is nothing in the theory that requires every language to have pivots, and a pivotless language would be able to realize all the major notional constructions, we should expect that pivotless languages exist.

We suggest that Choctaw/Chickasaw and Warlpiri are pivotless languages. We will examine their properties and show how they behave like pivotless languages. In the case of Choctaw/Chickasaw this may not be too surprising a conclusion, but we believe that it is a novel proposal for Warlpiri, which appears to be generally assumed to be a uniform-subject language. We will also speculate on the relationship between pivotlessness and morphological ergativity.

6.3.3.2   Choctaw/Chickasaw
We begin with Choctaw/Chickasaw. We will outline in this section the salient aspects of Choctaw/Chickasaw grammar, with an emphasis on the issue of pivothood. Our sources of information are Munro and Gordon (1982), Davies (1984), and Broadwell (in press). The examples are Chickasaw and taken from Munro and Gordon, unless otherwise noted.[7]

Perhaps the most discussed issue in Choctaw/Chickasaw grammar is the nature of the Case and agreement systems. The agreement system consists of three sets of affixes which, following Munro and Gordon, we will call Types I, II, and III. In a canonical transitive clause, agreement with the A is Type I and with the P is Type II.[8]

---

7 We follow Munro and Gordon and Davies in presenting the examples in an approximation of Choctaw/Chickasaw orthography, but marking nasality with a tilde instead of the orthographic underline. Broadwell uses the underline of the standard orthography.
8 There is no affix (or a ∅ affix) for third person Types I and II.

(19) a. Kisili-   li
         bite-   1SG.I
         'I bite him.'
      b. Sa-   kisili
         1SG.II- bite
         'He bites me.'

However, there are transitive verbs in which the A argument triggers II or III agreement, and ones in which the P triggers III agreement.

(20) a. Ofi' sa-   banna.
         dog   1SG.II- want
         'I want a dog.'
      b. Talowa' am-   alhkaniya- tok.
         song   1SG.III- forget-   PST
         'I forgot the song.'

(21) a. Chim-   ambi- li.
         2SG.III- beat- 1SG.I
         'I beat you (in a contest).'
      b. Chī-   hollo- li.
         2SG.III- love-   1SG.I
         'I love you.'

In an intransitive clause, any of the three types of agreement affix can be used, depending on the verb:

(22) a. Malili- li
         ran-   1SG.I
         'I ran.'
      b. Hotolhko- li
         coughed-   1SG.I
         'I coughed (on purpose).'

(23) a. Sa-   chokma
         1SG.II- good
         'I am good.'
      b. Sa-   hotolhko
         1SG.II- coughed
         'I coughed.'

(24) An-   takho'bi
      1SG.III- lazy
      'I am lazy.'

Clausal complements trigger II agreement (which is null, since clauses are third person).

Exactly how the type of agreement is determined is a matter of dispute in the literature. For example, Dixon (1994) cites this as an example of semantic marking, marking determined by thematic roles, while Davies (1984) considers this to be based on (sometimes non-surface) grammatical relations. Munro and Gordon show that while there are some thematic correlations there are also lexical idiosyncrasies, and state that the argument type must be marked lexically. In our framework, the relevant locus for describing idiosyncrasies of argument expression is the mapping of arguments to the syntax, so we propose that the agreement is triggered by grammatical functions – ĜF for Type I, OBJ and COMP for Type II, and OBJ$_\theta$ for Type III. This has as a consequence that Choctaw/Chickasaw must be analyzed as having an active system of argument mapping. In terms of subjecthood, an argument that triggers Type I agreement is thus subject in the sense of ĜF.

The Case-marking system works differently from agreement. One argument, the one that would correspond to the English subject, is marked with the suffix -V*t* regardless of which type of agreement it triggers, while other arguments optionally take a suffix -Ṽ or (less commonly) -V*k*. (In the examples, we gloss the *t* suffix as nominative and the nasal suffix as oblique.)

(25)   a. Hattak- at   malili.
              man-   NOM   run
              'The man runs.' (NOM triggers I agreement)

        b. Hattak- at   ihoo   pĩsa.
              man-   NOM   woman   see
              'The man sees the woman.' (NOM triggers I agreement)

        c. Hattak- at   an-   k-   ã   abi- tok.
              man-   NOM   my-   father-   OBL   kill-   PST
              'The man killed my father.' (NOM triggers I agreement)

        d. Hattak- at   chokma.
              man-   NOM   good
              'The man is good.' (NOM triggers II agreement)

        e. Hattak- at   in-   takho'bi.
              man-   NOM   3III-   lazy
              'The man is lazy.' (NOM triggers III agreement)

        f. Hattak- at   oho:yo (ã)   ĩ:-   nokšo:pa- h.   (Choctaw)
              man-   NOM   woman   OBL   3III-   afraid-   PRES
              'The man is afraid of the woman.' (NOM triggers II agreement)

The *t*-marked argument is clearly not the ĜF, thought it is called the "subject" by Munro and Gordon and by Broadwell. Davies (1984) considers both Type I

Universality 183

agreement and *t*-marking to be a consequence of bearing the 1 (subject) relation, and cites the mismatch between agreement-relevant grammatical relations and Case-relevant grammatical relations as evidence for multiple strata of grammatical relations. Dixon (1994) considers Choctaw/Chickasaw to be a language with a blend of semantically based marking (agreement) and syntactically based marking (Case).

The *t*-marked nominal is usually the highest argument on the relational hierarchy, but not always; Munro and Gordon mention the verb *alhkaniya* 'forget,' where the *t*-marked argument triggers III agreement and the other argument triggers II agreement.

(26) a. Talowa' am-   alhkaniya- tok.
        song   1SG.III- forget-   PST
        'I forgot the song.'

   b. Hakkat- at   talowa' im-   alhkaniya- tok.
      man-   NOM song   3III- forget-   PST
      'The man forgot the song.'

Under our analysis, the agreement markers show that the forgetter argument (the nominative one) is a restricted object (OBJ$_{Exp}$), while the non-nominative argument is a primary object (OBJ). In the case of this verb, the nominative argument is not the highest on the relational hierarchy, since OBJ outranks OBJ$_\theta$. On the other hand, at the thematic level the forgetter is Experiencer (a kind of undergoer) and the forgotten material is a Theme, so the *t*-marked argument is the highest on the thematic hierarchy: the $\hat{\theta}$.

It is even possible to get two or three *t*-marked nominals in a clause, primarily in the Possessor Raising construction.

(27) a. Larry ishkin- at   lakna.
        Larry eye-   NOM brown
        'Larry's eyes are brown.'

   b. Larry- at   ishkin- at   lakna.
      Larry- NOM eye-   NOM brown
      'Larry has brown eyes.'

(28) a. Jan ipāshi'- at   tapa.
        Jan hair-   NOM be.cut
        'Jan's hair was cut.'

   b. Jan- at   ipāshi'- at   tapa.
      Jan- NOM hair-   NOM be.cut
      'Jan got a haircut.'

(29)   Bonnie- at   in-   chokk- at   aboh- at   talhlha'pi.
       Bonnie- NOM 3III- house- NOM room- NOM five
       'Bonnie has a five-room house.'

Under our proposal concerning nominative marking, these would be analyzed as complex-predicate constructions.[9]

Formally, our proposal can be expressed by associating the nominative suffix with the following lexical information (where α is the mapping from a-structure to f-structure):

(30) $(\alpha(\hat{\theta}) \uparrow)$

Since the thematic and relational hierarchy usually match, it follows that most of the time the *t*-marked nominal will also be the highest on the relational hierarchy. The mapping of 'forget' is exceptional in that the hierarchies are reversed.[10] The f-structures of (25b,f) and (26b) are as follows (where the $\hat{\theta}$ is the leftmost argument in the verb's PRED):

(31) a. $\begin{bmatrix} \widehat{\text{GF}} & [\text{"man"}] \\ \text{OBJ} & [\text{"woman"}] \\ \text{PRED} & \text{'see} \langle (\uparrow \widehat{\text{GF}})(\uparrow \text{OBJ}) \rangle \text{'} \\ \text{TENSE} & \text{PRES} \end{bmatrix}$

   b. $\begin{bmatrix} \text{OBJ} & [\text{"man"}] \\ \text{OBJ}_\theta & [\text{"woman"}] \\ \text{PRED} & \text{'afraid} \langle (\uparrow \text{OBJ})(\uparrow \text{OBL}_\theta) \rangle \text{'} \\ \text{TENSE} & \text{PRES} \end{bmatrix}$

   c. $\begin{bmatrix} \text{OBJ} & [\text{"song"}] \\ \text{OBJ}_\theta & [\text{"man"}] \\ \text{PRED} & \text{'forget} \langle (\uparrow \text{OBJ}_\theta)(\uparrow \text{OBJ}) \rangle \text{'} \\ \text{TENSE} & \text{PAST} \end{bmatrix}$

We have now shown that the grammar of Choctaw/Chickasaw refers to $\widehat{\text{GF}}$ and $\hat{\theta}$. The question is whether there is any evidence for a PIV. We claim there is not. There does not seem to be any particular element that occupies a special structural position, as we would expect from a PIV. In fact, there seems to be no element that we could identify as the PIV in Choctaw/Chickasaw. The *t*-marked nominal comes first, but this could be thematically based order. Since a clause can have more than one *t*-marked nominal, it could not be the PIV

---

9 According to Munro and Gordon, the nominative marking on all but the highest $\hat{\theta}$ is optional.
10 According to Munro and Gordon, this is related to the fact that the verb is a derived form, based on a verb meaning 'go away' or 'lose.'

anyway. Furthermore, it does not have any cross-clausal continuity properties, and thus is not plausibly analyzed as functioning as the element of cross-clausal continuity.

Subordination and coordination in Choctaw/Chickasaw involve switch-reference markers rather than control or chaining.

(32) a. Aya- l- a'chi- kat ithaana- li.
go- 1SG.I- FUT- COMP.DIFF know- 1SG.I
'I know I am going.'

b. Ish- iyy- a'chi- kā ithanna- li.
2SG.I- go- FUT- COMP.DIFF know- 1SG.I
'I know you are going.'

(33) **Choctaw** (Davies 1984)
a. Tobi apa- li- cha/*na oka ishko- li- tok.
beans eat- 1SG.I- SAME/*DIFF water drink- 1SG.I- PST
'I ate beans and drank water.'

b. Tobi apa- li- na/*cha tāchi ish- pa- tok.
beans eat- 1SG.I- DIFF/*SAME corn 2SG.I- eat- PST
'I ate beans and you ate corn.'

The relevant notion of subject for switch-reference marking is the *t*-marked nominal, the $\hat{\theta}$ under our analysis.[11] As we have seen, this is one of the options that we expect to be available for switch-reference. The other one is $\widehat{GF}$. Davies (1984) reports that for some speakers of Choctaw either same-subject or different-subject marking can be used in coordination if, in our terms, the two $\hat{\theta}$s are not both $\widehat{GF}$s.

(34) a. Sa- hohchafo- cha/na tobi nonachi- li- tok.
1SG.II- hungry- SAME/DIFF beans cook- 1SG.I- PST
'I was hungry and cooked some beans.'

b. Soba sa- banna- cha/na chōpa- li- tok.
horse 1SG.II- want- SAME/DIFF buy- 1SG.I- PST
'I wanted a horse and bought it.'

Essentially following Davies' insight, we can characterize the coordination switch-reference marking in this idiolect of Choctaw as specifying that same-subject marking means the two clauses have coreferential $\hat{X}$s and different-subject marking means they have non-coreferential $\hat{X}$s. Since they have coreferential $\hat{\theta}$s but not $\widehat{GF}$s, both markings are possible. These multiclausal structures thus do not involve pivot-sensitive constructions.

---

11 Actually, the highest $\hat{\theta}$ in the clause, which is the only one obligatorily marked nominative.

186 *Subjects and their properties*

Relative clauses in Choctaw/Chickasaw are internally headed.

(35) a. Steve- at   [Dan- at   aaimpa' ikbi- tokã]   banna.
         Steve- NOM Dan- NOM table   make- PST.COMP.OBL want
         'Steve wants the table Dan made.'
      b. Choctaw (Broadwell in press)
         [Mary- at   páska' chãpóli' ikbi- tokã]   apa-
         Mary- NOM   bread sweet   make- PST.COMP.DIFF eat-
         li-   tok.
         1SG.I- PST
         'I ate the cake that Mary made.'

The language shows no evidence of externally headed relative clauses. Relative clauses are thus not long-distance dependency constructions. Similarly, elements with discourse prominence are not placed in a special position in the sentence. They remain in situ, with a special suffix indicating their discourse-prominent status.

Choctaw/Chickasaw thus appears to have the kinds of properties we expect of a pivotless language. It is a language which, given the constructions we have examined thus far, appears to lack pivot-sensitive constructions like functional control, chaining, long-distance dependencies, and the assignment of a special structural position to one element of the clause. It is instructive to compare these properties with those of languages like Acehnese – it is clear that, while both have been claimed to be pivotless, they are typologically very different. Our analysis captures this, by analyzing Acehnese as having a topic pivot and Choctaw/Chickasaw as being truly pivotless.

There is one potential problem for our analysis of Choctaw/Chickasaw as pivotless. This problem is the question construction. Alongside the expected in situ questions, Choctaw/Chickasaw also has questions with extraction:

(36) **Choctaw** (Broadwell in press)
      a. John- at   kata- h-   õ   pı́sa- tok?
         John- NOM who- TNS- PART.OBL   see- PST
      b. Kata- h-   õ   John- at   pı́sa- tok?
         who- TNS- PART.OBL John- NOM see- PST
         'Who did John see?'

This optional extraction of a question word can even cross clause boundaries:

(37) **Choctaw** (Broadwell in press)
Nata- h- ō   Pam- at   [Charles- at
what- TNS- PART.OBL Pam- NOM   Charles- NOM

honni- tok- ō]   hōkopa- tok?
cook-   PST- FOC.OBL   steal- PST
'What did Pam steal that Charles cooked?'

If this is really a long-distance dependency construction, it is the only one in the language. This construction has certain unusual properties for a long-distance dependency construction. As can be seen in the examples, the interrogative pronoun has verbal morphology, both in situ and fronted. The construction also lacks weak crossover effects. However, even if it is the long-distance dependency construction it appears to be, it is not really a problem for our analysis. We simply must hypothesize that it is licensed inside-out. We have seen that, although the inside-out licensing construction is marked, it is possible for a language to have inside-out licensing without the less marked outside-in construction. Since, under our analysis, Choctaw/Chickasaw has no PIV, inside-out functional uncertainty can license the extraction of all elements. It is significant that, unlike questions in other languages, there is no element which has a special status in terms of question-word extraction. There are no asymmetries in the ability to extract different elements. In this way, it differs from all cases of extraction we have seen up to this point. "Subjects" are neither easier nor more difficult to extract than non-"subjects." The extracted element need have no special discourse prominence (other than being the focus of a question) which is expressed syntactically. This is what we expect of inside-out licensing of long-distance dependencies in a language with no PIV.

Overall, Choctaw/Chickasaw gives the impression of a language which avoids pivot-sensitive constructions: it uses switch-reference instead of control, internally headed relative clauses, and has no structurally distinguished element. The only construction on which it fails, the interrogative, is the one we might least expect to find a language successfully avoiding such a construction. Furthermore, even the interrogative construction shows no evidence of a distinguished element that we could identify as PIV. The properties of Choctaw/Chickasaw are in marked contrast to languages such as Acehnese, which display the full range of pivot-sensitive constructions. We propose, therefore, that Choctaw/Chickasaw is a pivotless language.

6.3.3.3 Warlpiri

Warlpiri, one of the best known of the morphologically ergative languages, is a language whose syntax has many exotic features. It is best known for its wildly non-configurational structure. The basic phrase structure configuration of the clause in Warlpiri has one element, with discourse prominence, in the initial position, followed by an auxiliary (infl) element, followed by the rest of the elements of the clause in free order. The pre-aux element has no subject properties, so there is no reason to consider it a PIV.

As for subordinate clauses, Simpson (1983) concludes that Warlpiri has no (or few, see fn. 12) functional control constructions. Warlpiri has no raising construction (Hale 1983). Resultatives are often analyzed as optional functionally controlled arguments in languages like English. They are lexically restricted, and the choice of controller is governed by the argument structure of the verb: OBJ or unaccusative/passive SUBJ. However, in Warlpiri the class of verbs that can appear with resultatives is not lexically restricted, and the controller can be anything, including transitive SUBJ.

(38)   a. Janyungu   ka   nguna- mi   linji- karda.
               tobacco.ABS PRES lie-   NPST   dry-   TRANSL
               'The tobacco lies in the sun dry'. [= The tobacco lies in the sun, and as a result it is dry. ≈ 'The tobacco lies in the sun to dry.']

        b. Puluku-   rlu   kapu- lu   mama   nga- rni
               bullocks- ERG FUT- 3PL.SUBJ grass.ABS eat- NPST
               kuntukuntu- karda.
               fat-   TRANSL
               ' The bullocks will eat the grass fat.' [= The bullocks will eat grass, and as a result will be fat. ≈ 'The bullocks will eat themselves fat on the grass.']

In fact, the controller of the resultative need not be part of the sentence.

(39)   Yarlaparna- rlu   ka   parrka   munyurr- nga- rni
            caterpillar- ERG PRES leaf.ABS bare-   eat- NPST
            lirrki-lirrki- karda.
            defoliated- TRANSL
            'The caterpillar eats up all the leaves defoliated [i.e. until the tree is defoliated].'

These facts point to an analysis under which Warlpiri resultatives are anaphorically controlled adjuncts. Depictives are similar. Copular constructions are also typically functional control constructions. In Warlpiri, however, they differ from those in English, and other familiar languages, in that the copular verb and its complement form a single argument-taking domain; that is to say, Warlpiri copular constructions are complex predicates. For example, consider the following example:

(40)   Pakirdi   ka-   rla   karnta   nyina   wati- ki.
       in.love.ABS PRES-   DAT.OBJ   woman.ABS   sit.NPST   man- DAT
       'The woman is yearning for [literally: "sits in love with"] the man.'

The dative OBJ 'man,' even though it is an argument of the nominal 'in.love,' is registered on the aux as a clausal argument. This is evidence for a complex-predicate analysis.[12] Simpson also presents evidence that infinitival complements to jussive verbs are anaphorically controlled OBLS, and that the infinitives accompanying other classes of verbs (such as verbs of perception) are anaphorically controlled adjuncts.[13] Walrpiri thus is a language with no functional control constructions.

Walrpiri also has a complex system of complementizer suffixes with obviative (or switch-reference) features, discussed by Simpson (1983) and Simpson and Bresnan (1983). For example, the simultaneous-action suffix *-karra*, for most Warlpiri speakers, is a same-subject (or subject-control) marker. (Some speakers use it as a general complementizer, without its obviation function; for such speakers, [41c] is grammatical.)

(41)   a. Ngarrka   ka   wangka- mi   nyina- nja-   karra.
          man.ABS   PRES   talk-   NPST   sit-   INF-   SCONTR
          'The man is talking while sitting.'
       b. Turaki-   rli   puluku   winjarlu paka- rnu
          vehicle-   ERG   bullock.ABS   big.ABS   hit- PST
          parnka-   nja-   karra-   rlu.
          run-   INF-   SCONTR-   ERG
          'The moving car hit a big bullock.'
       c. *Ngarrka-   ngku ka   kurdu   paka- rni   wangka-
          man-   ERG PRES   child.ABS   hit- NPST   talk-
          nja- karra.
          INF- SCONTR
          'The man hits the child while it's talking.'

12 Simpson formalizes this as a type of functional control, but only because LFG at the time had no analysis of complex predicates. However, it is clear even from her formalization that what is involved is not functional control of the ordinary kind; it involves "control" of all the arguments, not just the SUBJ. It is thus not a pivot-sensitive construction. The other construction that Simpson identifies as involving functional control, the naming construction, could also be analyzed as a complex-predicate construction; in the absence of any other functional control construction, a complex-predicate analysis seems preferable. (Simpson also suggests that directional complements, as in *I ran to the zoo*, are functionally controlled XCOMPs, but these are OBLS in English and, presumably, in Walrpiri as well.)
13 It is not clear why Simpson analyzes these as adjuncts rather than arguments. It would be consistent with the evidence she presents to identify these clauses with the closed complement function COMP.

We argued in Chapter 2 that switch-reference marking is anaphoric in nature; Simpson and Simpson-Bresnan make the same claim for the Warlpiri obviation system. Unlike other switch-reference systems, the Warlpiri obviation system also has object-control (*-kurra*) and oblique-control (*-rlarni*) suffixes, instead of just picking out ĜF for reference. However, it is possible to analyze these other suffixes as "different-subject" suffixes, with the further proviso on the object-control suffix that the complement ĜF be coreferential with a matrix core argument. In other words, the lexical content of the suffixes will be (informally) as follows:

(42)   *karra:* ĜF is coreferential with upstairs clause's ĜF
       kurra: ĜF is non-coreferential with upstairs clause's ĜF
              ĜF is coreferential with a core argument in upstairs clause
       rlarni: ĜF is non-coreferential with any core argument in upstairs clause.

As predicted by this account (and by Simpson-Bresnan's [1983] similar analysis as well), the oblique-control complementizer *rlarni* can be used when there is an overt ĜF in the lower clause, and thus no control.

(43)   Yapa-   kari   ka-   rla   ngarrka   wangka-   mi
       man-   other.ABS   PRES-   datOBJ   man.ABS   speak-   NPST
       karnta-   ku,   [kalinyanu- ku   wirlinyi-   rlarni].
       woman-   DAT   husband-   DAT   hunting-   DIFF
       'Some man is speaking to the woman while her husband is out hunting.'

A sentence may have multiple adjuncts with different obviation markers:

(44)   Wati   rna   nya-   ngu   ngajulu-   rlu   marlu   [luwa-
       man.ABS   1sgSUBJ   see-   PST   I-   ERG   kangaroo.ABS shoot-
       rninja-   kurra]   [pama   nga-   rninja-   karra-   rlu].
       INF-   OCONTR   liquor.ABS   ingest- INF-   SCONTR-   ERG
       'I saw the man shooting the kangaroo while I was drinking liquor.'

The foregoing shows that Warlpiri's treatment of control-type constructions is what one would expect of a pivotless language. We turn now to long-distance dependency constructions. We begin with relative clauses. Warlpiri does not use LDDs for relative clauses. In fact, Warlpiri has been cited (Comrie 1989) as an unusual case of a language with no relative clause construction. Instead, a secondary predication construction is used.

(45) Ngajulu- rlu rna yankirri pantu- rnu kuja lpa ngapa
    I-   ERG 1SG.SUBJ emu   spear- PST COMP PST water
    nga-   rnu.
    drink-   PST
    'I speared the emu that was drinking water.'/'I speared the emu while it was drinking water.'

That is to say, the relative clause is an anaphorically controlled sentential adjunct. The f-structure is as follows:

(46) $\begin{bmatrix} \widehat{GF} & ["I"] \\ PRED & \text{'spear} \langle (\uparrow \widehat{GF})(\uparrow OBJ) \rangle \text{'} \\ TENSE & PAST \\ OBJ & ["emu"] \\ ADJ & \left\{ \begin{bmatrix} \widehat{GF} & [PRED \text{ 'PRO'}] \\ PRED & \text{'drink} \langle (\uparrow \widehat{GF})(\uparrow OBJ) \rangle \text{'} \\ TENSE & PAST \\ OBJ & ["water"] \end{bmatrix} \right\} \end{bmatrix}$

In other words, Warlpiri has adopted an unusual strategy to avoid using a long-distance dependency here.

The analysis of questions in Warlpiri, on the other hand, is controversial. The discussion here is based on Legate (2001), which is where all the examples will be drawn from. In a monoclausal structure, a *wh* element generally occupies the discourse-prominent pre-aux position. Unlike the comparable cases in a language like English, no weak crossover effects obtain, suggesting that it is not a conventional long-distance dependency construction.

(47) a. Ngana- ngku kurdu nyanungu- nyangu paka- rnu   ?
       who-   ERG child 3-   POSS   hit- NPST
       'Who$_i$ hit his$_i$ child?'
    b. Ngana ka   nyanungu- nyangu maliki- rli wajili-pi- nyi ?
       who   PRES 3-   POSS   dog-   ERG chase-   NPST
       'Who$_i$ is his$_i$ dog chasing?'

Furthermore, a *wh* element cannot be extracted from a subordinate finite clause. Instead, it is placed in the pre-aux position in its own clause, and a scope marker appears in the main clause.

(48) Nyarrpa ngku   yimi-   ngarru- rnu Jakamarra- rlu [kuja
      how   2SG.OBJ speech- tell-   PST Jakamarra- ERG COMP
      Nyarrpara- kurra Jampijinpa ya- nu]   ?
      where-   ALL   Jampijinpa go- PST
      'Where did Jakamarra tell you Jampijinpa went?'

Up to this point, it appears that, while Warlpiri has some mechanism for locally licensing grammaticized discourse functions, it has no long-distance dependencies. However, a *wh* element apparently can be extracted from a non-finite clause.

(49) Nyiya- kurra   ka-   npa   wawirri   nya- nyi
      what-   OCONTR PRES-   2SG.SUBJ   kangaroo.ABS see- NPST
      [nga- rninja- kurra]   ?
      eat- INF-   OCONTR
      'What do you see a kangaroo eating?'

Legate cites Simpson as proposing that, since non-finite clauses are nominal, this is not a true long-distance dependency structure, but rather a case of Warlpiri's rather free scrambling; an element of the subordinate nominal clause is generated non-adjacent to the clause. Legate argues, however, that this must be a true long-distance dependency construction, both because movement out of an adjunct is disallowed (50a), and because weak crossover effects appear in these long-distance cases (50b).

(50) a. *Nyiya- rlarni   ka   kurdu- ngku jarntu
         what- OCONTR   PRES   child- ERG   dog.ABS
         warru-   wajili-pi- nyi   karnta- ku, [purra- nja- rlarni]   ?
         Around-   chase-   NPST woman- DAT cook-   INF- OCONTR
         'What is the child chasing the woman's dog around while she is cooking?'

      b. *Ngana- kurra   npa   nyanungu- nyangu maliki
         who-   OCONTR   2SG.SUBJ   3-   POSS   dog.ABS
         nya- ngu   [paji- rninja- kurra]   ?
         see- PST   bite- INF-   OCONTR
         'Who$_i$ did you see his$_i$ own dog chasing?' (OK without coreference: 'Who$_i$ did you see his$_j$ dog chasing?')

It is beyond the scope of the present study to determine whether questions involving non-finite complement clauses are scrambling structures or conventional long-distance dependency constructions licensed by functional uncertainty. Like the Choctaw/Chickasaw case, the construction has properties that suggest that a long-distance dependency analysis is wrong. For example, the presence of the Case and complementizer suffixes of the lower clause on the fronted *wh* element gives the construction an uncanny resemblance to Warlpiri scrambling. However, the comments made earlier concerning Choctaw/Chickasaw apply here as well. The construction does not pick out a single nominal as PIV,[14] and it is possible to analyze Warlpiri, like Imbabura Quechua, as a language which only has (non-pivot-sensitive) inside-out (bottom-up) licensing of long-distance dependencies.

Whatever the correct analysis of Warlpiri questions, the overall picture is clear. Warlpiri is a language which avoids pivot-sensitive constructions. It conforms to the pattern that we expect from pivotless languages. Warlpiri thus appears to be another example of a language that does not make use of the PIV function.

6.3.3.4 Speculation on morphological ergativity

Our analysis of Warlpiri as a pivotless language raises the possibility of coming to a new understanding of the phenomenon of morphological ergativity. Specifically, we would like to suggest that it may be fruitful to examine other morphologically ergative languages for evidence of pivotlessness, as a possible explanation of the existence of this Case-marking pattern.

In our discussion of Case marking and pivothood in Chapter 3, we observed that there appear to be two primary factors in determining the distribution of unmarked Case (nominative/absolutive): pivothood and position on the animacy/definiteness hierarchy. The role of pivothood is clear in nominative-accusative languages: the S/A PIV invariably bears the unmarked Case. In syntactically ergative languages as well, despite the frequent split-marking properties, the S/P PIV is at least usually unmarked. This is illustrated in the following charts, where the parenthesized material is the effect of the animacy/definiteness dimension.

(51)   a. Nominative–accusative pattern
         PIV = S: unmarked   A: unmarked
                              P: accusative (marked)
       b. Syntactically ergative pattern
                              A: marked (ergative)
         PIV = S: unmarked   P: unmarked

Even topic-pivot languages like Acehnese seem to prefer not to Case-mark PIVs.

---

14 Weak crossover effects do not provide evidence of pivot status under the standard LFG account (Bresnan 1995). Weak crossover is based on such properties as linear order and relative prominence of arguments on the relational and thematic hierarchies.

194 *Subjects and their properties*

However, morphologically ergative languages are a puzzle under the usual assumption that they are uniform-subject languages. Ignoring possible animacy/definiteness-based splits, the conventional view of morphologically ergative languages can be charted as:

(52) Uniform-subject analysis of morphologically ergative pattern
   PIV = S: unmarked   A: ergative
                       P: unmarked

Pivothood appears to be completely irrelevant to the use of unmarked Case in morphologically ergative languages. This contradicts the usual trend for PIVs to bear unmarked Case, and calls out for explanation. It also raises the question of why there are no "morphologically nominative-accusative" languages: mixed-subject (syntactically ergative) languages with a basic nominative-accusative Case-marking system.

(53) Putative morphologically nominative-accusative pattern
                       A: unmarked
   PIV = S: unmarked   P: accusative

We speculate that pivothood is irrelevant for morphologically ergative languages because they are pivotless. Under this approach, neither (52) nor (53) is a possible Case-marking pattern: morphologically ergative languages (which usually have some sort of split marking) are languages whose Case-marking patterns are based purely on animacy/definiteness.

At this stage, this is mere speculation. More research is needed to determine whether pivotlessness is widespread among morphologically ergative languages. We note in passing that the morphologically ergative language Hindi has been claimed to be pivotless by Bickel and Yādava (2000), but they mention a raising (functional control) construction, which is possible as long as the raised element would have been nominative (or ergative) in the subordinate clause.

(54) a. Unko$_i$ maĩne [∅$_i$ ḍar- ā   hu-   ā]   pā-   yā.
         3SG.ACC   I.ERG (NOM)   fear- PERF   AUX- PERF find- PST.MSG
      b. *Unko$_i$ maĩne [∅$_i$ ḍar lag- ā   hu-   ā
         3SG.ACC   I.ERG (DAT)   fear feel- PERF   AUX- PERF
         pā-   yā.
         find- PST.MSG
         'I found him to be afraid.'

Under our theory of pivothood, then, Hindi presumably is not a pivotless language, but rather a uniform-subject (S/A pivot) language. The fact that there is a Case-based restriction on functional control is beside the point. However, Hindi is not a typical morphologically ergative language, so the fact that Hindi has a PIV does not necessarily invalidate our speculative analysis.

6.4 Conclusion

Our conclusions are thus very different from those of studies like Dixon (1994) and Van Valin and LaPolla (1997). They conclude that grammatical relations are not universal, and that, even in a specific language, notions like pivot are relativized to individual constructions (which we have talked about earlier). Our approach, based on a concept of grammatical functions rather than grammatical relations, and on the concept of parallel representations of different dimensions of language, has led us in a different direction. Our essential conclusions are the following:

- Argument functions are used in every language.
- The core argument functions $\widehat{\text{GF}}$ and OBJ appear to be used in every language, but the mapping from thematic roles is not uniform cross-linguistically. In non-subject languages, the mapping creates a closer link between thematic roles and grammatical functions. As a result, the Patient argument of an intransitive (unaccusative) verb maps as OBJ rather than $\widehat{\text{GF}}$ in such languages. We therefore reject a potential universal requirement that all verbs have a $\widehat{\text{GF}}$ argument.
- A subset of the topic-prominent languages, which we call topic-pivot languages, assigns the PIV function on the basis of discourse function rather than argument function. This creates the illusion that they lack a PIV, since (from the more familiar argument-based perspective) PIV properties are not uniquely the properties of one element of the clause. However, PIV properties exist in these languages, and are associated with an element which has syntactically encoded discourse prominence.
- Pivotless languages exist. In true pivotless languages, no element ever has PIV properties. While PIV is universal in the sense that Universal Grammar makes it available, it is not used in every language.[15]

---

15 In terms of the phonology analogy raised at the beginning of this chapter, $\widehat{\text{GF}}$ is like the feature [labial] and PIV is like the feature [±distributed]. The feature [labial] is needed to formally characterize the labial sounds that every language has, irrespective of whether it is needed to state any phonological rules. Similarly, argument functions like $\widehat{\text{GF}}$ are needed to characterize the syntactic expression of arguments. On the other hand, the feature [±distributed] is made available by UG but not necessarily used in the grammar of every language, just like PIV.

The approach we take here to non-subject languages is more explanatory. A wide range of properties that a language has follows from the parametric choices that it makes on how to map arguments to the syntax, whether to use the PIV function, and whether to choose a PIV on the basis of syntactic expression of argumenthood or syntactically expressed discourse prominence. Our approach also opens interesting questions for further typological investigation concerning morphological ergativity.

7 Competing theories

7.1 Other approaches

The issues we have examined in this study have been discussed in a wide range of theoretical frameworks, with varying conclusions. In some respects, most of these analyses share a certain family resemblance to each other and to the proposals made here. This is not surprising; all typologically aware analyses of subjecthood work with the same phenomena. Given the properties of mixed-subject languages, the conclusion that subject needs to be factored into two distinct grammatical functions, as we have done here, seems inescapable.

Nevertheless, our analysis differs from the others, if not in its basic outline, in the implementation and the conceptualization of grammatical functions. We believe that, while other approaches may (or may not) describe subjecthood as well as the theory proposed here, none of them can explain subjecthood as well.

The advantages of our approach begin with the underlying assumptions we have made. The theory proposed here is based on a formal theory embodying a multidimensional architecture in which constituent structure, grammatical functions, and argument structure are distinct parallel levels of representation. This kind of theoretical architecture has allowed us to seriously consider questions of function within a formal syntactic system, rather than dealing only with formal structure or only with function. We have taken the functionality of elements within the formal syntactic system to be the crucial element in understanding the behavior of $\widehat{GF}$ and PIV.

We have also made a crucial distinction between notional constructions, what one wants to do with syntax, and formal constructions, how one does it. This distinction, which is made possible by the multidimensional approach, has turned out to be crucial. Originally drawn in Chapter 3 in the discussion of coordination chaining, it has turned out to be crucial in understanding the properties of long-distance dependencies and, especially, control constructions. This distinction has not been fully understood in previous work, and has led to what we believe are misunderstandings about the nature of syntactic constructions.

This chapter will explore some of the differences between the analysis proposed here and the other major analyses in the literature. Given the mass of work on subjecthood, we cannot review each alternative analysis individually. Instead, we will discuss the major families of analyses. We will discuss, in turn, typological, functionalist, and inverse and multistratal approaches. The bulk of the chapter will be a detailed look at the leading formal approach to syntax, the constituent structure–based approach, showing how our function-based approach is superior both at describing and explaining the facts. We will focus on the question of how our ĜF and PIV functions are analyzed in these alternatives. Throughout, we will use the terms "ĜF" and "PIV" in discussing other theories as a way to refer to the elements we have referred to by those names in the present study.

7.2 Typological approach

Much of the research into subjecthood on which the present study is based has been undertaken from a perspective that can best be described as typologically oriented. The typological literature has been invaluable in bringing to light important facts from less-known languages. However, despite the deep debt that the current study owes to typological studies, particularly Dixon (1994), there are crucial differences.

One difference between the typological approach and ours is in the treatment of the typology itself. Typical typological approaches begin by classifying languages along various dimensions. Within the context of subjecthood, the relevant dimension is Case marking: nominative-accusative vs. ergative. Since Case marking is only one indication of grammatical function, and a relatively poor one, the result is a poor foundation on which to base a theory of subjecthood. The Case-marking dimension is often described as a scale of ergativity, and languages are conceived of as adopting varying amounts of ergativity. As Comrie (1989: 114) puts it, "it is misleading to classify a language as being either ergative or not, rather one must ask: to what extent, and in what particular constructions is the language ergative, i.e. where does its syntax operate on an ergative-absolutive basis." Nominative-accusative languages are classified as being at the lowest end of the scale, morphologically ergative languages are somewhere in the lower half, and syntactically ergative languages are in the upper half. The pervasiveness of this approach is illustrated by the fact that in Plank (1979), a volume entitled *Ergativity*, most of the articles address the question of "how ergative" a language is.

In the present approach, there is no intrinsic significance to the notion ergative language. Our typological organization of languages is the following:

(1) Languages with PIV
        Argument-pivot languages
            Uniform-subject languages
            Mixed-subject (including "syntactically ergative" and
                "Philippine-type") languages
        Topic-pivot languages
Languages without PIV

This organization is based directly on the nature of pivot assignment in the language, instead of indirect measures, such as the type of Case marking. This has allowed us to explore the nature of pivothood more directly, including the discovery that the morphologically ergative language Warlpiri is pivotless.

In contrast to the usual typological approach, we do not recognize a notion of degrees of ergativity. This notion is the result of two confusions. First of all, it is the result of confusing pivot choice with Case marking. Case-marking patterns, while related in part to pivot choice, are not a direct indication of it. It is instructive that Dixon (1994: 16f.), in defining ergativity, distinguishes morphological and syntactic ergativity as if they were two distinct phenomena which happen to have been given the same name. That is precisely the position we are taking here. Morphologically ergative languages like Warlpiri and Hindi are not less ergative than Dyirbal – if anything, since Warlpiri uniformly uses ergative Case marking, one might want to say that it is more ergative – but they differ from Dyirbal (and from each other) in pivot choice. The other confusion behind the notion of degrees of ergativity is the failure to recognize the distinction between notional constructions and formal constructions. Yidin^y is not less ergative than Dyirbal because coreference in coordination is consistently along S/P lines in the latter but not the former; Yidin^y simply differs from Dyirbal in not making use of the PIV-based chaining construction for coordination. The concept of degrees of ergativity tends to obscure the true issues.

More generally, while the work done by typologists in sorting out types of languages is extremely valuable, the "types" tend to be assigned a theoretical significance they do not deserve. Labels like "ergative" are useful shorthand for some property or combination of properties, and should be used to the extent that they are found to be useful. However, languages are not exhaustively divided into a series of such types; if the nominative-accusative/ergative distinction is irrelevant for languages like Tagalog, like Acehnese, or like Choctaw-Chickasaw, there is no reason why one should feel obligated to make them relevant.

Arguments over whether Tagalog, for example, is nominative-accusative or ergative are pointless. What is important is to understand how a particular language deploys the grammatical tools made available to it by Universal Grammar. Typological study is invaluable for reaching an understanding of what these tools are, but the focus on *typ*ology is misplaced.

The view that we take of conventional typological views of ergativity is essentially that of Manning (1996). As he points out, the usual view leads to a situation where "Dyirbal has tended to stand alone as the one true syntactically ergative language" (1996: 10). Under Manning's approach, and ours, many languages which have been claimed to be ergative only in their morphology turn out to be mixed-subject ("syntactically ergative") languages.

Within the context of a discussion of typologically based approaches, we should mention that an interesting but highly problematic approach to argument grammatical functions is taken by Dixon (1994). He recognizes the existence of core argument functions as primitive syntactic elements, but instead of our ĜF and OBJ, he has three: S, A, and P.[1] Dixon's P corresponds roughly to our OBJ, but our ĜF is factored into S (the ĜF of an intransitive verb) and A (the ĜF of a transitive verb). As a descriptive device, this distinction is useful, and we have employed it in this study. However, Dixon ascribes to them a theoretical content which most researchers do not, and defines subject (ĜF) in terms of S and A. He justifies this on the basis of the existence of a semantic basis for A (i.e., it expresses Agent-like thematic roles) and the absence of such a basis for S (it can express any thematic role). Furthermore, since some languages (our uniform-subject languages) have an S/A pivot, while others (syntactically ergative languages) have an S/P pivot, Dixon considers S and A to be two distinct types of syntactic entities. He also mentions acquisition evidence that shows that children learning the Papuan language Kaluli generalize the ergative suffix, which goes on some As, to all As but never to Ss. None of Dixon's arguments are sufficient to establish S and A as distinct primitive grammatical argument functions. The lack of semantic uniformity in the case of ĜF of an intransitive verb is due to the hierarchy-alignment nature of argument mapping, as we saw in Chapter 2. Syntactically ergative languages use ĜF as the PIV in an intransitive clause because there is no OBJ. And it is plausible that children acquiring a language operate under the assumption that, since Case serves to distinguish arguments of a verb, Case marking is unnecessary on the sole argument of an intransitive. Against these arguments for

---

1 Dixon uses O instead of P. I prefer the P used in much of the typological literature because it is parallel to A: A evoking Agent and P evoking Patient.

splitting ĜF we offer a counterargument. S cannot be a primitive notion in syntax because it is based on (in)transitivity. Transitivity is a property of argument mapping: an intransitive verb maps one core argument and a transitive verb maps more than one. Transitivity is thus a description of the type of argument mapping. The grammatical argument functions are the result of argument mapping. (This appears to be the case in Dixon's system as well.) Transitivity is thus a more basic concept than Dixon's distinction between S and A. It is therefore unclear in what sense S could be a primitive, as Dixon claims. One also wonders why Dixon didn't make a similar distinction in the case of ditransitive verbs: why use P for both the non-A argument of (mono)transitives and one of the non-A arguments of ditransitives? There are differences in properties there, too.

7.3 Functionalism

The typological approach discussed in the previous section is often grounded in a functionalist[2] view of syntax. Functionalist linguistics is grounded in the idea that the properties of language are grounded in the communicative function of language, and is broadly in contrast with formalist linguistics, the leading idea of which is that the properties of language are a consequence of the formal properties of the linguistic system.

Semantics and pragmatics have an obvious role in a communicative perspective on language, and therefore play a major role in functionalist description. Syntax, on the other hand, as it does not have any direct relationship to communication and information, is appealed to much less, often being seen as something of a last resort when semantics and pragmatics fail to provide a solution.

The functionalist approach contrasts sharply with the approach we have taken here, which takes both the function and the formal expression to be part of linguistic description. The distinction we have drawn between notional constructions and formal constructions is, in a sense, a functionalist–formalist distinction: notional constructions are constructions in the functionalist sense, and formal constructions are constructions in the formalist sense. In our view, the subjecthood functions are part of the formal syntactic expression, so subject properties are primarily a consequence of the formal aspect.

A functionalist study that addresses much of the same material we have dealt with in the present study is Van Valin and LaPolla (1997), and our survey here will be based on Van Valin and LaPolla. In Chapter 6, we discussed claims

---

2 We use the term "functionalist" here rather than "functional" to avoid confusion with the (formal) notion of *grammatical function*.

made by functionalists that grammatical functions/relations are not universal. We will not repeat the discussion here, but the central point bears reiterating in the present context. The view expressed by Van Valin and LaPolla that grammatical relations represent restricted neutralizations of semantic or pragmatic relations, and that in the absence of such a restricted neutralization there are no grammatical relations, is diametrically opposed to the view of grammatical functions that we are adopting in this study.

Consider the status of ĜF in functionalist studies. Van Valin and LaPolla discuss the classification of arguments primarily from a semantic/thematic perspective. After discussing thematic roles, they introduce the "macroroles" Actor and Undergoer, which group together different thematic roles. While they claim that these macroroles are based on semantics, they are in fact defined by syntactic properties: the macrorole Actor includes those arguments which are mapped to the syntax as ĜF, while the macrorole Undergoer includes those which can map as either ĜF or OBJ.[3] This is made clear when they refer to the fact that languages can differ in which thematic roles are subsumed under the macroroles; the evidence for this is in the nature of the argument mapping. Even more crucially, in Van Valin and LaPolla's analysis of the Raising-to-Object construction (1997: 574), the raised object, which is not a thematic argument of the matrix verb, is said to have a macrorole in the main clause. In our terms, Van Valin and LaPolla's macroroles are core arguments – but core argumenthood is syntactic, not semantic.

Van Valin and LaPolla do not have a direct analog to ĜF in their system, as argument linking is directly to PIV. However, Dixon (1994) does; our ĜF corresponds to what he calls the subject. However, following the general tendency in functionalist work, Dixon treats ĜF primarily in semantic (thematic) terms, and he explains ĜF properties on semantic grounds. We have attempted to show here that, while semantic considerations have a role to play in understanding such properties as being the addressee of imperatives and being the controllee in control constructions, they cannot be the full explanation.

Perhaps the most glaring difference between our approach to subjecthood and that of the functionalist literature is in the treatment of pivots: specifically the recurrent claim in the functionalist literature that a language may have different pivots for different constructions. We have discussed examples of this in previous chapters, and concluded that the appearance of different pivots for

---

3 From the perspective of LFG, the macroroles Actor and Undergoer correspond to the a-structure classifications [−o] (when it is also θ̂) and [−r] respectively. Thus, while Van Valin and LaPolla are correct in stating that they are not grammatical functions, it does not follow that they must be semantic rather than syntactic in nature.

different constructions is the result of the use of different syntactic constructions, some of which are pivot-sensitive and others of which are not. For example, as we have seen, a (notional) control construction can be realized syntactically by argument sharing (functional control) licensed outside-in, by argument sharing licensed inside-out, and by the use of null anaphora (anaphoric control): the first of these is PIV-sensitive and the last is generally limited to $\widehat{GF}$. We simply note here that the claim that different constructions can have different pivots empties the concept PIVOT of all significance: it is not clear how it is revealing to say that different constructions refer to different grammatical functions. The question is to explain how this happens, and what the possible choices are. An explanatory theory has to account for the fact, for example, that constructions like reflexivization and imperatives can be sensitive to $\widehat{GF}$ status but not PIV status (and thus will not target S/P in any language). Van Valin and LaPolla's theory cannot do this; ours can.

7.4 Inverse mapping and multistratal subjects

In Chapter 2, we contrasted the theory of subjecthood developed here with the inverse mapping theory (Marantz 1984, Kroeger 1993, Manning 1996, Wechsler and Arka 1998). We will expand on this contrast in this section.

To review from our discussion in Chapter 2, the basic idea of inverse mapping is that there is a parametric difference in argument mapping between different types of languages. In nominative-accusative languages the argumenthood hierarchy is preserved in the mapping to syntactically realized grammatical functions,[4] while in ergative languages the hierarchy is reversed, at least for the two most prominent arguments. Thus, while in a canonical transitive in a nominative-accusative language the Agent is realized as SUBJ and the Patient as OBJ, in an ergative language the Patient is SUBJ and the Agent OBJ. Adapting the notation slightly from Manning (1996), the argument structure and functional structure of a sentence like (2a) in a syntactically ergative language would look like (2b) and (2c) respectively.

---

4 In Marantz's version of the Inverse Mapping approach, this is pushed back one level. He has argument structure (which he calls logico-semantic structure) mapped inversely from thematic roles, so the argumenthood hierarchy and the hierarchy of grammatical functions match, with P outranking A at both levels. As pointed out by Manning and others, this makes it difficult to account for phenomena, such as binding theory properties, in which syntactically ergative languages have the same properties as nominative-accusative languages. In this section, we will consider only those versions of the Inverse Mapping approach which place the inversion at the argument structure-grammatical function mapping.

(2) a. The baby saw the toy.

b.
$$\underset{a\text{-}structure}{\left[\begin{array}{ll} \text{see} & \\ \text{SUBJ} & [\text{"the baby"}] \\ \text{ARG} & [\text{"the toy"}] \end{array}\right]}$$

c.
$$\underset{f\text{-}structure}{\left[\begin{array}{ll} \text{PRED} & \text{"see"} \\ \text{SUBJ} & [\text{"the toy"}] \\ \text{OBJ} & [\text{"the baby"}] \end{array}\right]}$$

At a-structure, as in nominative-accusative languages, the A argument is SUBJ (Manning's actual notation is A-SB, for *a-structure subject*) and the P is a lesser argument (Manning is non-committal as to the existence of the function OBJ at a-structure). At f-structure, on the other hand, it is the P which is SUBJ, and the A is OBJ.[5] Philippine-type languages have both types of mapping: the Agentive voice is a nominative-accusative construction and the Direct Object voice is an ergative construction. This is made most explicit in the HPSG analysis of Wechsler and Arka (1998), discussed in Chapter 2.

In a system like this, those subject properties which are shared by uniform-subject languages and mixed-subject languages are identified as a-structure properties, and those which differ are f-structure properties. To put it slightly differently, our ĜF is identified as a-structure SUBJ, and our PIV as f-structure SUBJ. In fact, Manning uses the grammatical function name PIVOT for the f-structure SUBJ (see Manning 1996: 48). However, other studies that adopt Inverse Mapping use SUBJ for f-structure subject, and we will do the same here to distinguish Manning's concept of pivot from ours.

To put it slightly differently, the Inverse Mapping theory claims that there are subjects at two different syntactic levels: a-structure SUBJ and f-structure SUBJ, the former corresponding to our ĜF and the latter to our PIV. This approach overlaps with what we can call the Multistratal Subject approach, an approach most clearly exemplified by Bell's (1983) analysis of the Philippine-type language Cebuano. Bell's analysis is framed within the framework of Relational Grammar, a multistratal theory, and characterizes ĜF as an initial 1 (RG terminology for subject) and PIV as a final 1, where 1 is characterized as an argument relation.

Characterizing ĜF and PIV as kinds, or strata, of subject, is thus a central part of the Inverse Mapping and Multistratal Subject approaches. Calling

---

5 Manning's notations for grammatical functions in f-structure are a little different; we will return to this below.

them different types of SUBJ implies that they are essentially the same type of entity, with similar properties. Since subject is taken by these approaches to be an argument function/relation, this view of PIV contrasts sharply with our theory. In the theory developed here, PIV is an overlay function, an extra grammatical function held by an element which is locally licensed. It is not an argument function. We claim that the identification of the pivot function as an argument function represents an important drawback of Inverse Mapping/Multistratal Subject. We have argued here (particularly in Chapter 3) that the properties of PIV are not argumenthood properties, and are disjoint from the properties of ĜF. Even the property of being a controllee, which appears to be a shared ĜF/PIV property, is revealed not to truly be a shared property. However, a multistratal approach would lead us to expect that there is no difference in principle between ĜF properties and PIV properties. This is especially true in the Relational Grammar version of the Multistratal Subject approach, under which there is no difference between grammatical relations at the initial stratum and grammatical relations at the final stratum. There is no reason to expect anaphora to be defined in terms of the initial stratum and Raising in terms of the final stratum, for example.

In Manning's implementation, the situation is a little better, but not much. In laying out his approach, Manning states that ĜF properties are "semantic" in nature, where by "semantic" he means that they have some basis in thematic roles. As we saw in Chapter 2, the characterization of these constructions as semantic is incomplete; however, we can reinterpret Manning's view as being that the constructions are related to notions of argumenthood. That this is a valid reading of Manning is shown by the fact that he uses the level of argument structure as the locus of these properties. So the properties of ĜF are predicted by Manning to be argument-related. But since the f-structure SUBJ (PIV) is also an argument function in Manning's approach, pivot properties should also be argumenthood-related. Aside from a semantic/thematic aspect to ĜF, there should be no basic difference between the properties of ĜF and PIV. The fact that they are totally disjoint sets of properties is a problem. At the outset, we argued that a theory of grammatical functions should explain the properties of syntactic elements; as we have shown, the properties of PIV are not argumenthood properties. The Inverse Mapping/Multistratal Subject theory can stipulate that, for example, in certain languages only "surface/grammatical" subjects can extract, but it cannot explain this. Our theory explains this and other properties.

The analysis of pivot selection as part of argument mapping is also typologically untenable. It is, of course, unproblematic in uniform-subject languages.

As we discussed in Chapter 2, it is problematic but feasible in mixed-subject languages (for an explicit account of argument mapping under an Inverse Mapping theory, see Arka [1998] on the Philippine-type language Balinese). However, as we saw in Chapter 6, these two language types, although the most commonly discussed, do not exhaust the possibilities. In a topic-pivot language like Acehnese or Mandarin, pivothood is transparently unrelated to argument mapping. Pivotless languages like Choctaw/Chickasaw and Warlpiri are even more problematic. The illusion that pivothood is a type of argumenthood is a result of considering only argument-pivot languages.

To this line of criticism we can add points we have made earlier in this study. In Chapter 2, we criticized this approach on the grounds that it is inadequate as a theory of argument mapping. In the first place, it is implausible, as the universal trend appears to be to maintain hierarchies across dimensions of language. There are clear reasons why language would work this way, and the alignment of hierarchies is a recognized concept in Optimality Theory. As a design feature, it appears unlikely that Universal Grammar would allow Inverse Mapping as the basic mapping principle in a language.[6] Secondly, this approach conflates our $\widehat{GF}$ and $\hat{\theta}$. To the extent that they can be shown to differ (as in our discussion of anaphora in Chapter 2), a theory which conflates them is empirically inadequate.

There are grammatical phenomena that are more straightforward to describe using the pivot theory proposed here than under the inverse mapping theory. One example is the nature of the controlled clause in Balinese, discussed in Chapter 5. As we saw there, the Inverse Mapping theory requires one to allow functional control of clauses with the grammatical function SUBJ in languages

---

6 Chris Manning (personal communication) has objected to this objection on the grounds that identifying PIV with OBJ, as I claim syntactically ergative languages do, also involves a mismatch of prominence across different linguistic dimensions. While Manning's point does have some validity, and this may explain the rarity of languages in which PIV is not automatically associated with $\widehat{GF}$, there is a fundamental conceptual difference between inverse mapping and our theory of pivots. Mapping involves representing essentially the same relations at different dimensions of linguistic structure. An argument is the most prominent argument ultimately because of its position in conceptual structure. The most sensible system of mapping, and what I claim is the only available one, will maintain this prominence through to the syntax. Being a PIV, does not involve mapping from one level to another – it simply assigns a second function to an element which is already part of the f-structure. Manning also observes, quite correctly, that despite the apparent negative reading that his theory gets here, there are some fundamental issues on which we are in complete agreement. Foremost among these is that he and I both reject an analysis of syntactically ergative languages in which all sentences are intransitive, with the ergative argument being similar to a passive *by* phrase.

like Balinese. This is a problem for many theories of control, motivated on the basis of the properties of control constructions in many languages. (LFG-internally, functionally controlled clauses bear the function XCOMP.) Under the theory of pivots proposed here, however, there is no need for any theory to recognize a special kind of subject control which behaves like complement control. Another example comes from a consideration of certain phenomena in Indonesian which have been discussed using the Inverse Mapping theory by Arka and Manning (1998). Much of their analysis can be translated in a straightforward manner into the theory proposed here. However, certain aspects of their analysis are problematic under their assumptions and simple under ours. In particular, consider the structural realization of arguments. Arka and Manning identify the following as Philippine-type Agent voice and Direct Object voice:

(3) a. Amir mem- baca buku itu.
    Amir AGT- read book that
    'Amir read the book.'

 b. Buku itu dia baca.
    book that he/she read.DO
    '(s)he read that book.'

Under the analysis we have proposed, the f-structures of these two sentences are as follows:

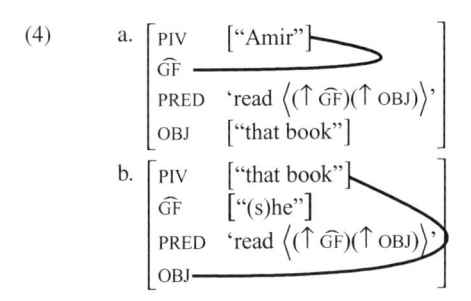

(4) a. $\begin{bmatrix} \text{PIV} & [\text{"Amir"}] \\ \widehat{\text{GF}} & \\ \text{PRED} & \text{'read} \langle (\uparrow \widehat{\text{GF}})(\uparrow \text{OBJ}) \rangle\text{'} \\ \text{OBJ} & [\text{"that book"}] \end{bmatrix}$

 b. $\begin{bmatrix} \text{PIV} & [\text{"that book"}] \\ \widehat{\text{GF}} & [\text{"(s)he"}] \\ \text{PRED} & \text{'read} \langle (\uparrow \widehat{\text{GF}})(\uparrow \text{OBJ}) \rangle\text{'} \\ \text{OBJ} & \end{bmatrix}$

We can state the word order facts simply: the PIV in Indonesian appears clause-initially, in [SPEC, IP]. Within the VP, the verb is followed by non-PIV arguments other than the (non-PIV) $\widehat{\text{GF}}$ (Agent). The $\widehat{\text{GF}}$ appears initially in the VP, either as a pronoun or a clitic on the verb. Under the Inverse Mapping theory, non-PIV Agents and non-PIV Patients both bear the function OBJ, even though they have completely disjoint distributional properties. The f-structures under the inverse mapping theory are the following:

(5) a. $\begin{bmatrix} \text{SUBJ} & [\text{``Amir''}] \\ \text{PRED} & \text{`read} \langle(\uparrow \text{SUBJ})(\uparrow \text{OBJ})\rangle\text{'} \\ \text{OB} & [\text{``that book''}] \end{bmatrix}$

b. $\begin{bmatrix} \text{SUBJ} & [\text{``that book''}] \\ \text{PRED} & \text{`read} \langle(\uparrow \text{OBJ})(\uparrow \text{SUBJ})\rangle\text{'} \\ \text{OBJ} & [\text{``(s)he''}] \end{bmatrix}$

The phrase structure rules therefore need to refer to thematic roles. As Arka and Manning (1998: 14) state:

> All the verbal clitic positions, including the preceding full pronouns, must be immediately adjacent to the verb and are reserved for words with pronominal meaning that express the OBJECT/Term-complement of the clause. These are used when the verb remains transitive.... *[T]he preverbal positions are positions for agent term complements only.* When these positions are occupied, the clause is in the objective voice. [italics added]

Under the account proposed here, only Patients are OBJ; Agents are $\widehat{\text{GF}}$. Our account of Indonesian word order is more straightforward.

Our theory of pivots is thus preferable to the Inverse Mapping/Multistratal Subject theory. It has stronger conceptual grounding, is more explanatory, provides more adequate descriptions of linguistic facts, is typologically superior, and is more consistent with theoretical assumptions in LFG.

7.5 Constituent structure approaches

The leading approach to grammatical functions (and syntax in general) in generative theory has been a constituent-structure-based (henceforth structural) approach. We will discuss what appear to be the primary trends in this kind of theory, and show that the grammatical-function-based approach that we have developed here is preferable and more explanatory. This is important particularly because proponents of the structural approach often claim a higher degree of explanatoriness. We have already addressed this in a preliminary way in Chapter 1; here we will look at specific analyses.

In an insightful survey of the history of approaches to subjecthood in the structural tradition, McCloskey (1997) describes it as a progressive "deconstruction" of the notion of subject. In this, it does not differ from what we have done here, nor from what has been done in other approaches. The theory developed here "deconstructs" SUBJ into the two distinct, inherently unrelated functions $\widehat{\text{GF}}$ and PIV (and, if we want to extend this, the traditional notion "logical subject" corresponds to our $\hat{\theta}$). Of course, unlike our grammatical-function-based approach, the structural tradition identifies the functions with structural positions which are derivationally related to each other.

At the very least, subjects are associated in structural analysis with two positions: one internal to the VP (either [SPEC, VP] or adjoined to VP) and one in the specifier position of a higher functional projection (which we will refer to as [SPEC, IP]). As McCloskey points out, in a version of the structural approach which factors IP into multiple functional phrases, there may be more such positions (McCloskey appears to favor two: a higher [SPEC, AGR$_S$P] and a lower [SPEC, TP]), but for our purposes we will limit our attention to one [SPEC, IP] position. Our $\widehat{\text{GF}}$ corresponds to the VP-internal position in such a theory, and our PIV to [SPEC, IP]. Baker (1997: 82–83) gives a very clear overview of how such a system is supposed to work:

> For reasons that are quite independent of ergativity, it has become standard to assume that the agent argument of a transitive verb in English is a subject in (at least) two ways: it is base-generated as the specifier of a VP projection where it is directly theta-marked; it then raises to the specifier of an Inflectional head to receive (or check) its nominative Case. Thus, the agent is both the subject of VP and the subject of IP. However, these two distinct senses of subject may diverge, resulting in a "deep ergative" language. Thus, suppose that the basic projection of arguments is the same [as English] in languages like Dyirbal or Inuit, but the verbs in these languages cannot license accusative Case on the underlying object. Then, it is the patient argument of the verb, not the agent, that must move to the specifier position of IP to receive/check nominative Case and trigger agreement on I . . . . The agent NP, on the other hand, remains in the specifier of VP and receives ergative Case by some other means (researchers vary on the exact mechanisms here). Simple versions of the two basic clause structures are compared [below], where I leave open the possibility that there are additional functional categories and/or a more complex VP-internal structure.

Baker's sample structures, adapted slightly, are the following.

(6) a. **English**

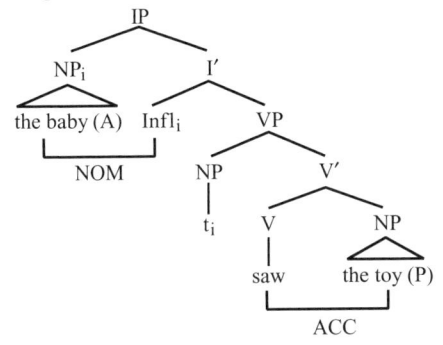

```
                IP
              /    \
           NP_i     I'
          /   \    /  \
   the baby (A) Infl_i  VP
       |_____|     /  \
          NOM         NP   V'
                      |   /  \
                      t_i V    NP
                          |   /  \
                         saw the toy (P)
                          |_____|
                             ACC
```

b. **Dyirbal/Inuit**

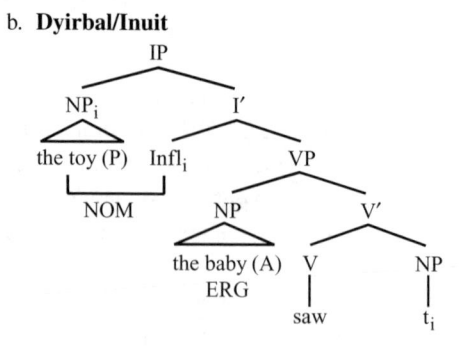

```
              IP
         ┌────┴────┐
        NPᵢ         I'
       ╱  ╲    ┌────┴────┐
  the toy (P) Inflᵢ      VP
       └──NOM──┘     ┌────┴────┐
                    NP         V'
                   ╱  ╲    ┌───┴───┐
              the baby(A) V       NP
                   ERG    │        │
                         saw       tᵢ
```

As Baker makes clear, the key technical mechanism for licensing movement to [SPEC, IP] is Case theory. In uniform-subject languages, the A argument in [SPEC, VP] (or adjoined to VP) undergoes this movement, whereas in mixed-subject languages it is some other element. The notion of Case here is what is known in the structural tradition as abstract Case, not necessarily related to morphological Case.

We will examine this approach by taking a closer look at GB (single IP, government-based Case marking) and MP (exploded IP, SPEC–head Case checking) implementations. We will first outline the technical aspects of each of these versions, and then take a look at an overview at the explanatoriness of this type of account.

Based on data from Malagasy, Tagalog, Cebuano, and Malay/Indonesian, Guilfoyle et al. (1992) (henceforth GHT) argue for a version of the [SPEC, IP]/ [SPEC, VP] analysis. As noted above, in such an analysis [SPEC, IP] is the structural equivalent of the function PIV, while [SPEC, VP] is ĜF. Inexplicably, GHT refer to both positions as subject positions and explicitly refer to the [SPEC, IP] (i.e., PIV) as an argument position.

GHT assume a basic GB-style theory of clause structure (with a single functional category Infl) and a government-based approach to Case marking. Within the framework that they assume, a nominal becomes PIV (moves to [SPEC, IP]) by virtue of not being assigned Case. They work out the analysis in detail for Malagasy, where the prefix *an-* appears on A-pivot (AGT) verbs, the suffix *-na* on P-pivot (DO) verbs, and both appear on the verb if the pivot is something else specified in the lexical entry of the verb.

(7)   (Guilfoyle et al. [4] and [6])
    a. M-   an-   sasa (manasa)   ny lamba amin' ny savony
       TNS- AGT- wash   the clothes with the soap
       ny   zazavavy.
       the   girl

b. Sasa- na (sasan') ny zazavavy amin' ny savony ny lamba.
   wash- DO   the girl   with the soap the clothes

c. An- sasa- na (anasan') ny zazavavy ny lamba ny savony.
   ACT- wash- DO   the girl   the clothes the soap
   'The girl washes the clothes with soap.'

The analysis is that the prefix is part of the verb and assigns Case to the P, while the suffix is part of INFL and assigns Case to the A in [SPEC, VP]. Unlike in standard versions of GB, the verb itself does not assign Case. The argument that is not assigned Case moves to [SPEC, IP], where it can be marked nominative through SPEC–head agreement. The attractiveness of this proposal comes from the combination of prefix and suffix: in such a case, both Agent and Patient are assigned Case and something else must move instead. An alternative analysis must treat the circumfix *an-*... *-na* as a third morphological element, unrelated to the Agentive-voice prefix and DO-voice suffix. Furthermore, constituent order facts in Malagasy support this analysis: the trace of the verb (which moves to INFL) intervenes between the Agent and the Patient, so the Patient is in a position adjacent to the verb if it is Case marked. Schematic structures, adapted from GHT, are as follows (these structures do not show V-to-I movement):

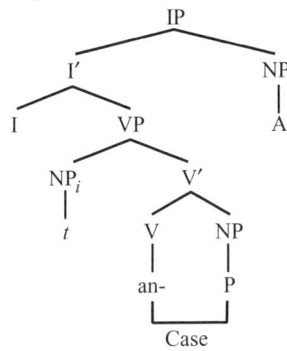

(8)   a. A-pivot

```
                    IP
                 /      \
               I'        NP_i
              /  \        |
             I    VP       A
                 /  \
              NP_i   V'
               |    /  \
               t   V    NP
                   |    |
                  an-   P
                   └────┘
                    Case
```

b. P-pivot

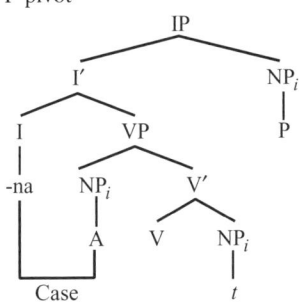

```
                    IP
                 /      \
               I'        NP_i
              /  \        |
             I    VP       P
             |   /  \
            -na NP_i  V'
                 |   /  \
                 A  V    NP_i
                 └──┘    |
                         t
                Case
```

c. Other pivot

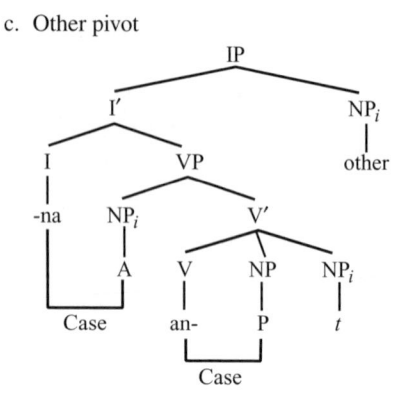

```
           IP
          /  \
         I'   NP_i
        / \    |
       I   VP  other
       |   / \
      -na NP_i V'
           |  / \
           A V   NP  NP_i
           | |   |   |
          Case an-  P   t
               └──┬──┘
                Case
```

Attractive as it is at first glance, this account faces some problems. Some of these problems are apparent in the analysis of Malagasy. In the first place, it requires an approach under which transitive verbs do not have the inherent ability to assign Case. This contradicts most approaches to Case in the GB tradition. Second, the fact that both Agent and Patient are assigned Case if the circumfix appears on the verb is not enough to explain the movement of another argument to [SPEC, IP]. As GHT observe (1992: 382 fn. 7), the preposition must be assumed to incorporate into the verb as well. If it did not, it would surface and assign Case to the nominal. This incorporation must be stipulated, and, though GHT claim that it is similar to an applicative construction, in the Malagasy case there is no morphological indication of the alleged incorporation.

Further problems emerge when the analysis is extended to other Austronesian languages. Unlike Malagasy, languages like Tagalog do not combine the AGT voice affix and the DO voice affix if an oblique argument becomes the pivot. This may indicate that, messy though it may be for Malagasy, the correct treatment of oblique-pivot affixes is simply as separate affixes. The word order facts are also less cooperative in other languages, as GHT point out and discuss in detail for Tagalog by Kroeger (1993). Finally, it is unclear how the GHT analysis would extend to syntactically ergative languages.

Bittner and Hale (1996a, 1996b) propose a theory of Case that shares some of the features of GHT's analysis: there is a VP-internal subject position (adjoined to VP in their implementation) corresponding to our ĜF and [SPEC, IP] corresponding to PIV. Their theory of Case is rather involved, and we will not discuss it here. As in GHT's account, inability to be assigned Case causes a DP to move to [SPEC, IP]. Under normal circumstances (and contrary to the standard GB Case theory), the A can be assigned Case[7] but the P cannot, so it moves

---

[7] This is a simplification of Bittner and Hale's theory, since the movement or government transparency about to be mentioned are necessary to allow I to assign Case to the A. For details, see Bittner and Hale (1996a, 1996b).

to [SPEC, IP] resulting in a syntactically ergative structure, or is allowed to remain in situ through some mechanism rendering the VP and IP transparent to government,[8] resulting in a morphologically ergative structure. (For Bittner and Hale, morphologically ergative languages never raise an argument to [SPEC, IP], and are thus pivotless.) To allow Case to be assigned to P, a D (sometimes realized overtly as object agreement) must be adjoined to the verb to create a Case competitor. It is then the A that is left without Case. The A either raises to [SPEC, IP] or gets governed in situ by C through government transparency. In an intransitive clause, since there is no competition for Case,[9] the S cannot be assigned Case, so it behaves like the Caseless A of nominative-accusative languages and P of ergative languages. As for Philippine-type languages, Bittner and Hale adapt GHT's analysis. For Bittner and Hale, the AGT voice affix (*an-* in Malagasy) is a D adjoined to V, resulting in a nominative-accusative construction where the P can be assigned Case but the A cannot and must move to [SPEC, IP]. This is similar to GHT's analysis. The DO voice affix (Malagasy *-na*) is not discussed; Bittner and Hale gloss it as INFL but do not explain why it is absent in AGT voice sentences.

The GB-style Case-theoretic analyses have a strange quality to them. We will focus on the more straightforward GHT account. Removing the technicalities of both our theoretical assumptions and GHT's, the two approaches to Philippine-type languages can be compared in the following way. In both ours and theirs, the essence of Philippine-type languages is in the voice affix. This works as follows.

(9)   a. Analysis proposed in this book
        AGT affix: "pivot is A"
        DO affix: "pivot is P"
        INSTR affix: "pivot is instrumental"
      b. GHT analysis
        AGT affix: "pivot is not P"
        DO affix: "pivot is not A"
        INSTR affix: "pivot is neither A nor P"

The GB Case-theoretic analysis is based not on identifying what the pivot is, but rather what it is not. Pivothood is something of an accident under such an

---

8 Either verb movement or coindexation of C, I, and V.
9 Bittner and Hale's (1996a, 1996b) notion of Case assignment being the result of competition between two nominals is interesting, and it is a shame that it has not been taken up in subsequent structural theories of Case assignment. It is a formal expression of the functionalist concept that Case exists to distinguish arguments: one argument is unmarked, and the others bear some sort of marking of their grammatical function (or thematic role). The problem with Bittner and Hale's approach is its complexity: in an era when structural-transformational theory aspires to minimalism in its formal devices, Bittner and Hale's theory has something of a "maximalist" feel to it.

account, a booby prize for the loser of the musical chairs of Case assignment. The basic theoretical machinery of Case marking itself needs to be rewritten to create a system which will achieve the correct results. Aside from the technical problems cited above and explanatory problems to be discussed below, this is a conceptual weakness of this type of account of subjecthood.

Murasugi (1992) proposes a theory of ergativity within the framework of early MP. Murasugi hypothesizes a clausal architecture in which Infl is decomposed into two functional categories: Tense and Transitivity. Case is checked in the specifier positions of these functional categories when they have a positive value for the feature they host: the unmarked Case (nominative/absolutive) in [SPEC, TP] when T is [+tense] and the marked Case (accusative/ergative) in [SPEC, TrP] when Tr is [+trans]. In an intransitive clause, the S moves to [SPEC, TP] to check its Case (since Tr is [−trans], it cannot check Case). For this reason, S has the unmarked Case in all types of languages. On the other hand, there are two possibilities for NP movement in transitive clauses: either A moves to the higher position [SPEC, TP] and P to the lower [SPEC, TrP], or P moves to the higher position [SPEC, TP] and A to the lower [SPEC, TrP]. The former is the pattern in nominative-accusative languages, and the latter in ergative languages. The reason for the different NP-movement properties is taken to be feature strength: one of the functional categories has strong Case features, requiring overt movement, and for reasons of Economy the closest NP (the A) has to move there. The P moves to the other specifier position at LF. Schematically:

(10) Nominative-accusative languages
    a. D-structure

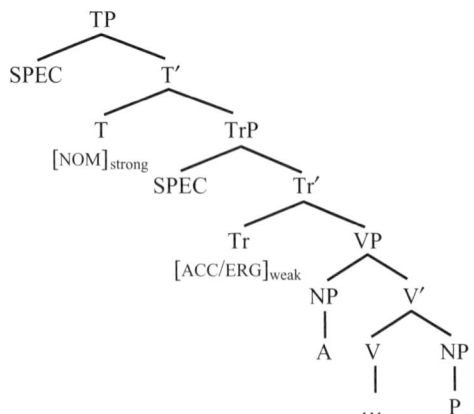

```
            TP
           /  \
        SPEC   T'
              /  \
             T    TrP
      [NOM]strong / \
                SPEC  Tr'
                     /  \
                    Tr   VP
            [ACC/ERG]weak / \
                         NP  V'
                         |  / \
                         A V   NP
                           |   |
                          ...  P
```

b. S-structure

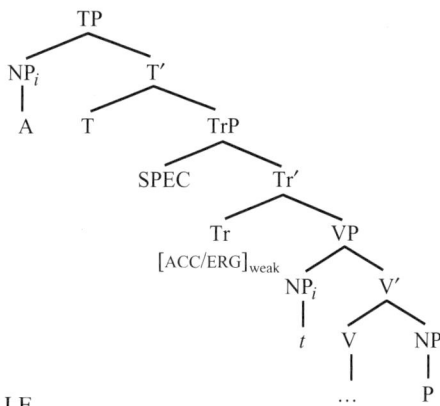

```
            TP
           /  \
        NPᵢ    T'
         |    /  \
         A   T    TrP
                 /   \
              SPEC    Tr'
                     /  \
                    Tr   VP
              [ACC/ERG]_weak
                        /  \
                      NPᵢ   V'
                       |   /  \
                       t  V    NP
                          |    |
                          ...  P
```

c. LF

```
            TP
           /  \
        NPᵢ    T'
         |    /  \
         A   T    TrP
                 /   \
              NPⱼ    Tr'
               |    /  \
               P   Tr   VP
                        /  \
                      NPᵢ   V'
                       |   /  \
                       t  V    NPⱼ
                          |    |
                          ...  t
```

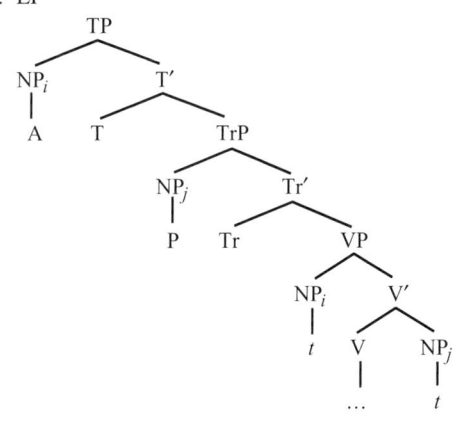

(11)   Ergative languages
       a. D-structure

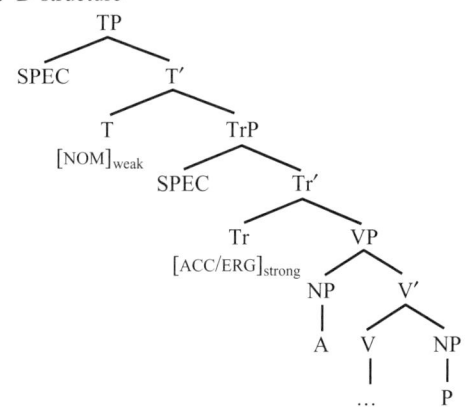

```
              TP
             /  \
          SPEC   T'
                /  \
               T    TrP
          [NOM]_weak
                    /   \
                 SPEC    Tr'
                        /  \
                       Tr   VP
                 [ACC/ERG]_strong
                            /  \
                          NP    V'
                           |   /  \
                           A  V    NP
                              |    |
                              ...  P
```

b. S-structure

```
         TP
        /  \
     SPEC   T'
           /  \
          T    TrP
       [NOM]weak  / \
                NPᵢ  Tr'
                 |   / \
                 A  Tr  VP
                       / \
                     NPᵢ  V'
                      |  / \
                      t V   NP
                        |   |
                       ...  P
```

c. LF

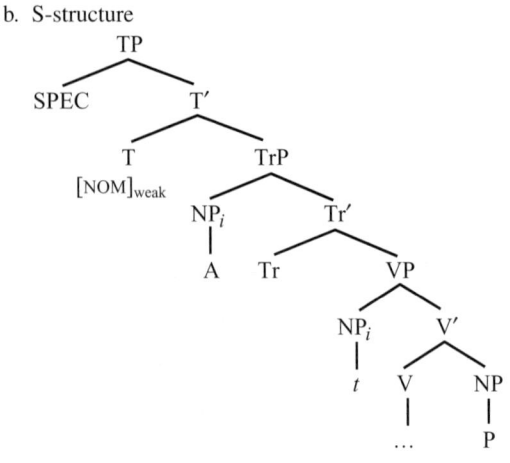

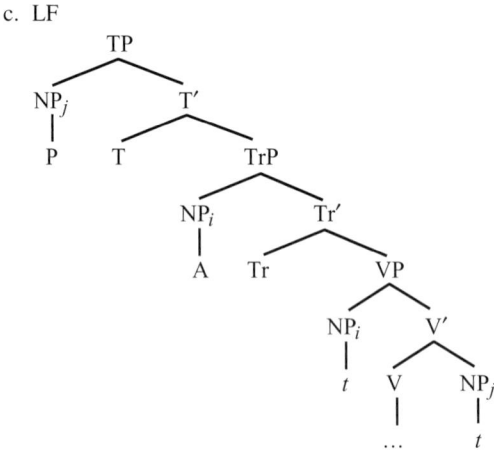

```
            TP
           /  \
         NPⱼ   T'
          |   / \
          P  T   TrP
                / \
              NPᵢ  Tr'
               |   / \
               A  Tr  VP
                     / \
                   NPᵢ  V'
                    |  / \
                    t V   NPⱼ
                      |   |
                     ...  t
```

Thus, the [SPEC,VP] position is the representation of ĜF and the [SPEC, TP] position (corresponding to [SPEC, IP] in Baker's trees) is PIV.

In Murasugi's (1992) account, the difference between uniform-subject languages and mixed-subject languages is a technical question of feature strength in the functional layer of clausal structure. The resultant PIV, with its array of properties, is a by-product of the requirements of feature-checking. In this respect it is (unsurprisingly) similar to the GB accounts: pivothood is an accident; the grammar specifies what is not a pivot.

The only mixed-subject language type that Murasugi discusses explicitly is ergative. It is unclear how she would account for Philippine-type languages; plausibly, the choice of strong feature would be variable and linked to the voice morphology, but it is unclear what sort of feature configuration would be responsible for voices other than Agent or Direct Object. Even more mysterious is how Murasugi would account for active languages and pivotless languages.

The critical question is how well structural theories explain the properties of ĜF and PIV. The answer is, not very well. Part of the problem has been discussed in earlier chapters: the theory requires all languages to have the highly configurational constituent structures typical of languages like English, and the structural constraints which are supposed to explain the properties of ĜF and PIV are themselves arbitrary. The proposal here avoids both of these pitfalls: the crucial level for our theory is functional structure, not constituent structure; and the nature of the grammatical functions is independently based on their functionality, and then used to explain the properties of ĜF and PIV, including the constituent structure properties of PIV in configurational languages. However, even within the assumptions of the structural theory, the prediction of properties is not particularly successful.

Consider, for example, the extraction properties of PIV. Both GB-type analyses that we have reviewed suggest that the prominent structural position is somehow involved. GHT (1992) suggest that some sort of locality may be involved, and Bittner and Hale (1996a, 1996b) argue that, since [SPEC, IP] is an Ā position, its prominence should manifest itself mostly in Ā dependencies. However, neither GHT nor Bittner and Hale propose a mechanism for achieving this, so it is not clear that they have explained anything.

Murasugi (1992) focuses on relative clauses (taking the position that other long-distance dependency constructions that appear to be limited to PIV are types of relative clauses), and argues that in a [−tense] clause relativization should be restricted to the nominative argument (PIV) because it can't check its Case in [SPEC, TP], so it has to move to [SPEC, CP]. However, in finite clauses anything should be able to relativize, because everything can check its Case clause-internally, so movement to [SPEC, CP] is just ordinary Ā movement, not Case-motivated movement. She then discusses the fact that in some Mayan languages, such as Jakaltek, finite ([+tense]) relatives seem to be limited to relativizing the PIV (S/P), with antipassive (A→S) being used to relativize A arguments. While this appears to be a counterexample, she suggests that this may not be a structural (i.e., syntactic) restriction, but simply a "pragmatic" preference. Her only evidence for this is that other Mayan languages allow anything to be relativized but use antipassive as a disambiguating device, or a way to get a slightly different meaning. This is irrelevant for languages like Jakaltek, however; she appears to be left with no explanation of the PIV restriction.

218 *Subjects and their properties*

Control constructions also appear to pose problems for structural accounts. The existence of both ĜF and PIV controllees is not recognized by everyone: Bittner and Hale (1996a, 1996b) appear to believe that only ĜF can be controlled. Strangely, they attribute this to Chomsky (1981), even though Chomsky's PRO-must-be-ungoverned account applies to [SPEC, IP], the PIV position. GHT assume the standard Chomsky (1981) analysis that PRO must be ungoverned, which in their analysis (correctly) accounts for PIV controllees, as [SPEC, IP] is ungoverned if Infl is non-finite. As for ĜF controllees, they suggest that PRO is possible in that position because of some relation between control and binding theory.[10] Since Binding Theory is sensitive to argumenthood, as discussed in Chapter 2 of this book,[11] and [SPEC, VP] is an argument position, PRO is possible there. However, the nature of the relation to Binding Theory is not specified and, as they point out, the analysis also entails that government of [SPEC, VP] by Infl is optional – a problematic concept. They do not discuss Raising, nor do they mention languages in which the controllee is limited to either ĜF or PIV. Murasugi (1992) suggests that the only true cases of PRO control involve PIV, for reasons of Case, and that apparent cases of ĜF controllees are either finite or involve *pro* instead of PRO. The latter approach bears some resemblance to our distinction between functional control (which would be the equivalent of Murasugi's PRO) and anaphoric control (*pro*), although in the case of the account here the distinction is one independently motivated in the theory. The lack of independent motivation renders her account more stipulative and less explanatory than one would like. Murasugi also has nothing to say about Raising.

Another point that needs to be made about the structural analyses is that they do not seem to provide a way to account for topic-pivot languages like Acehnese. Bittner and Hale's (1996a, 1996b) is the only account even to attempt this, but in their analysis of Acehnese the ĜF is always the PIV (they hypothesize a null expletive ĜF for unaccusative clauses). They do not motivate this on grounds of

---

10 The idea that control is related to Binding Theory is intuitively plausible, but it violates the leading idea behind control theory in GB, which is that, since PRO is a pronominal "anaphor," it cannot be subject to the principles of Binding Theory.

11 In the interests of fairness, I should point out that the binding-theoretic prominence of ĜF can be accounted for within the structural theory if one accepts the assumption that ĜF is structurally higher than other arguments in all languages. The explanation works best in Bittner and Hale's (1996a, 1996b) account. They observe, correctly, that under the VP-internal Subject Hypothesis, [SPEC, IP] is an Ā position, and thus irrelevant for Binding Theory. All Binding Theory can see is that [SPEC, VP] (or distinguished adjunct of VP in their implementation) c-commands the other arguments. This does not change the fact that other subject properties are not explained under structural accounts.

pivot behavior, which is striking since the Core Topic (PIV) figures prominently in Durie (1985). Topic-pivot languages appear to pose a serious problem for any Case-theoretic account of pivothood, since Case is linked to argumenthood, and topic-pivot languages do not pick the pivot on the basis of argumenthood.

The structural analyses are similar to ours in recognizing ĜF and PIV as two distinct elements, but require all languages to have the same c-structure configurations, and cannot provide analyses of pivothood in languages like Acehnese. Instead of directly addressing the question of grammatical functions, they create complex webs of c-structural conditions which conspire to create the surface grammatical relations that the analysis proposed here creates directly. The essential properties of the two kinds of subject, which are predicted by the current proposal by virtue of the nature of the two distinct grammatical functions, are not predicted by the structural accounts.

7.6   Final thoughts

The theory of subjecthood that we have proposed in the present study has certain properties that distinguish it from other, similar theories. We have taken a multidimensional functionally informed formalist approach, and we claim that this provides a better basis for understanding and explaining the properties of subjects than other approaches. In previous chapters, we have made this argument by showing how our theory, which factors the grammatical function SUBJ into the argument function ĜF and the overlay function PIV, explains the cross-linguistic properties of subjects. We have even explained typologically strange facts, such as the differences between languages in choice of controllee in control constructions.

In this, the final chapter, we have contrasted our approach with related approaches based on different assumptions. We have argued that these other approaches, while they share certain features with ours, fall short of accounting for the full range of subject-related phenomena which we account for.

There are several broader issues which are raised by the present study, in particular the formalist–functionalist divide, the explanatory potential of a theory based on grammatical functions, approaches to typology, the relation between explanation and description, and parallel architecture in linguistic theory. We will discuss these briefly here.

We believe the distinction between formalism and functionalism which pervades linguistics today to be a harmful sociological phenomenon. While one can (perhaps inevitably) approach language from one perspective or the other, ultimately language is built out of both form and function. The functions of language are expressed in form, and the forms of language serve functions (Falk 1992). In the present study, although our perspective has been primarily formalist, we have made use of observations from the functionalist side of the linguistics world. It is only through such a mixed perspective that true progress can be achieved.

Related to the breaking down of the formalist–functionalist barrier is the notion of grammatical functions: functionality based not on extrasyntactic dimensions but on the formal syntactic system itself. This notion of grammatical function has been the foundation on which the present analysis has been built. Such a concept is only truly possible if the formalist–functionalist distinction is rejected, and it is our contention that the generative goal of explaining linguistic phenomena requires a serious consideration of the formal syntactic functionality of linguistic elements. This was discussed in a preliminary way in Chapter 1, and the rest of this book can be seen as a case study in grammatical-function-based explanation. Further studies based on formal syntactic functionality will probably result in other explanations of phenomena that have resisted non-circular explanation in the past. This view of grammatical functions and explanatoriness runs counter to what is often assumed in the generative literature, particularly in the transformational literature; in fact, Chomsky (1981) argues explicitly against a role for grammatical functions in syntactic theory. Our approach is obviously different.

A second artificial division in contemporary linguistic research is the one between approaches to typology, as described in the following quotation from Comrie (1989: 1–2):

> On the one hand, some linguists have argued that in order to carry out research on language universals, it is necessary to have data from a wide range of languages; linguists advocating this approach have tended to concentrate on universals statable in terms of relatively concrete rather than abstract analyses, and have tended to be open, or at least eclectic, in the kinds of explanations that may be advanced for the existence of language universals. On the other hand, some linguists have argued that the best way to learn about language universals is by the detailed study of a small number of languages; such linguists have also advocated stating language universals in terms of abstract structures and have tended to favor innateness as the explanation for language universals. The first of these two approaches is perhaps most closely associated with the work of Joseph H. Greenberg and those inspired by his work. . . . The second is most closely associated with the work of Noam Chomsky and those directly influenced by him, and might be regarded as the orthodox generative position.

The approach we have taken here is neither "Greenberg" typology nor "Chomsky" typology. We take it to be self-evident that a study of this kind could not be undertaken without a sufficiently broad sample of languages. In this way, we differ from the "Chomsky" approach, which advocates taking a smaller set of languages. We do not believe that *any* meaningful typological work can be accomplished by comparing, say, French and English. On the other hand, we differ with the "Greenberg" approach that linguistic universals must be stated in relatively surfacy terms. We believe that the correct approach to typology has to rely on relatively detailed analysis of a wide range of languages, a combination of "Greenberg" typology and "Chomsky" typology. It is only through detailed analysis that we can find the explanations for the illusion of mixed-pivot languages, by recognizing the existence of both functional control and anaphoric control, or different ways of sharing participants between coordinated clauses. And we see nothing undesirable in expressing universals in abstract formal terms; our Pivot Condition is a formal universal condition on rules (or constraints), not on directly observable data.

A third problematic distinction often found in contemporary linguistic work is the distinction between explanation and description. This distinction is often drawn by researchers in the transformational tradition, with the associated implication that explanation is superior to "mere" description. Obviously, we do not wish to denigrate the idea that the goal of linguistics is explanation; the present study has been devoted to the concept of explanation. But explanation must be grounded in accurate description. Without a full understanding of the facts, any alleged explanation is useless. The present study has been solidly grounded in language description – in our view, the only possible way to do explanatory linguistics.

Finally, we have relied on a parallel-architecture multidimensional approach to language, the kind championed by LFG. We believe, with Bresnan (2001), that the multidimensionality of language holds the explanation for much of language variation. Such a multidimensional approach runs counter to the spirit of many other theoretical frameworks, which prefer to express all (or most) generalizations in terms of one type of linguistic representation. A multidimensional approach is a more realistic approach to language (Jackendoff 1997, 2002), and we take this to be one of the advantages of the theory proposed here.

The theory of subjecthood that we have proposed here, distinguishing $\widehat{\text{GF}}$ and PIV as functional elements with formal properties, and using a broad typological range of languages as its basis, is thus superior to other types of theories of subjecthood and ergativity in achieving the goal of explaining subjecthood.

References

Aissen, Judith L. 1983. "Indirect Object Advancement in Tzotzil." In David M. Perlmutter, ed., *Studies in Relational Grammar* vol. I. Chicago: University of Chicago Press. 272–302.

Aissen, Judith L. 1999. "Markedness and Subject Choice in Optimality Theory." *Natural Language and Linguistic Theory* 17: 673–711.

Aissen, Judith L. 2003. "Differential Object Marking: Iconicity vs. Economy." *Natural Language and Linguistic Theory* 21: 435–483.

Alsina, Alex. 1992. "On the Argument Structure of Causatives." *Linguistic Inquiry* 23: 517–555.

Alsina, Alex, and Smita Joshi. 1991. "Parameters in Causative Constructions." *CLS* 27: 1–15.

Andersen, Torben. 1988. "Ergativity in Päri, a Nilotic OVS Language." *Lingua* 75:289–324.

Andrews, Avery. 1985. "The Major Functions of the Noun Phrase." In Timothy Shopen, ed., *Language Typology and Syntactic Description*, vol. I, *Clause Structure*. Cambridge: Cambridge University Press. 62–154.

Arka, I Wayan. 1998. "From Morphosyntax to Pragmatics in Balinese: A Lexical-Functional Approach". Ph.D. dissertation, University of Sydney.

Arka, I Wayan, and Christopher D. Manning. 1998. "Voice and Grammatical Relations in Indonesian: A New Perspective." In Miriam Butt and Tracy Holloway King, eds., *Proceedings of the LFG98 Conference*, The University of Queensland, Brisbane. Online: CSLI Publications. http://cslipublications.stanford.edu/LFG/3/lfg98.html

Arka, I Wayan, and Jane Simpson. 1998. "Control and Complex Arguments in Balinese." in Miriam Butt and Tracy Holloway King, eds., *Proceedings of the LFG98 Conference*, The University of Queensland, Brisbane. Online: CSLI Publications.

Austin, Peter. 1981. "Switch-Reference in Australia." *Language* 57: 309–334.

Baker, Mark C. 1988. *Incorporation: A Theory of Grammatical Function Changing*. Chicago: University of Chicago Press.

Baker, Mark C. 1997. "Thematic Roles and Syntactic Structure." In Liliane Haegeman, ed., *Elements of Grammar: Handbook of Generative Syntax*. Dordrecht: Kluwer. 73–137.

Bell, Sarah J. 1983. "Advancements and Ascensions in Cebuano." In David M. Perlmutter, ed., *Studies in Relational Grammar* vol. I. Chicago: University of Chicago Press. 143–218.

Besnier, Nikko. 1988. "Semantic and Pragmatic Constraints on Tuvaluan Raising." *Linguistics* 26: 747–778.
Bhat, D.N.S., and M.S. Ningomba. 1997. *Manipuri Grammar*. München: Lincom Europa.
Bickel, Balthasar, and Yogrenda P. Yādava. 2000. "A Fresh Look at Grammatical Relations in Indo-Aryan." *Lingua* 110: 343–373.
Bittner, Maria. 1994. *Case, Scope, and Binding*. Dordrecht: Kluwer.
Bittner, Maria, and Ken Hale. 1996a. "Ergativity: Towards a Theory of a Heterogeneous Class." *Linguistic Inquiry* 27: 531–604.
Bittner, Maria, and Ken Hale. 1996b. "The Structural Determination of Case and Agreement." *Linguistic Inquiry* 27: 1–68.
Bouchard, Denis. 1984. *On the Content of Empty Categories*. Dordrecht: Foris.
Bouma, Gosse, Robert Malouf, and Ivan A. Sag. 2001. "Satisfying Constraints on Extraction and Adjunction." *Natural Language and Linguistic Theory* 19: 1–65.
Bresnan, Joan 1982. "Control and Complementation." In Joan Bresnan, ed., *The Mental Representation of Grammatical Relations*. Cambridge, Mass.: MIT Press. 282–390.
Bresnan, Joan 1995. "Linear Order, Syntactic Rank, and Empty Categories: On Weak Crossover." In Mary Dalrymple, Ronald M. Kaplan, John T. Maxwell III, and Annie Zaenen, eds., *Formal Issues in Lexical-Functional Grammar*. Stanford, Calif.: CSLI Publications. 241–274.
Bresnan, Joan. 2001. *Lexical-Functional Syntax*. Oxford: Blackwell.
Bresnan, Joan, and Sam Mchombo. 1987. "Topic, Pronoun, and Agreement in Chicheŵa." *Language* 63: 741–782.
Bresnan, Joan, and Annie Zaenen 1990. "Deep Unaccusativity in LFG." In Katarzyna Dziwirek, Farrell Patrick, and Errapel Mejías-Bikandi, eds., *Grammatical Relations: A Cross-Theoretical Perspective*. Stanford, Calif.: CSLI Publications. 45–57.
Broadwell, George Aaron. In press. *A Choctaw Reference Grammar*. Lincoln, Nebr.: University of Nebraska Press.
Burzio, Luigi. 1986. *Italian Syntax: A Government-Binding Approach*. Dordrecht: D. Reidel.
Butt, Miriam. 1993. "Object Specificity and Agreement in Hindi/Urdu." *CLS* 29: 89–103.
Chapin, Paul G. 1970. "Samoan Pronominalization." *Language* 46: 366–378.
Chomsky, Noam. 1965. *Aspects of the Theory of Syntax*. Cambridge, Mass.: MIT Press.
Chomsky, Noam. 1980. "On Binding." *Linguistic Inquiry* 11: 1–46.
Chomsky, Noam. 1981. *Lectures on Government and Binding*. Dordrecht: Foris.
Chomsky, Noam. 1982. *Some Concepts and Consequences of the Theory of Government and Binding*. Cambridge, Mass.: MIT Press.
Chomsky, Noam. 1986. *Barriers*. Cambridge, Mass.: MIT Press.
Chomsky, Noam. 1995. *The Minimalist Program*. Cambridge, Mass.: MIT Press.
Chomsky, Noam 2000. "Minimalist Inquiries: The Framework." In Roger Martin, David Michaels and Juan Uriagereka, eds., *Step by Step: Essays on Minimalist Syntax in Honor of Howard Lasnik*. Cambridge, Mass.: MIT Press. 89–155.

Chomsky, Noam, and Howard Lasnik 1993. "The Theory of Principles and Parameters." In Joachim Jacobs, Arnim von Stechow, Wolfgang Sternefeld, and Theo Vennemann, eds., *Syntax: An International Handbook of Contemporary Research*. Berlin: Walter de Gruyter. 506–569.

Chung, Sandra. 1978. *Case Marking and Grammatical Relations in Polynesian*. Austin: University of Texas Press.

Chung, Sandra, and William J. Seiter. 1980. "The History of Raising and Relativization in Polynesian." *Language* 56: 622–638.

Clements, George N., James McCloskey, Joan Maling, and Annie Zaenen. 1983. "String-Vacuous Rule Application." *Linguistic Inquiry* 14: 1–17.

Cole, Peter. 1982. *Imbabura Quechua*. Amsterdam: North Holland.

Cole, Peter 1983. "Switch-Reference in Two Quechua Languages." In John Haiman and Pamela Munro, eds., *Switch Reference and Universal Grammar*. Amsterdam: John Benjamins. 1–15.

Cole, Peter. 1987. "Null Objects in Universal Grammar." *Linguistic Inquiry* 18: 597–612.

Comrie, Bernard 1978. "Ergativity." In Winfred P. Lehmann, ed., *Syntactic Typology: Studies in the Phenomenology of Language*. Austin: University of Texas Press. 329–394.

Comrie, Bernard 1979. "Degrees of Ergativity: Some Chukchee Evidence." In Frans Plank, ed., *Ergativity: Towards a Theory of Grammatical Relations*. New York: Academic Press. 219–240.

Comrie, Bernard 1983. "Switch-Reference in Huichol: A Typological Study." In John Haiman and Pamela Munro, eds., *Switch Reference and Universal Grammar*. Amsterdam: John Benjamins. 18–37.

Comrie, Bernard. 1989. *Language Universals and Linguistic Typology* (2nd edition). Chicago: University of Chicago Press.

Cooreman, Ann. 1988. "Ergativity in Dyirbal Discourse." *Linguistics* 26: 717–746.

Cooreman, Ann M., Barbara Fox, and Talmy Givón 1988. "The Discourse Definition of Ergativity: A Study of Chamorro and Tagalog Texts." In Richard McGinn, ed., *Studies in Austronesian Linguistics*. Athens, Ohio: Ohio University Center for International Studies. 387–425.

Dalrymple, Mary. 1993. *The Syntax of Anaphoric Binding*. Stanford, Calif: CSLI Publications.

Dalrymple, Mary. 2001. *Lexical-Functional Grammar* (Syntax and Semantics, vol. xxxiv). New York: Academic Press.

Dalrymple, Mary, and Ronald M. Kaplan. 2000. "Feature Indeterminacy and Feature Resolution." *Language* 76: 759–798.

Dalrymple, Mary, Ron Kaplan, and Tracy Holloway King. 2001. "Weak Crossover and the Absence of Traces." In Miriam Butt and Tracy Holloway King, eds., *Proceedings of the LFG01 Conference*, University of Hong Kong. Online: CSLI Publications. 66–82. http://cslipublications.stanford.edu/LFG/6/lfg01.html

Davies, William D. 1984. "Antipassive: Choctaw Evidence for a Universal Characterization." In David M. Perlmutter and Carol G. Rosen, eds., *Studies in Relational Grammar* vol. II. Chicago: University of Chicago Press. 331–376.

References

Déchaine, Rose-Marie, and Martina Wiltschko. 2002. "Decomposing Pronouns." *Linguistic Inquiry* 33: 409–442.
Dixon, R.M.W. 1972. *The Dyirbal Language of North Queensland*. Cambridge: Cambridge University Press.
Dixon, R.M.W. 1977. *A Grammar of Yidiɲ* Cambridge: Cambridge University Press.
Dixon, R.M.W. 1979. "Corrections and Comments Concerning Heath's 'Is Dyirbal Ergative?'." *Linguistics* 17: 1003–1015.
Dixon, R.M.W. 1994. *Ergativity*. Cambridge: Cambridge University Press.
Dowty, David. 1991. "Thematic Proto-Roles and Argument Selection." *Language* 67: 547–619.
Dryer, Matthew S. 1986. "Primary Objects, Secondary Objects and Antidative." *Language* 62: 808–845.
Durie, Mark. 1985. *A Grammar of Acehnese on the Basis of a Dialect of North Aceh*. Dordrecht: Foris.
Durie, Mark. 1987. "Grammatical Relations in Acehnese." *Studies in Language* 11: 365–399.
Durie, Mark. 1988. "The So-Called Passive of Acehnese." *Language* 64: 104–113.
Falk, Yehuda N. 1983. "Subjects and Long-Distance Dependencies." *Linguistic Analysis* 12: 245–270.
Falk, Yehuda N. 1992. "Suppress α." *Linguistics* 30: 999–1030.
Falk, Yehuda N. 1994. "A New Look at Agreement." *Proceedings of the Ninth Annual Meeting of the Israel Association for Theoretical Linguistics*, Ben-Gurion University of the Negev, Beersheva, June 21–22, 1993.
Falk, Yehuda N. 1996. "Case Typology and Case Theory." Department of English, The Hebrew University of Jerusalem.
Falk, Yehuda N. 1999. "Philippine Subjects in a Monostratal Framework." Sixth annual conference of the Austronesian Formal Linguistics Association, April 16–18, 1999, University of Toronto.
Falk, Yehuda N. 2000. "Pivots and the Theory of Grammatical Functions." In Miriam Butt and Tracy Holloway King, eds., *Proceedings of the LFG00 Conference*, University of California, Berkeley. Online: CSLI Publications. 122–138. http://cslipublications.stanford.edu/LFG/ 5/lfg00.html
Falk, Yehuda N. 2001. *Lexical-Functional Grammar: An Introduction to Parallel Constraint-Based Syntax*. Stanford, Calif.: CSLI Publications.
Falk, Yehuda N. 2002. "Resumptive Pronouns in LFG." In Miriam Butt and Tracy Holloway King, eds., *Proceedings of the LFG 02 Conference*, National Technical University of Athens, Athens. Online: CSLI Publications. 154–173. http://cslipublications.stanford.edu/LFG/ 7/lfg02.html
Falk, Yehuda N. 2005. "Open Argument Functions." In Miriam Butt and Tracy Holloway King, eds., *Proceedings of the LFG 05 Conference*, University of Bergen. Online: CSLI Publications. http://cslipublications.stanford.edu/LFG/10/ lfg05.html
Farrell, Patrick, Stephen A. Marlett, and David M. Perlmutter. 1991. "Notions of Subjecthood and Switch Reference: Evidence from Seri." *Linguistic Inquiry* 22: 431–456.
Finer, Daniel L. 1985. "The Syntax of Switch-Reference." *Linguistic Inquiry* 16: 35–55.

Foley, William A., and Robert D. Van Valin, Jr. 1984. *Functional Syntax and Universal Grammar*. Cambridge: Cambridge University Press.

Gazdar, Gerald. 1981. "Unbounded Dependencies and Coordinate Structure." *Linguistic Inquiry* 12: 155–184.

Ginzburg, Jonathan, and Ivan A. Sag. 2000. *Interrogative Investigations: The Form, Meaning, and Use of English Interrogatives*. Stanford, Calif.: CSLI Publications.

Givón, T. 1990. *Syntax: A Functional-Typological Introduction*, vol. II. Philadelphia: John Benjamins.

Gordon, Lynn 1983. "Switch Reference, Clause Order, and Interclausal Relationships in Maricopa." In John Haiman and Pamela Munro, eds., *Switch Reference and Universal Grammar*. Amsterdam: John Benjamins. 83–104.

Guilfoyle, Eithne, Henrietta Hung, and Lisa Travis. 1992. "SPEC of IP and SPEC of VP: Two Subjects in Austronesian Languages." *Natural Language and Linguistic Theory* 10: 375–414.

Haiman, John, and Pamela Munro 1983. "Introduction." In *Switch-Reference and Universal Grammar*. Amsterdam: John Benjamins. ix–xv.

Hale, Ken. 1983. "Warlpiri and the Grammar of Non-Configurational Languages." *Natural Language and Linguistic Theory* 1: 5–47.

Hale, Ken 1992. "Subject Obviation, Switch Reference, and Control." In Richard K. Larson, Sabine Iatridou, Utpal Lahiri, and James Higginbotham, eds., *Control and Grammar*. Dordrecht: Kluwer. 51–77.

Hawkins, John A. 1999. "Processing Complexity and Filler-Gap Dependencies Across Grammars." *Language* 72: 244–285.

Heath, Jeffrey. 1979. "Is Dyirbal Ergative?." *Linguistics* 17: 401–463.

Hornstein, Norbert. 1999. "Movement and Control." *Linguistic Inquiry* 30: 69–96.

Huang, C.-T. James. 1984. "On the Distribution and Reference of Empty Pronouns." *Linguistic Inquiry* 15: 531–574.

Huang, C.-T. James 1989. "Pro-Drop in Chinese: A Generalized Control Theory." In Osvaldo Jaeggli and Ken Safir, eds., *The Null Subject Parameter*. Dordrecht: Kluwer. 185–214.

Huddleston, Rodney. 1984. *An Introduction to the Grammar of English*. Cambridge: Cambridge University Press.

Jackendoff, Ray. 1972. *Semantic Interpretation in Generative Grammar*. Cambridge, Mass.: MIT Press.

Jackendoff, Ray. 1987. "The Status of Thematic Relations in Linguistic Theory." *Linguistic Inquiry* 18: 369–411.

Jackendoff, Ray. 1990. *Semantic Structures*. Cambridge, Mass.: MIT Press.

Jackendoff, Ray. 1997. *The Architecture of the Language Faculty*. Cambridge, Mass.: MIT Press.

Jackendoff, Ray. 2002. *Foundations of Language*. Oxford: Oxford University Press.

Jaeggli, Osvaldo, and Ken Safir 1989. "The Null Subject Parameter and Parametric Theory." In Osvaldo Jaeggli and Ken Safir, eds., *The Null Subject Parameter*. Dordrecht: Kluwer. 1–44.

Johnson, David E., and Paul M. Postal. 1980. *Arc Pair Grammar*. Princeton, N. J.: Princeton University Press.

Kaplan, Ronald M., and Joan Bresnan 1982. "Lexical-Functional Grammar: A Formal System for Grammatical Representation." In Joan Bresnan, ed., *The Mental Representation of Grammatical Relations*. Cambridge, Mass.: MIT Press. 173–281.

Kaplan, Ronald M., and John T. Maxwell, III 1995. "Constituent Coordination in Lexical-Functional Grammar." In Mary Dalrymple, Ronald M. Kaplan, John T. Maxwell III, and Annie Zaenen, eds., *Formal Issues in Lexical-Functional Grammar*. Stanford, Calif.: CSLI Publications. First published in 1988, Proceedings of the 12th International Conference on Computational Linguistics (COLING88), Budapest, vol. I. 199–210.

Kaplan, Ronald M., and John T. Maxwell, III. 1996. *Grammar Writer's Workbench (Technical Report)*. Palo Alto, Calif.: Xerox Palo Alto Research Center. ftp://ftp.parc.xerox.com/pub/lfg/lfgmanual.ps

Kaplan, Ronald M., and Annie Zaenen 1989. "Long-Distance Dependencies, Constituent Structure, and Functional Uncertainty." In Mark R. Baltin and Anthony S. Kroch, eds., *Alternative Conceptions of Phrase Structure*. Chicago: University of Chicago Press. 17–42.

Keenan, Edward L. 1976. "Towards a Universal Definition of "Subject." In Charles Li, ed., *Subject and Topic*. New York: Academic Press. 303–333.

Keenan, Edward L., and Bernard Comrie. 1977. "Noun Phrase Accessibility and Universal Grammar." *Linguistic Inquiry* 8: 63–99.

Kibrik, A. E. 1987. "Constructions with Clause Actants in Daghestanian Languages." *Lingua* 71: 133–178.

King, Tracy Holloway. 1995. *Configuring Topic and Focus in Russian*. Stanford, Calif.: CSLI Publications.

Kroeger, Paul. 1993. *Phrase Structure and Grammatical Relations in Tagalog*. Stanford, Calif.: CSLI Publications.

Langdon, Margaret, and Pamela Munro. 1979. "Subject and (Switch-)Reference in Yuman." *Folia Linguistica* 13: 321–344.

Larsen, Thomas W. 1987. "The Syntactic Status of Ergativity in Quiché." *Lingua* 71: 33–59.

Legate, Julie Anne. 2001. "The Configurational Structure of a Nonconfigurational Language." *Linguistic Variation Yearbook* 1: 61–104.

Levin, Beth, and Malka Rappaport Hovav. 1995. *Unaccusativity: At the Syntax–Lexical Semantics Interface*. Cambridge, Mass.: MIT Press.

Li, Charles N., and Sandra A. Thompson. 1981. *Mandarin Chinese: A Functional Reference Grammar*. Berkeley: University of California Press.

Li, Charles N., and Sandra A. Thompson 1976. "Subject and Topic: A New Typology of Language." In Charles N. Li, ed., *Subject and Topic*. New York: Academic Press.

Lødrup, Helge 2000. "Underspecification in Lexical Mapping Theory: The Case of Norwegian Existentials and Resultatives." In Miriam Butt and Tracy Holloway King, eds., *Argument Realization*. Stanford, Calif.: CSLI Publications. 171–188.

Lynch, John 1983. "Switch-Reference in Lenakel." In John Haiman and Pamela Munro, eds., *Switch Reference and Universal Grammar*. Amsterdam: John Benjamins. 209–221.

McCloskey, Jim 1997. "Subjecthood and Subject Positions." in Liliane Haegeman, ed., *Elements of Grammar: Handbook of Generative Syntax*. Dordrecht: Kluwer. 197–235.

Mallinson, Graham, and Barry J. Blake. 1981. *Language Typology: Cross-Linguistic Studies in Syntax*. Amsterdam: North-Holland.

Manning, Christopher D. 1996. *Ergativity: Argument Structure and Grammatical Relations*. Stanford, Calif.: CSLI Publications.

Marantz, Alec 1982. "Grammatical Relations and Explanation in Linguistics." In Annie Zaenen, ed., *Subjects and Other Subjects: Proceedings of the Harvard Conference on the Representation of Grammatical Relations*. Bloomington, Ind.: Indiana University Linguistics Club. 1–24.

Marantz, Alec. 1984. *On the Nature of Grammatical Relations*. Cambridge, Mass.: MIT Press.

Mohanan, K.P. 1982. "Grammatical Relations and Clause Structure in Malayalam." In Joan Bresnan, ed., *The Mental Representation of Grammatical Relations*. Cambridge, Mass.: MIT Press. 504–589.

Mohanan, K.P. 1983. "Functional and Anaphoric Control." *Linguistic Inquiry* 14: 641–674.

Moore, John, and David M. Perlmutter. 2000. "What Does it Take to be a Dative Subject?" *Natural Language and Linguistic Theory* 18: 373–416.

Mosel, Ulrike, and Even Hovdhaugen. 1992. *Samoan Reference Grammar*. Oslo: Scandinavian University Press.

Munro, Pamela, and Lynn Gordon. 1982. "Syntactic Relations in Western Muskogean: A Typological Perspective." *Language* 58: 81–115.

Murasugi, Kumiko G. 1992. "Crossing and Nested Paths: NP Movement in Accusative and Ergative Languages". Ph.D. dissertation, MIT.

Nordlinger, Rachel. 1998. *Constructive Case: Evidence from Australian Languages*. Stanford, Calif.: CSLI Publications.

Palmer, F.R. 1994. *Grammatical Roles and Relations*. Cambridge: Cambridge University Press.

Perlmutter, David M. 1978. "Impersonal Passives and the Unaccusative Hypothesis." *BLS* 4.

Perlmutter, David M., ed., 1983. *Studies in Relational Grammar*, vol. I. Chicago: University of Chicago Press.

Perlmutter, David M. 1984. "The Inadequacy of Some Monostratal Theories of Passive." In David M. Perlmutter and Carol G. Rosen, eds., *Studies in Relational Gramma*, vol. II. Chicago: University of Chicago Press.

Perlmutter, David M., and Paul M. Postal 1983. "Towards a Universal Characterization of Passivization." In David M. Perlmutter, ed., *Studies in Relational Grammar*, vol. I. Chicago: University of Chicago Press.

Plank, Frans, ed., 1979. *Ergativity: Towards a Theory of Grammatical Relations*. New York: Academic Press.

Pollard, Carl, and Ivan A. Sag. 1994. *Head-Driven Phrase Structure Grammar*. Stanford, Calif.: CSLI Publications.

Pullum, Geoffrey K. 1997. "The Morpholexical Nature of English to Contraction." *Language* 73: 79–102.
Radford, Andrew. 1997. *Syntactic Theory and the Structure of English: A Minimalist Approach*. Cambridge: Cambridge University Press.
Rappaport Hovav, Malka, and Beth Levin (2003) "Deconstructing Thematic Hierarchies." Ms., The Hebrew University of Jerusalem and Stanford University.
Rizzi, Luigi. 1986. "Null Objects in Italian and the Theory of *pro*." *Linguistic Inquiry* 17: 501–557.
Rizzi, Luigi. 1990. *Relativized Minimality*. Cambridge, Mass.: MIT Press.
Sadler, Louisa. 1999. "Non-Distributive Features in Welsh Coordination." In Miriam Butt and Tracy Holloway King, eds., *Proceedings of the LFG 99 Conference*, The University of Manchester. Online: CSLI Publications. http://cslipublications.stanford.edu/LFG/4/lfg99.html
Sag, Ivan A., and Carl Pollard. 1991. "An Integrated Theory of Complement Control." *Language* 67: 63–113.
Saiki, Mariko. 1985. "On the Coordination of Gapped Constituents in Japanese." *CLS* 21: 371–387.
Schachter, Paul 1976. "The Subject in Philippine Languages: Topic, Actor, Actor-Topic, or None of the Above." In Charles Li, ed., *Subject and Topic*. New York: Academic Press. 493–518.
Schachter, Paul 1987. "Tagalog." In Bernard Comrie, ed., *The World's Major Languages*. New York: Oxford University Press. 936–958.
Seiter, William J. 1983. "Subject–Direct Object Raising in Niuean." In David M. Perlmutter, ed., *Studies in Relational Grammar*, vol. I. Chicago: University of Chicago Press. 317–359.
Sells, Peter. 1984. "Syntax and Semantics of Resumptive Pronouns". Ph.D. dissertation, University of Massachusetts, Amherst.
Shlonsky, Ur. 1988. "Complementizer-Cliticization in Hebrew and the Empty Category Principle." *Natural Language and Linguistic Theory* 6: 191–205.
Simpson, Jane. 1983. "Aspects of Warlpiri Morphology and Syntax". Ph.D. dissertation, MIT.
Simpson, Jane. 1991. *Warlpiri Morpho-Syntax: A Lexicalist Approach*. Dordrecht: Kluwer.
Simpson, Jane, and Joan Bresnan. 1983. "Control and Obviation in Warlpiri." *Natural Language and Linguistic Theory* 1: 49–64.
Sobin, Nicholas. 1987. "The Variable Status of COMP-Trace Phenomena." *Natural Language and Linguistic Theory* 5: 33–60.
Vainikka, Anne, and Yonata Levy. 1999. "Empty Subjects in Finnish and Hebrew." *Natural Language and Linguistic Theory* 17: 613–671.
Van Valin, Robert D., Jr., and Randy J. LaPolla. 1997. *Syntax: Structure, Meaning, and Function*. Cambridge: Cambridge University Press.
Wechsler, Stephen, and I Wayan Arka. 1998. "Syntactic Ergativity in Balinese: An Argument Structure Based Theory." *Natural Language and Linguistic Theory* 16: 387–441.

Williams, Edwin. 1984. "Grammatical Relations." *Linguistic Inquiry* 15: 639–673.
Woolford, Ellen. 1997. "Four-Way Case Systems: Ergative, Nominative, Objective and Accusative." *Natural Language and Linguistic Theory*. 181–227.
Ziv, Yael 1976. "On the Reanalysis of Grammatical Terms in Hebrew Possessive Constructions." In Peter Cole, ed., *Studies in Modern Hebrew Syntax and Semantics: The Transformational-Generative Approach*. Amsterdam: North-Holland.

Language index

Acehnese (Austronesian, Malayic) 12, 166, 167–170, 171–175, 177, 179, 186, 187, 193, 199, 206, 218–219
Avar (North Caucasian) 8

Balinese (Austronesian) 11, 40, 45, 136–137, 143–144, 145, 152–154, 161, 206–207
Basque (isolate) 8, 9, 66

Cebuano (Austronesian, Meso Philippine) 204, 210
Chichewa (Niger-Congo, Bantu) 41
Chimwiini (Niger-Congo, Bantu) 63–64
Choctaw/Chickasaw (Muskogean) 180–187, 192, 193, 199, 206
Chukchee (Chukotko-Kamchatkan) 58, 112, 161

Daghestanian languages (North Caucasian) 157
Dargwa (North Caucasian) 66
Diyari (Australian, Pama-Nyungan) 4, 66, 68, 69
Dyirbal (Australian, Pama-Nyungan) 8, 9, 48, 58, 70–71, 85, 89–90, 91, 92–93, 161, 199, 200, 209–210

English (Indo-European, [West] Germanic) 3, 4–5, 30, 40, 47, 52, 54, 55, 56, 57, 80, 84, 85, 89, 99, 101–102, 106, 109, 119–120, 121, 122, 131, 133, 141–142, 209
Eskimo languages (Eskimo-Aleut) 71
see also Inuit

French (Indo-European, Romance) 52, 84

Gokana (Niger-Congo, Benue-Congo) 68–69, 70
Greek (Indo-European) 52, 66

Hebrew (Afro-Asiatic, Semitic) 31, 34, 49–50, 52–53, 54, 55, 57, 84, 102–103, 118, 130–131, 133
Hindi-Urdu (Indo-European, Indo-Iranian) 100–101, 194–195, 199
Huichol (Uto-Aztecan) 68

Icelandic (Indo-European, [North] Germanic) 121
Indonesian (Austronesian, Malayic) 161, 207–208, 210
Inuit (Eskimo-Aleut) 8, 9, 12–14, 42, 64–65, 80, 99, 111, 136–137, 143, 144, 161, 209–210
see also Eskimo languages
Italian (Indo-European, Romance) 54, 55, 57

Jakaltek (Mayan) 93–94, 146, 217
Japanese (classification uncertain) 63, 126–128, 176, 177

Kalkatungu (Australian, Pama-Nyungan) 8
Kaluli (Trans-New Guinea) 200
Korean (classification uncertain) 54, 176

Lahu (Sino-Tibetan, Tibeto-Burman) 176
Lakhota (Siouan) 11, 166
Latin (Indo-European, Italic) 31, 40
Lenakel (Austronesian, Oceanic) 67

Malagasy (Austronesian) 210–212
Malay (Austronesian, Malayic) 210
Malayalam (Dravidian) 51, 65
Mam (Mayan) 112

231

Language index

Mandarin (Sino-Tibetan, Chinese) 54, 57, 176, 177–178, 179, 206
Manipuri (Sino-Tibetan, Tibeto-Burman) 11, 166
Marathi (Indo-European, Indo-Iranian) 65
Maricopa (Hokan) 67
Mayan languages 9
  see also Jakaltek, Mam, Quiché
Mojave (Hokan) 67–68

Nadëb (Maku) 60, 95–96
Nez Perce (Penutian) 8
Niuean (Austronesian, Polynesian) 158
Norwegian (Indo-European, [North] Germanic) 31, 36, 62–63

Päri (Nilo-Saharan) 96–97
Pashto (Indo-European, Indo-Iranian) 53

Quechua, Imbabura (Quechuan) 54, 115–116, 120–121, 180, 193
Quiché (Mayan) 104

Rotuman (Austronesian, Oceanic) 159
Russian (Indo-European, [East] Slavic) 19–20, 43, 64–65, 109

Samoan (Austronesian, Polynesian) 4, 98, 160
Sanskrit (Indo-European, Indo-Iranian) 64
Seri (Hokan) 69–70
Spanish (Indo-European, Romance) 52, 56, 84

Tagalog (Austronesian, Meso Philippine) 10, 12, 14–15, 48, 57–58, 59, 81, 99, 109, 111, 147–152, 155, 156–157, 159–160, 161, 173, 199–200, 210, 212
Thai (Tai-Kadai, Kam-Tai) 54
Toba Batak (Austronesian) 61–62, 161
Tongan (Austronesian, Polynesian) 160
Tsimshian (Penutian) 60
Turkish (Altaic) 40
Tuvaluan (Austronesian, Polynesian) 160
Tzotzil (Mayan), *see* Mayan languages

Wambaya (Australian, West Barkly) 18
Warlpiri (Australian, Pama-Nyungan) 9, 18, 180, 187–193, 199, 206
Waurá (Arawakan) 46

Yidin^y (Australian, Pama-Nyungan) 90, 91–92, 93, 161, 199

Author index

Aissen, Judith L. 9, 38, 104
Allen, Cynthia 102
Alsina, Alex 41
Andersen, Torben 96
Andrews, Avery 2–3, 23, 48
Arka, I Wayan 11, 40, 45, 136, 143, 152–154, 161, 203, 204, 206, 207–208
Austin, Peter 4–5, 66, 68

Baker, Mark C. 18, 63, 209
Bell, Sarah J. 204
Besnier, Nikko 159, 160
Bhat, D.N.S. 11
Bickel, Balthasar 194
Bittner, Maria 8, 13, 14, 99, 212–213, 217, 218
Blake, Barry J. 8, 11
Bouchard, Denis 51
Bouma, Gosse 118
Bresnan, Joan 3, 23, 24, 33, 35, 36, 40, 47, 55, 62, 74, 75, 77, 113, 117, 119, 141, 142, 145, 150, 155, 156, 189–190, 193, 221
Broadwell, George Aaron 180, 182, 186
Burzio, Luigi 32
Butt, Miriam 100

Chapin, Paul G. 4
Chomsky, Noam 3, 7, 17, 19, 40, 50, 51, 61, 107, 129, 136, 218, 220
Chung, Sandra 158, 160
Clements, George N. 121
Cole, Peter 54, 66, 115, 121
Comrie, Bernard 3, 7, 36, 58, 68, 70, 74, 85, 91, 104, 111, 112, 115, 118, 161, 190, 198, 220
Cooreman, Ann M. 48

Dalrymple, Mary 24, 26, 36, 52, 56, 62, 65, 86, 113, 117, 122
Davies, William D. 180, 182, 185
Déchaine, Rose-Marie 67
Dixon, R.M.W. 7, 8, 11, 28, 29, 46, 58, 59, 60, 66, 70–71, 74, 83, 85, 88, 89, 90–92, 93, 95, 96, 104, 139, 161, 167, 171, 182, 183, 195, 198, 199, 200–201, 202
Doron, Edit 134
Dowty, David 33
Dryer, Matthew S. 30
Durie, Mark 12, 167–168, 169, 171, 173, 186

Falk, Yehuda N. 24, 35, 47, 103, 113, 117, 119, 127, 128, 132, 141, 154, 156, 220
Farrell, Patrick 69
Finer, Daniel L. 67, 71
Foley, William A. 74
Fox, Barbara 48

Gazdar, Gerald 119
Ginzburg, Jonathan 117, 129
Givón, Talmy 48, 131–132
Gordon, Lynn 67, 180, 182
Guilfoyle, Eithne 14, 210–212, 217, 218

Haiman, John 69
Hale, Kenneth 8, 66, 67, 212–213, 217, 218
Hawkins, John A. 106
Heath, Jeffrey 92
Hornstein, Norbert 51
Hovdhaugen, Even 98, 160
Huang, C.-T. James 49, 51, 53, 57
Huddleston, Rodney 48
Hung, Henrietta 14, 210–212, 217, 218

233

Author index

Jackendoff, Ray 23, 33, 34, 37, 61, 137, 139, 164, 169, 221
Jaeggli, Oswaldo 54
Johnson, David E. 19
Joshi, Smita 41

Kaplan, Ronald M. 24, 77, 78, 86, 109, 117, 122
Keenan, Edward L. 2, 36, 74, 111, 115, 118
Kibrik, A. E. 157
King, Tracy Holloway 109, 117
Kroeger, Paul 15, 57, 109, 111, 139, 147, 148, 149, 150, 152, 156, 159, 203, 212

LaPolla, Randy J. 5, 20, 29, 83, 93, 146, 165, 167–168, 170, 171, 178, 195, 201–203
Langdon, Margaret 67, 68
Lasnik, Howard 107, 136
Legate, Julie Anne 18, 191–192
Levin, Beth 32, 33
Levy, Yonata 55
Li, Charles N. 175, 177
Lødrup, Helge 31
Lynch, John 67

McCloskey, James 18, 121, 208, 209
Maling, Joan 121
Mallinson, Graham 8, 11
Malouf, Robert 118
Manning, Christopher D. 12, 29, 30, 42, 44, 61, 64, 65, 66, 71, 72, 79, 96, 99, 111, 112, 136, 143–144, 161, 200, 203–204, 205, 207–208
Marantz, Alec 8, 17, 21, 44, 72, 80, 203
Marlett, Stephen A. 69
Maxwell, John T., III 78, 122
Mchombo, Sam A. 55
Mohanan, K. P. 51, 65
Moore, John 43
Mosel, Ulrike 98, 160
Munro, Pamela 67, 68, 69, 180, 182
Murasugi, Kumiko G. 214–217, 218

Ningomba, M. S. 11
Nordlinger, Rachel 18, 95, 113, 163

Palmer, F. R. 21, 31, 33, 71, 85
Perlmutter, David M. 19, 32, 36, 38, 39, 40, 43, 69
Plank, Frans 198
Pollard, Carl 36, 137–138, 141, 148
Postal, Paul M. 19, 39, 40
Pullum, Geoffrey K. 118

Radford, Andrew 52
Rappaport Hovav, Malka 32, 33
Rizzi, Luigi 54, 57, 129

Sadler, Louisa 86
Safir, Ken 54
Sag, Ivan A. 36, 117, 118, 129, 137–138, 141, 148
Saiki, Mariko 126
Schachter, Paul 10, 12, 13, 14, 28, 59, 81–82, 99, 111, 147
Seiter, William J. 158
Sells, Peter 132
Shlonsky, Ur 130
Simpson, Jane 9, 18, 143, 152–154, 188, 189–190, 192
Sobin, Nicholas 131, 133

Thompson, Sandra A. 175, 177
Travis, Lisa 14, 210–212, 217, 218

Vainikka, Anne 55
Van Valin, Robert D., Jr. 5, 20, 29, 74, 83, 93, 146, 165, 167–168, 170, 171, 178, 195, 201–203

Wechsler, Stephen 45, 203, 204
Williams, Edwin 19, 21
Wiltschko, Martina 67
Woolford, Ellen 8

Yādava, Yogrenda P. 194

Zaenen, Annie 47, 77, 109, 121
Ziv, Yael 103

General index

active languages 1, 11–12, 46–47, 166, 167, 168, 182, 217
  see also non-subject languages
Agent, *see* thematic roles
agreement 100–103, 104–105
  see also pronouns, incorporated
alignment, harmonic 38, 45–46, 48, 63, 200, 206
anaphora
  null, *see* pronouns, null
  prominence in 4, 12, 13, 14, 19–20, 24, 61–66, 218
  see also switch reference
argument
  core 35, 36, 38, 169–170
  functions 30, 35
  locality of 77
  mapping 30, 34, 36, 37–38, 44, 45–47, 168, 195, 200
    see also inverse mapping
  most prominent, *see* ĜF *and* θ̂
  non-thematic 34, 36
  structure 35

c-command 62
Case
  in transformational theory 17, 136, 210, 213–214, 219
  in typological analysis 198
  unmarked 7, 100–104, 193
  see also ergativity
causative, *see* complex predicates
chaining 88–89, 177, 179
  see also coordination, shared elements in *and* multifunctionality
complex predicates 41–42, 63–64

constructions, notional and formal 84–85, 89–92, 94, 115–116, 121–122, 140, 141, 197, 199, 201
control 5, 13, 14, 17, 136–137, 140, 161–162, 217–218, 219
  adjuncts 155
  anaphoric 140, 141–142, 144–145, 146, 147–150, 188, 189, 191, 221
  functional 141–142, 145–146, 154, 160–161, 179, 188, 189, 206–207, 221
  subjects 154–155
  see also raising *and* semantics, of control
coordination
  extraction from 122–128
  shared elements in 5, 85–89, 221
  in Dyirbal 89–90, 92–93
  in English 89
  in Yidin^y 90, 91–92
  see also Lexical-Functional Grammar, coordination in

definiteness 6, 99
distributed (phonological feature) 164

equi, *see* control
ergativity 1, 7–9, 79–80
  morphological 9, 104, 193–195, 196, 198, 199, 213
  scale of 198, 199
  split 8, 104
  syntactic 10, 44, 193, 198, 200, 203, 212, 213, 216
  see also mixed-subject languages
experiencer 44
external structural position 6, 17, 18–19, 24, 95–98, 175

formalist linguistics 1, 2, 3, 23, 28, 201, 219–220
Functional Locality Condition 77
functionalist linguistics 1, 2, 23, 29, 83, 161, 165, 201–203, 219–220

ĜF 29, 39, 45, 47, 62, 65, 66, 70, 72, 165–166, 169, 170, 182, 185, 195, 200–201, 202, 206, 209, 212, 219
Government/Binding theory, *see* transformational grammar
grammatical functions 21–24, 30, 35, 75, 163–165, 169, 195, 197, 220
  see also relational hierarchy
grammatical relations 19–21, 169, 182, 195

Head-driven Phrase Structure Grammar 45, 117–118, 129–130, 204

imperative addressee 3, 13, 14, 59–60
inverse mapping 44–46, 65, 66, 72, 82, 147, 203–208
inversion 43, 64–65

labial (phonological feature) 164
Lexical-Functional Grammar 21, 24–28, 49, 55, 62, 75, 94, 98, 117, 141, 157, 162, 168, 170, 187, 221 *et passim*
  coordination in 86, 122–123
  functional uncertainty 108–109
  inside-out licensing 112–115, 116, 119, 157–159, 161, 179
  Lexical Mapping Theory of 35, 47
long-distance dependencies 5, 13, 14, 174–175, 178, 179, 186–187, 190, 191–193, 217
  across-the-board 122–128
  and relational hierarchy 118
  displacement 107, 108
  empty categories (traces) 116–119
  in LFG, *see* Lexical-Functional Grammar, functional uncertainty
  multifunctionality 107–109
  subject-related properties 106–107
  that-trace effect 5, 128–134

Minimalist Program, *see* transformational grammar

mixed-subject languages 12, 15–16, 29, 44, 72, 73–74, 79–80, 134, 175, 178, 210, 216
  and anaphora 61, 66
  and control 136–137, 146, 147–152, 161
  and external position 95
  and imperatives 59
  and null pronouns 57–58
  and switch-reference 71
modularity, *see* parallel architecture
multidimensional architecture, *see* parallel architecture
multifunctionality 90–91, 107–108, 141
multistratalism vs. monostratalism 18, 20, 22–23, 32, 40, 47, 168, 204–205, 209

non-configurationality 18, 95, 163
non-subject languages 12, 163, 170, 195

obligatoriness of subject 6, 98, 170
Optimality Theory 9, 104, 206

parallel architecture 23, 39, 60, 84, 94, 141, 164, 195, 197, 219, 221
  and mismatches 39
passive 3, 19–20, 39–41, 64–65
Philippine-type languages 10–11, 45, 80–82, 204, 216
  see also mixed-subject languages
pivot 29, 74, 83, 132–133, 154, 170–171, 172, 173–175, 199, 202–203, 205, 209, 212, 213, 216, 217, 219
  characterization of 76
  condition 77–78, 88, 110–111, 113–114, 119, 145, 157, 178, 179, 221
  in topic-prominent languages 177–178, 179, 186, 195, 206, 218–219
  lack of 179–180, 184–185, 186, 193–195, 199, 206, 217
pro-drop, *see* pronouns, null *and* pronouns, incorporated
pronouns
  incorporated 52, 56, 86–88, 90–91
  null 3–4, 49–52, 56–58, 86–88, 90–91, 144, 149–150
  PRO and pro 29, 140

quantifiers
  floating 6
  scope 6, 13, 14, 99

raising 5, 15, 17, 155–159, 161, 173, 178, 188, 194
  copy 159–160
Relational Grammar 19–20, 32, 75, 98, 170, 204, 205
relational hierarchy 36, 37, 41, 47, 48, 56, 59, 60, 62, 63, 118
Role and Reference Grammar 20–21, 201–203
relative clauses, *see* long-distance dependencies

S, A, and P 7, 200–201
semantics
  and imperative addressees 59, 60
  coerced readings 60, 138–139, 146
  of control 137–139, 148–150
structure
  subjecthood based on 16–19, 29

switch-reference 4, 66–71, 136, 179, 185, 189–190

that-trace, *see* long-distance dependencies
thematic hierarchy 33–34, 36, 37, 41, 62
thematic roles 3, 31, 32–33, 63, 168, 182
  hierarchy of, *see* thematic hierarchy
  $\hat{\theta}$ 35, 36, 40, 45, 62, 63–64, 65, 66, 69, 70, 183, 185, 206
topichood, and subjects 6, 48
transformational grammar 16–19, 32, 55, 61, 75, 95, 98, 107, 128–129, 136, 161, 163, 170, 208–219, 220
typology, "Greenberg" vs. "Chomsky" 220–221

unaccusativity 32, 47
uniform-subject languages 12, 44, 72, 79, 82, 175, 178, 193, 210, 216
  and control 146
  and switch-reference 71

wh-movement, *see* long-distance dependencies